A Bibliography
Of
Canadian Theatre History

1583 • 1975

John Ball • Richard Plant

General Editor: Anton Wagner

The compilers wish to acknowledge the assistance of the Ontario Arts Council and the Humanities Research Council of Canada. We also wish to thank Heather McCallum and Anton Wagner for their many comments and suggestions, the Canadian Theatre History Research Programme, Professor Mavor Moore and all those, too numerous to mention, who have corresponded with us over the past few years. The seemingly endless typing was undertaken by Penelope Vardy and Gillian Ball.

Published by:

The Playwrights Co-op,
8 York Street,
Toronto, Ontario,
Canada,   M5J 1R2

Design and Production:

Gwen Dempsey, Page Publications

First printing: May 1976
Second printing: January 1978
Paper **ISBN** 0-919834-03-5
Cloth **ISBN** 0-919834-02-7

Contents

A Bibliography of Canadian Theatre History

1583 - 1975: A Preface

As theatre researchers can readily testify, there has been, to this point, no extensive bibliography of published materials relating to Canadian theatre history. The present work grew out of an earlier bibliography, published in *Canadian Literature* in 1962,[1] which was in turn based on a bibliographic thesis for the Diploma in Librarianship at the University of London.[2] A number of other limited sources exist, such as the various bibliographies of Canadian literature which have sections on drama, and books on the theatre which contain selected references to Canadian theatre history, but these are of only marginal use to the growing number of researchers in Canadian theatre study.

With the growth in theatrical activity during the 1960's and early 1970's, people have developed an interest in our native theatre and drama — even to the point of digging into its past with a faint awareness that the present and the future exist only as an extension of the past. In light of these developments, it is hoped that this bibliography, by serving as a companion to Heather McCallum's *Theatre Resources in Canadian Collections,* the Brock bibliographies of published Canadian stage plays, and other existing bibliographies in related areas of Canadian scholarship, will help stimulate Canadian theatre history research, and thereby play a part in articulating Canada's theatrical past.

Previously, much of the information now made available by this bibliography was accessible only to a small number of specialists in the area. Apart from the factual aspect of presenting theatre history documents, the bibliography offers through its geographical and chronological arrangement, the possibility of tracing the development of Canadian theatre. This overview reveals the topics of special interest and importance at different times in the history of Canadian theatre. The movement from imported touring companies to local resident ones in the 19th. century, the striving for a national indigenous theatre, the evolution from amateur little theatre to professional, and the development of regional theatres are all represented, as well as larger issues such as the function of the theatre in society over the years.

The *Bibliography of Canadian Theatre History* contains approximately 2,000 entries which span a period of some 400 years beginning with an item from 1583 which makes brief reference to entertainments held on shipboard off the coast of Canada. The most current items are as recent as mid-1975, the official cut-off date. The entries are arranged in 13 sections, "A" to "M", determined by period, region, and topic. In 11 of the 13 sections, (excluding section K: Theses and L: Periodicals) the arrangement is chronological by year of publication, and within each chronological year, the items are subsequently arranged alphabetically. The sections entitled "Theses" and "Periodicals" are simply arranged alphabetically by author or title, respectively, without attention to publication dates. As the name implies, Section A, "General Surveys", offers a list of works which provide historical overviews of Canadian theatrical activity and works which are of value in understanding the development of Canadian dramatic activity. Section C, "Twentieth Century — English Canada: general comment and surveys at particular periods", lists items which provide a survey of or comment on Canadian theatre and dramatic activity during a specific period of the twentieth century. In Sections G, "Stratford Festival", and E, "Little Theatre Movement", a subdivision entitled "General" is included in which are listed those articles on the subject of a general nature. The information in the bibliography is made more easily accessible by an index which lists the entries by author and specific topic headings.

A special word must be said about the French-Canadian sections. Our aim in collecting French-Canadian items has largely been to provide a record of those materials which supplement the study of English-Canadian theatre history. We have not attempted to be exhaustive, especially since French-Canadian theatre is sufficiently large to require a bibliography unto itself, (researchers will quickly become aware of the admirable bibliographical work already done in Quebec), but we have included those items which bear special significance to the English-Canadian theatre; for example, items which help to outline periods in the development of Canadian theatre that are not accounted for by English-Canadian activity alone. As well, we have listed materials which are complementary to English-Canadian theatre and shed light in some way on English-Canadian activity. It should be noted that articles on the English-speaking theatre in Quebec are also listed in the French Canadian sections.

As a general rule, the items listed in all sections, excluding "Theses", have been published in one form or another. However, a few items, such as the microfilm of *Theatre Journey: Ramblings of an Adjudicator* by Malcolm Morley, (F 13), the C.B.C. tapes, *Canadian Theatre: Fact and Fancy*, (A 12), and the Royal Alexandra scrapbooks, (C 379), also on microfilm, have been included. Further information on these and other items of this nature may be obtained by consulting Heather McCallum's

Theatre Resources in Canadian Collections, (M 28), and the recent edition of the *Union List of Manuscripts in Canadian Repositories* published by the Public Archives, (M 41). Unpublished studies, such as the manuscript of *Thunderbird* by Richard Courtney, which explores the dramatic implications of the ceremonies of native Indians on Vancouver Island, have not been listed.[3] Ballet, music, and opera have been excluded, as have radio drama, for the most part, and articles in newspapers. An exception in regard to newspapers has been made concerning the *Financial Post* which is not an obvious source for most theatre researchers, yet has consistently provided articles relating to Canadian theatre, and offers valuable insight into the relationship between theatre and business. No attempt has been made to list published Canadian plays, although sources are listed in Section M. In this case, a researcher is advised to refer to such sources as the Brock bibliographies, (M 15, M 25). For a variety of reasons, there are a few items, designated by an asterisk, which we have entered in an incomplete form. These entries show all of the information we were able to collect as of the date of publication; they are included in the hope that subsequent research will be able to complete them.

As might be expected, the problems encountered in this project have been many, not all of which have been solved. As a result, we are only too aware of the limitations of the bibliography and the possibilities of error. We hope that errors have been kept to a minimum. A section such as "Tours and Visits", for example, is especially problematical since information is continually being uncovered in accounts of artists in early Canada. Many of these accounts are to be found in the biographies and autobiographies of the artists concerned, and as a result those which we have been able to include are often listed in the "Biography and Criticism" section. In addition, there are sources of information, the large number of local history journals, for example, which we have not been able to record fully, but which will eventually yield a wealth of material on Canadian theatre. We have not fully indexed the invaluable *Saturday Night* or *Canadian Forum,* although a significant number of items from each is included. Some mysteriously evasive works, like James Fearnside's *Showman's Guide for Canada*[4] and Franklin Graham's *Kings of Tragedy*[5] are unaccounted for at this time, and await discovery by subsequent researchers.

Since it has not been possible for us to include locations for the items in the bibliography, a brief note on sources may be of value, especially for beginning researchers. Generally, theatre history materials are widely scattered throughout Canada in various public libraries, archives, and museums, university repositories, and private collections. In many cases, materials exist only in small numbers, virtually hidden as parts of larger collections which often bear little relationship to the theatre. The largest amount of published material is contained in periodicals, both contemporary and from the past. Consequently, libraries with extensive periodical holdings are of particular value; for example, major universities and large public systems.

A number of repositories are now making a determined effort to collect Canadian theatre materials, and it is to these sources a person might turn first. What is probably the largest collection is held in the Theatre Section of the Metropolitan Toronto Central Library, where its extensive holdings are supplemented by other Metropolitan Toronto Central Library departments, such as History, the Baldwin Room, and the Toronto Room. The Public Archives and the National Library, both in Ottawa, are also important sources of information and have valuable collections. In Quebec, Les Archives du Québec and La Bibliothèque Nationale du Québec have extensive collections. Outside Canada, the large collections of Brown and Harvard Universities and the New York Public Library are of special importance for Canadian material.

Of Canadian universities, the University of Toronto (Robarts and Thomas Fisher Rare Book libraries) has a valuable collection and the University of Alberta in Edmonton has holdings in Canadian drama worthy of note. Apart from these special collections, as is the case with public libraries, each university has at least a small collection of Canadian theatre and drama material, often documenting local theatre history.

In the past, Canadian theatres, both professional and amateur, have often failed to maintain records of their activities, while many of those which did keep records saw them destroyed by fire or lost in the general instability of the Canadian theatre world. As a result, the theatres themselves are not always as valuable a source as they might be. A number of larger bodies, such as the Stratford Festival which established the post of archivist in 1971, and the D.D.F./Théâtre Canada, Le Théâtre du Rideau Vert, Le Théâtre du Nouveau Monde, the Shaw Festival, and the Neptune Theatre, have kept extensive records. But for the most part, theatres, especially the smaller ones, have been limited by insufficient staff and funds. It is encouraging to note that many of our present theatres are now able to undertake at least small archival projects and have the awareness to do so.

Of particular note as a source of information is the Canadian Theatre History Research Programme established in the fall of 1975 and located administratively in the Robarts Library at the University of Toronto. Among its aims, and as one of its necessary early priorities, the Programme is working at drawing together a nation-wide network of theatre historians in an attempt to promote the orderly investigation of Canadian theatre history. A continual up-dating of this present bibliography is also one of the many projects the Programme has embarked on.

There are a number of published works which are of assistance in locating theatre materials. Previously mentioned, *Theatre Resources in Canadian Collections* (M 28) and the *Union List of Manuscripts in Canadian Repositories* (M 41) are invaluable. Reginald Watters' *A*

Checklist of Canadian Literature and Background Materials 1628-1960 (M 20) is of special importance as a bibliography because it includes locations, as does Dorothy Sedgwick's *Bibliography of English-Language Theatre and Drama in Canada 1800-1914* published in 1976 by *Nineteenth Century Theatre Research.* The four volumes of Juge G. Edouard Rinfret's mammoth study, *Le Théâtre Canadien, d'expression française; répertoire analytique des débuts de la colonie à nos jours,* added to those bibliographies already in Quebec, will be of extraordinary value for researchers.

Out of the collecting of material for this bibliography has emerged an affirmation of our belief that a sizeable amount of valuable information is extant which chronicles Canada's theatrical past. What is equally exciting is the suspicion that a wealth of similar material exists which is still to be uncovered. We hope this bibliography will contribute in some small way to that future discovery.

John Ball
Richard Plant
April, 1976

---

[1] Ball, John L. Theatre in Canada — a bibliography. *Canadian Literature* no. 14, autumn 1962. p. 85-100.

[2] Ball, John L. *Theatre in Canada* — a bibliography submitted in part requirement for the University of London, Diploma in Librarianship. 1960. 42 l.

[3] *Thunderbird* is available to interested readers by permission of Richard Courtney at the Ontario Institute for Studies in Education, Toronto.

[4] Published 1874 c. in Hamilton, Ontario. Apart from our own work, Professor Mary Brown, University of Western Ontario, has conducted a thorough search for this item and is the most knowledgeable person on the subject.

[5] Mentioned by Mr. Graham in *Histrionic Montreal* (B 45, Prologue, n.p.) as his "initial effort . . . published in 1888". We speculate that it may have been a series of newspaper articles carried in a Montreal newspaper.

John Ball

John Ball is College Librarian at Scarborough College, University of Toronto. His initial bibliography, "Theatre in Canada", was published in *Canadian Literature* in 1962. Mr. Ball worked with the Drao Players in 1961 and 1962 when they won the Dominion Drama Festival with their production of *Rashomon* and opened the Central Library Theatre in Toronto with *Six Days and a Dream*. Since 1962, he has been a member of Theatre Aurora, formerly the Aurora Drama Workshop.

Richard Plant

Richard Plant is a PhD candidate at the Centre for Graduate Studies in Drama at the University of Toronto and has received MA's from Northwestern University, Evanston, Illinois, and the University of Toronto. He has acted and directed in the theatre as well as teaching courses in Canadian literature, drama and theatre history. In 1974, he directed the Canadian premiere of Merill Denison's *Marsh Hay* at Hart House Theatre in Toronto.

Abbreviations

bibl.	bibliography
bibl. f.	bibliographic footnotes
diagr.	diagram(s)
ed.	edition
enl.	enlarged
front.	frontispiece
illus.	illustration(s)
l.	leaves
n.s.	new series
no.	number
p.	page(s)
port.	portrait(s)
rev.	revised
sect.	section
ser.	series
v.	volume(s)
+	continuing publication

A

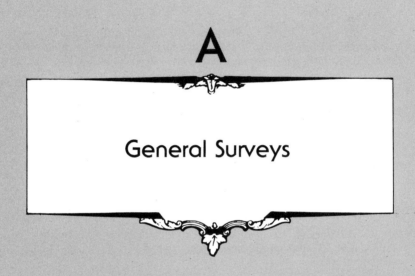

General Surveys

A1. **Poirier, Pascal.** Le théâtre au Canada. *Nouvelles Soirées Canadiennes.* V: 193-200, 1886.

A2. **Middleton, Jesse Edgar.** Theatre in Canada. In Adam Shortt and A.G. Doughty, eds. *Canada and Its Provinces.* Toronto, Glasgow Brook, 1914. v.12, p. 651-661.

A3. **Lassalle, Eugène.** *Comédiens et amateurs.* Montréal, Imprimerie du Devoir, 1919. 235 p.

A4. **Rhodenizer, Vernon Blair.** Canadian drama. In his *Handbook of Canadian literature.* Ottawa, Graphic, 1930. p. 152-159.

A5. **Bullock-Webster, Llewelyn.** *Transcript of an address on the development of Canadian drama,* given at Loretto Hall, Victoria. February 23rd, 1943. Victoria, B.C., Department of Education, 1943. 17 p.

A6. **Leonard, Agatha.** Theatre. In *Encyclopedia of Canada.* Toronto, University Associates of Canada, 1948. v.6, p. 132-135. bibl.

A7. **Glasstone, Victor.** Canadà — teatro drammatico. In *Enciclopedia dello spettacolo.* Rome, Casa editrice le maschere, 1954. v.2, p. 1612-1618. bibl.

A8. **Béraud, Jean.** 350 ans de théâtre au Canada français. In *Encyclopédie du Canada français.* Montréal, Le Cercle du Livre de France, 1958. v.1, 321 p. illus., ports., facsims., bibl.

A9. **Blum, Daniel.** *A pictorial history of the American theatre 100 years 1860-1960.* N.Y., Chilton, 1960. 384 p.

A10. **Watt, Frank.** The growth of proletarian literature in Canada: 1872-1920. *Dalhousie Review* 40: 157-173, summer 1960.

A11. **Hamelin, Jean.** *Le renouveau du théâtre au Canada français.* Montréal, Editions du Jour, 1962. 160 p. illus.

A12. *Canadian theatre: fact and fancy.* Toronto, Canadian Broadcasting Corporation, 1964. 13 tape reels broadcast weekly by C.B.C. from Sunday January 26, 1964, for 13 weeks.

A13. **Whittaker, Herbert.** Shakespeare in Canada before 1953. In Shakespeare Seminar, Stratford, Ont. *Stratford papers on Shakespeare.* Toronto, Gage, 1964. p. 71-89.

A14. **Tait, Michael.** Drama and theatre 1920-1960. In Klinck, Carl ed. *Literary history of Canada.* Toronto, University of Toronto Press, 1965. p. 633-657.

A15. **Houle, Renée.** *Le théâtre au Canada.* Canada. Royal Commission on Bilingualism and Biculturalism. Research Studies. Series E. Ottawa, October 1966. 193 p.

A16. **Tougas, Gérard.** *History of French Canadian literature.* 2nd ed. tr. by Alta Lind Cook. Toronto, Ryerson Press, 1966. ix, 301 p. bibl.

A17. **Beaulne, Guy.** *Notre théâtre, conscience d'un peuple.* Québec, Ministère des Affaires Culturelles, 1967. 18 l.

A18. **Hartnoll, Phyllis.** ed. *Oxford companion to the theatre.* 3rd ed. London, Oxford University Press, 1967. xv, 1088p. illus.

A19. **Story, Norah.** *Oxford companion to Canadian history and literature.* Oxford University Press, 1967. xi, 935 p.

A20. **Stratford, Ont. Shakespeare Festival.** *100 years of theatre in Canada.* (Stratford, Ont.) (1967). 18 p. illus.

A21. **Tougas, Gérard.** *Histoire de la littérature canadienne-française.* 4th ed. Paris, Presses Universitaires de France, 1967. xii, 312 p. (1st ed. 1960, 2nd ed. 1964, 3rd ed. 1967).

A22. **Edwards, Murray D.** *A stage in our past. English language theatre in Eastern Canada from the 1790's to 1914.* Toronto, University of Toronto Press, 1968. xii, 212 p. illus., ports., bibl.

A23. **Novick, Julius.** *Beyond Broadway; the quest for permanent theatres.* N.Y. Hill & Wang, 1968. xiv, 393 p. illus., ports.

A24. **Ontario Council for the Arts.** *The awkward stage. The Ontario theatre study report.* Toronto, Methuen, 1969. xvi, 244 p. illus., bibl.

A25. **Godin, Jean Cléo.** *Le théâtre québecois* by Jean Cléo Godin and Laurent Mailhot. Montréal, Editions HMH, 1970. 254 p. bibl.

A26. **Whittaker, Herbert.** Canada - Theatre. In *Encyclopedia Americana.* Canadian edition. Toronto, Americana Corporation of Canada, (c.1970) v.5, p. 435-437.

A27. **Angus, William.** Theatre. In *Encyclopedia Canadiana.* Toronto, Grolier Society of Canada, (c.1972) v.10, p. 61-67. illus.

A28. **Atwood, Margaret.** *Survival.* Toronto, House of Anansi, 1972. 280 p.

A29. **Hartnoll, Phyllis** ed. *The concise Oxford companion to the theatre.* London, Oxford University Press, 1972. 640 p.

A30. **Waller, Adrian.** *Theatre on a shoestring.* Toronto, Clarke, Irwin, 1972. 158 p. illus. bibl.

A31. **Denham, Paul.** ed. *The evolution of Canadian literature in English, 1945-1970.* Toronto, Holt, Rinehart and Winston, 1973, 288 p. bibl.

A32. **Doat, Jan.** ed. *Anthologie du théâtre québecois, 1606-1970.* Québec, Editions la liberté, 1973. 505 p.

A33. **Fulford, Robert.** General perspectives on Canadian culture. *American Review of Canadian Studies* 3:115-121, spring 1973.

A34. **Hull, R.** This writing business: literary contests. *Canadian Author and Bookman* 48:11, fall, 1973.

A35. **McLuhan, Marshall.** Politics as theatre. *Performing Arts* 10:14-15, winter, 1973, illus.

A36. **New, William H.** Introduction: Canada: annual bibliography of Commonwealth literature. *Journal of Commonwealth Literature* 8:59-64, December, 1973.

A37. **Parkin, Andrew.** Theatre and drama in Canada: an emerging tradition. In *Stage One.* Toronto, Van Nostrand-Reinhold, 1973. p. ix-xvi.

A38. **Pride, Leo B.** *International theatre directory: a world directory of the theatre and performing arts.* New York, Simon and Schuster, 1973. 577 p.

A39. **Toye, William.** ed. *Supplement to the Oxford companion to Canadian history and literature.* Toronto, Oxford University Press, 1973. 318 p.

A40. **Wagner, Anton.** Theatre and national identity, French Canadian political theatre, 1606-1971. *Alive* 31:17-21, 1973.

A41. **Waterston, Elizabeth.** Theatrical colours in the dark. In *Survey: a short history of Canadian literature.* Toronto, Methuen, 1973. p. 155-156.

A42. **Blackwell, Florence King.** Puppetry is much too good to be wasted on the young. *Performing Arts* 11:16-17, fall, 1974. illus.

A43. Canadian professional theatres: a checklist. *Canadian Theatre Review* CTR 1:138-144, winter, 1974.

A44. **Dafoe, Christopher.** Theatre in Winnipeg: a brief history. *Canadian Theatre Review* CTR 4:11-12, fall, 1974.

A45. **Lister, Rota.** Canada's Indians and Canadian drama. *American Review of Canadian Studies* 4:54-74, spring, 1974.

A46. **McKay, K.** Puppets old and new. *Canadian Antique Collector* 9:7-11, March-April, 1974,. illus.

A47. **Wagner, Anton.** Nationalism and the French-Canadian drama. *Canadian Theatre Review* CTR 1:22-27, winter, 1974.

A48. **Kaplan, Beth.** Women in theatre. *Communiqué* 8:30-31, 50-51, May, 1975. port.

A49. **Stuart, Euan Ross.** Theatre in Canada: an historical perspective. *Canadian Theatre Review* CTR 5:6-15, winter, 1975.

A theatrical performance given by the Officers of the Garrison at Halifax, assisted by lady amateurs, to re-open the Soldier's Institute in October, 1872. The scene is from *The Lady of Lyons Burlesque,* one of the plays on this occasion, and attention should be drawn to "Mr. Rowe's clever impersonation of the love-worn widow", (last on the right). See items listed in Index under Garrison Theatricals.

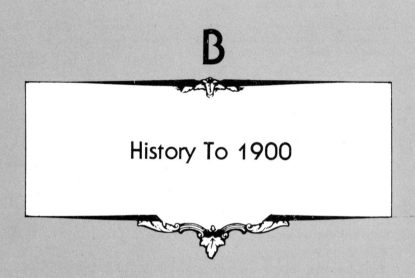

B

History To 1900

B1. **Hakluyt, Richard.** *Voyages and Documents*, edited by Janet Hampden. Oxford University Press. 1958. p. 250.

B2. **Saint Vallier, Jean Baptiste De La Croix Chevrières De, Bp. of Quebec.** Mandement au sujet des comédies. In *Mandements des Evèques de Québec.* Québec, Coté, 1887. v.1, p. 302-4.

B3. **Journal des Jésuites.** 2. ed. Montréal, Valois, 1892. (References to dramatic performances: février 1647, décembre 1651, avril 1652, janvier 1657, juillet 1658, août 1659, février 1668, mars 1668.)

B4. *Réception de Monseigneur le vicomte d'Argenson par toutes les nations du pays de Canada à son entrée au gouvernement de la Nouvelle France.* Publiée par Pierre-Georges Roy. Québec, Brousseau, 1890. 23 p.

B5. *Jesuit relations and allied documents.* ed. by Reuben Gold Thwaites. Cleveland, Burrows, 1894-1901. 73v. (Items in index v. 73-73.)

B6. **Roy, Joseph Edmond.** Le Baron de Lahontan. *Transactions of Royal Society of Canada.* 1. ser; v.13, sect. 1:63-192, 1894. (References to performances in 1691-2.)

B7. **Gosselin, August.** Un épisode de l'histoire de théâtre au Canada. *Transactions of Royal Society of Canada.* 2 ser., v.4, sect. 1:55-72, 1898. (Episode of Tartuffe-1694.)

B8. **Hicks, Rivers Keith.** Le théâtre de Neptune. *Queen's Quarterly* 34:215-223, October 1926.

B9. **Bullock-Webster, Llewelyn.** Early drama in Canada. *Drama* 18:11-12, 30. October 1927.

B10. **Lescarbot, Marc.** *The Theatre of Neptune in New France* with a translation and introduction by Harriette Taber Richardson. Boston, Houghton Mifflin, 1927. xxii, 28 p.

B11. **Roquebrune, Robert De.** Le théâtre au Canada en 1694; l'affaire du "Tartuffe". *Revue de l'Histoire des Colonies Françaises* 24: 181-194, mars/avril 1931.

B12. **Cameron, Margaret M.** Play acting in Canada during the French regime. *Canadian Historical Review* 11:9-19. 1930. bibl.f.

B13. **Waldo, Lewis Patrick.** French drama in Canada in the seventeenth and eighteenth centuries. In his *French drama in America in the eighteenth century and its influence on the American drama of that period, 1701-1800.* Baltimore, Johns Hopkins Press, 1942. p. 19-49. bibl.f.

B14. **Paquet, André.** Les origines du théâtre au collège. *Canadien Français* 32:99-118, Octobre 1944.

B15. **Bonenfant, Jean Charles.** Théâtre au collège. *Revue Dominicaine* 52: 27-32, janvier 1946. (Jesuits and the theatre.)

B16. **Lescarbot, Marc.** *Marc Lescarbot's Theatre of Neptune,* tr. by Rivers Keith

Hicks with an introduction by W.L. Grant. Lower Granville, N.S., Abanaki Press, 1947. 12 p. (Reprinted from *Queen's Quarterly* 1926).

B17. **MacDougall, Angus J.** An historical sidelight - Quebec 1658. *Culture* 11:15-28, January 1950. (Performance to welcome governor of New France 1658.)

B18. **Marion, Séraphin.** Le Tartuffe et Mgr. de Saint Vallier. In *Les Lettres Canadiennes d'Autrefois.* Ottawa, L'Eclair, 1954. v.8, p. 15-37.

B19. **Bond, Frank Fraser.** America's premier "first night" - 1606. *Dalhousie Review* 36:392-398, winter 1957.

B20. **Wetmore, Donald.** The first play produced in North America. *Journal of Education* Ser. 5, v.2: 47, January 1953.

B21. **Bond, Frank Fraser.** "First night" - 1606. *Performing Arts* 3:57-59, fall 1964.

B22. **Auger, Colette.** Tartuffe à Québec: Jamais! *Magazine Maclean* 5:24-25, 52-56, septembre 1965. illus., ports.

B23. **Pichette, Robert.** Marc Lescarbot et son théâtre de Neptune. La Société Historique Acadienne. *Cahier* 8:21-32, mai 1965.

ATLANTIC PROVINCES 1700-1900

B24. **Howe, Jonas.** A theatrical interlude 100 years ago. *Acadiensis* v:102-114, April-July, 1905. (Saint John.)

B25. **Jewitt, Arthur Russell.** Early Halifax theatres. *Dalhousie Review* 5:444-459, January 1926.

B26. **Mullane, George.** *The professional drama of yesterday in Halifax 1787-1870.* Halifax, Nova Scotia Historical Society. Paper, 1926. 49p.

B27. **Blakeley, Phyllis R.** The theatre and music in Halifax. *Dalhousie Review* 29:8-20, April 1949 bibl.f.

B28. **Fergusson, C. Bruce.** The rise of the theatre in Halifax. *Dalhousie Review* 29:419-427, January 1950.

B29. **Harper, J. Russell.** The theatre in Saint John 1789-1817. *Dalhousie Review* 34: 260-269, autumn 1954.

B30. **Harper, J. Russell.** Showmen, tinsel and tanbark. *Atlantic Advocate* 48: 49, 51, 53, 55, 57, November 1957. illus.

B31. **McGowan, Elizabeth.** Early theatre in Canada. *Performing Arts* 1, no. 2:36-37, October 1961. (Prince Edward Island.)

B32. **Blakeley, Phyllis.** A Royal patron of the theatre. *Atlantic Advocate* 58: 42, January 1968. (Duke of Kent c. 1800.)

B33. **Best, James Linden.** Box, pit, and gallery: the Theatre Royal at Spring Garden. *Dalhousie Review* 53:520-528, autumn, 1973. bibl., f.

B34. **Lambert, John.** *Travels through Lower Canada and the United States of North America in the years 1806, 1807, and 1808.* London, Richard Phillips, 1810, 3 vol. See Vol. I, Ch. XV, pp. 299-304 and Vol. II, Ch. XXV, pp. 73-74.

B35. Theatre. *Canadian Magazine and Literary Repository.* 1:220-221, September 1823.

B36. On the influence of a well regulated English theatre in Montreal. *Canadian Magazine and Literary Repository.* 1: 221-226, September 1823.

B37. **Bosworth, Newton** ed. *Hochelaga depicta or the early history and present state of the city and island of Montreal.* Montreal, W. Greig, 1839. 284p. (Reprint: Rexdale, Ont., Coles, 1974.)

B38. **Alexander, J.E.** *Burning of the St. Louis theatre, Quebec.* Quebec, 1846. n.p.

B39. **Gaisford, John.** *Theatrical thoughts and conundrums.* Montreal, 1848, n.p.

B40. **Poirier, Pascal.** Papineau: drame historique canadien en quatre actes et neuf tableaux par M. Louis M. Frechette. *Revue Canadienne* xvii:279-287, 356-366, 1881.

B41. **Graham, Franklin Thomas.** *Histrionic Montreal: annals of the Montreal stage together with biographical and critical notices of the plays and players of a century.* n.p. 1897. 179 p. index in MSS.

B42. **Sulte, Benjamin.** The miscellaneous and historical literature of Quebec. *Transactions of Royal Society of Canada* 2. ser., v.3, sect. 2:269-278, 1897. (References to Quesnel and performances in Quebec 1790-92.)

B43. **Massicotte, Edouard Zotique.** Elzéar Roy, directeur des soirées de familles au Monument National. *Le Monde Illustré* 15 ème année, no. 769:611, 28 janvier 1899. port.

B44. **Massicotte, Edouard Zotique.** Les soirées de famille. *Le Monde Illustré* 16 ème année, no. 824:675, 17 février 1900.

B45. **Graham, Franklin Thomas.** *Histrionic Montreal; annals of the Montreal stage with biographical and critical notices of the plays and players of a century 1804-1898* 2. ed. Montreal, Lovell, 1902. 306, viii p. front. illus. (Reprint N.Y., Blom, 1969.)

B46. **Tremblay, Ernest.** Notre théâtre: histoire de sa fondation. *Le Terroir* janvier-septembre 1909:205-214.

B47. **Atherton, William Henry.** *History of Montreal.* Montreal, Clarke, 1914. 3v. (See especially: v.2 Chap. 29. and chapters headed: "Supplemental Annals and Sidelights of Social Progress".)

B48. **Berthelot, Hector.** *Le bon vieux temps;* compilé, revue et annoté par E-Z Massicotte. 2. série. Montréal, Beauchemin, 1916. (Articles from *La Patrie* 1884-5.)

B49. **Massicotte, Edouard Zotique.** Le premier théâtre de Montréal? *Bulletin des Recherches Historiques* 23: 373-376, décembre 1917.

B50. **Massicotte, Edouard Zotique.** Soirée d'amateurs, à Montréal, en 1831. *Bulletin des Recherches Historiques* 24: 134-136, mai 1918.

B51. **Massicotte, Edouard Zotique.** Le théâtre à Montréal en 1787. *Bulletin des Recherches Historiques* 25: 154, mai 1919.

B52. **Massicotte, Edouard Zotique.** Un théâtre à Montréal en 1789. *Bulletin des Recherches Historiques* 23:191-192, juin 1919.

B53. **Massicotte, Edouard Zotique.** Soirée d'amateurs à Montréal en 1816. *Bulletin des Recherches Historiques* 26:256, août 1920.

B54. **Gale, George.** *Historic tales of old Quebec.* Quebec, Telegraph Printing Co., 1920. (Theatres see p. 40, 46, 58-59), (Rev. enl. ed., 1923. See chapter XV: Music and drama in Quebec in the ancient days. p. 256-268.)

B55. **Massicotte, Edouard Zotique.** Recherches historiques sur les spectacles à Montréal de 1760 à 1800. *Transactions of Royal Society of Canada.* 3. ser., v.26, sect. 1:113-122, 1932.

B56. **Roy, Pierre-Georges.** Le Cirque Royal ou Théâtre Royal (Québec). *Bulletin des Recherches Historiques* 42:641-66, novembre 1936.

B57. **Roy, Pierre-Georges.** Le Théâtre Patagon à Québec. *Bulletin des Recherches Historiques* 42:300-303, mai 1936.

B58. **Roy, Pierre-Georges.** Le Théâtre Saint-Louis à Québec. *Bulletin des Recherches Historiques* 42:174-188, mars 1936.

B59. **Roy, Pierre-Georges.** Une tragédie de Voltaire à Québec en 1839. *Bulletin des Recherches Historiques* 42:640, octobre 1936.

B60. **Roy, Pierre-Georges.** Le Théâtre Champlain à Près-de-Ville, rue Champlain, Québec. *Bulletin des Recherches Historiques* 42:705-9, décembre 1936.

B61. Vaudeville de l'Hon. F-G. Marchand. *Bulletin des Recherches Historiques* 42: 488-489, août 1936. (Member of Quebec Parliament. Presented in 1872.)

B62. **Roy, Pierre-Georges.** L'Hôtel Union ou Saint-George à Québec. *Bulletin des Recherches Historiques* 43:3-17, janvier 1937.

B63. **Roy, Pierre-Georges.** Le Théâtre du Marché à Foin à Québec. *Bulletin des Recherches Historiques* 43:33-45, février 1937. 65-70, mars 1937. 97-101, avril 1937.

B64. **Morley, Malcolm.** Theatre Royal, Montreal. *The Dickensian* 45:39-44, winter 1948-9.

B65. **Marion, Séraphin.** Notre première tragédie. In *Origines littéraires du Canada français.* Ottawa, Editions de l'Université, 1951. p. 13-29.

B66. Workers theatre: Quebec in the 1830's. *New Frontiers* 3:27-28, summer 1954.

B67. **Denison, Merrill.** *The barley and the stream: the Molson story.* Toronto, McClelland and Stewart, 1955. xiv, 398 p. (Theatre Royal Montreal p. 149-151.)

B68. **Wyczynski, Paul.** Dans les coulisses du théâtre de Frechette. *Archives des Lettres Canadiennes* 1:230-258, 1961.

B69. **Burger, Baudoin.** *L'activité théâtrale au Québec, 1765-1825.* Montréal, Les Editions Parti Pris, 1974. 410 p. illus.

B70. **Gourlay, Robert.** *A statistical account of Upper Canada.* London, Simpkin and Marshall, 1822. (See Vol 1, Sketch xxxiii, p. 247-250.)

B71. *Descriptive catalogue of the Provincial Exhibition at Toronto, September, 1858.* 2nd. ed. Toronto, 1858. See p. 79. (Description of Apollo Saloon; concert room. Royal Lyceum theatre.)

B72. **MacGeorge, Robert Jackson.** Amateur histrionics. In his *Tales, sketches and lyrics* Toronto, A.H. Amour, 1858. p. 239.

B73. **Scadding, Henry.** *Toronto of old.* Toronto, Adam, Stevenson & Co. 1873. xii, 594p.

B74. The church and theatre. *Belford's Monthly Magazine* 1, no. 2:320-321, January 1877.

B75. **Young, James.** *Reminiscences of the early history of Galt and the settlement of Dumfries.* Toronto, Hunter, Rose and Co., 1880. (See p. 129-131, 191-193. Galt Thespian Amateurs.)

B76. Life at Rideau Hall. *Harper's Magazine* 63:213-223, July, 1881. illus. See p.221.

B77. **Harrington, George M.** Toronto and its early theatrical entertainments. *Canadian Monthly* 8:600-613, June 1882.

B78. **Mulvany, C. Pelham.** *Toronto: past and present until 1882.* Toronto, W.E. Caiger Publishing, 1884, 320 p. (section entitled "Social Life in Toronto", p. 116-127.) Reprint by Ontario Reprint Press, Toronto, 1970.

B79. **Robertson, John Ross.** The theatres of the town; theatrical reminiscences from 1793 to 1893; the plays and players. In his *Landmarks of Toronto; a collection of historical sketches* . . . . Toronto, Robertson, 1894. 1. series, p. 478-491. illus.

B80. **Taylor, Conyngham Crawford.** *Toronto "called back" from 1897 to 1847.* Toronto, William Briggs, 1897. x, 398p.

B81. **Yeigh, Frank.** Drama of Hiawatha or Mana-Bozho. *The Canadian Magazine* 17:207-217, July, 1901, illus.

B82. **Morgan, Henry James.** *Canadian life in town and country.* London, George Newnes, 1905. xii, 266p.

B83. **Colgate, William G.** Toronto theatres in the eighties. *Canadian Magazine* 57: 279-282, August 1921.

B84. **Ham, George H.** *Reminiscences of a raconteur between the '40s and the '20s.* Toronto, Musson Book Co., 1921. xvi, 330 p. (Toronto).

B85. **Middleton, Jesse Edgar.** (Theatre) In his *Municipality of Toronto, a history.* Toronto, Dominion Publishing Co., 1923. v.2, p. 679-681.

B86. **Charlesworth, Hector Willoughby.** *Candid chronicles.* Toronto, Macmillan, 1925. 404 p. (Stars of other times 1880's-1890's).

B87. **Charlesworth, Hector Willoughby.** *More candid chronicles.* Toronto, Macmillan, 1928. xv, 429 p.

B88. **Campbell, Mrs. William.** *Toronto theatres in old days.* York Pioneer and Historical Society - Annual Report for the year 1930. Toronto, 1931. p. 13-15.

B89. **Guillet, Edwin Clarence.** *Early life in Upper Canada.* Toronto, Ontario Publ. Co., 1933. 782 p.

B90. **Guillet, Edwin Clarence.** Theatre. In his *Toronto from trading post to great city.* Toronto, Ontario Publishing Co., 1934. p. 400-414, 420-425, 442-444, 459-464. illus.

B91. **Middleton, Jesse Edgar.** (Theatre) In his *Toronto's 100 years.* Toronto Centennial Committee, 1934. p. 107-109.

B92. **Brault, Lucien.** (Theatres) In his *Ottawa old and new.* Ottawa, Historical Information Institute, 1946. p. 92, 291-292.

B93. **Wingfield, Alexander H.** ed. *The Hamilton Centennial, 1846-1946.* Hamilton, Ont., Hamilton Centennial Committee, 1946. 122 p.

B94. **Masters, Donald Campbell.** *The rise of Toronto 1850-1890.* Toronto, University of Toronto Press, 1947. xi, 239 p.

B95. **Brault, Lucien.** (Theatres) In his *Hull 1800-1950.* Ottawa, Université d'Ottawa, 1950. p. 163-164.

B96. **Klinck, Carl F.** Early theatres in Waterloo County. In Waterloo Historical Society. *Thirty-ninth Annual Report.* May 1951, p. 14-17.

B97. **Tait, Michael.** Playwrights in a vacuum. English Canadian drama in the nineteenth century. *Canadian Literature* no. 16: 3-18, spring 1963.

B98. **Walker, Frank Norman.** *Sketches of Old Toronto.* Toronto, Longmans, 1965. 350 p.

B99. **Glazebrook, George P. de T.** *Life in Ontario; a social history.* Toronto, University of Toronto Press, 1968. 316 p.

B100. **Spurr, John W.** The Kingston garrison, 1815-1870. *Historic Kingston* 20:14-34, February, 1972.

B101. **Tait, Michael.** Playwrights in a vacuum: English Canadian drama in the nineteenth century. In New, William H. ed. *Dramatists in Canada: selected essays.* Vancouver, University of British Columbia Press, 1972. p. 13-26. (Reprinted from: *Canadian Literature* no. 16:3-18, spring 1963.)

B102. **Spurr, John W.** Theatre in Kingston, 1816-1870. *Historic Kingston* 22:37-55, March, 1974.

MANITOBA

B103. **An Old Timer.** *The early playhouses of Winnipeg.* Winnipeg, Feb. 18-19, 1907. (Pamphlet to mark the opening of Walker Theatre, Winnipeg.)

B104. **Craig, Irene.** Grease-paint on the prairies; an account of the theatres, the plays and the players of Winnipeg from 1866-1921. *Historical and Scientific Society of Manitoba. Papers.* 3. ser., no. 3:38-55, 1947.

B105. **Harvey, Ruth Walker.** *Curtain time.* Boston, Houghton Mifflin, 1949. 310 p. (Walker Theatre, Winnipeg.)

THE WEST

B106. **Booth, Michael, R.** Gold Rush theatre: the Theatre Royal Barkerville, British Columbia. *Pacific Northwest Quarterly* 51: 97-102, July 1960.

B107. **Booth, Michael, R.** Pioneer entertainment: theatrical taste in the early Canadian west. *Canadian Literature* no. 4:52-58, spring 1960.

B108. **Booth, Michael R.** Theatrical boom in the Kootenays. *Beaver* 292:42-46, autumn 1961. illus.

B109. **Booth, Michael R.** The beginnings of theatre in British Columbia. *Queen's Quarterly* 68:159-168, spring 1961.

B110. **Ernst, Alice Henson.** *Trouping the Oregon country.* Portland, Oregon Historical Society, 1961. xviii, 197 p. illus. (Late 19th and early 20th centuries - includes accounts of Vancouver and Victoria, B.C.)

B111. **Booth, Michael R.** Gold rush theatres of the Klondike. *Beaver* 292:32-37, spring 1962. illus.

B112. **Barkerville, B.C. Theatre Royal.** *Tintypes from Barkerville B.C.* Quesnel, B.C., Cariboo Observer, 1963. 14 p. illus.

B113. **Ludditt, Fred W.** *Barkerville days.* Vancouver, Mitchell Press, 1969. illus. (See p. 4, 82, 84-7, 155, 174. Cariboo Dramatic Society.)

TOURS AND VISITS

B114. **(Rhys, Charles Horton)** *A theatrical trip for a wager through the United States and Canada* by Morton Price pseud. London, Dudley, 1861. iv, 128 p. (Reprint N.Y., Blom, 1969.)

B115. **Smith, Solomon Franklin.** *Theatrical management in the west and south for thirty years.* N.Y. Harper & Brothers, 1868. (See p. 40-42 Canada.)

B116. **Macready, William Charles.** *Reminiscences and selections from his diaries and letters.* ed. Sir Frederick Pollock. London, Macmillan 1875. 2 v.

B117. **Colombier, Marie.** (Canada) In her *Le voyage de Sarah Bernhardt en Amérique.* Paris, Dreyfous, 1881. p. 165-178.

B118. **Leman, Walter M.** *Memories of an old actor.* San Francisco, Roman & Co., 1886. (p. 167-68 Montreal, p. 373-74 Garrison theatre in Vancouver.)

B119. **Forster, John.** *Life of Charles Dickens.* ed. Gadshill London, Chapman & Hall, 1899. 2 v.

B120. **Macready, William Charles.** *Macready's reminiscences* ed. Sir Frederick Pollock. London, Macmillan, 1906. Vol. XI p. 746.

B121. **Bernhardt, Sarah.** (Canada and America.) In her *Memories of my life; being my personal, professional and social recollections as woman and artist.* New York, Appleton, 1907. p. 402-456.

B122. **Fitzgerald, Shafto Justin Adair.** *Dickens and the Drama.* London, Chapman & Hall, 1910. 352 p. (Reprint: N.Y. Benjamin Blom 1969.)

B123. **Toynbee, William.** *The diaries of William Charles Macready 1833-1851.* London, 1912. Vol. II, p. 272.

B124. **Taverner, Albert.** *The Taverner collection of scrapbooks in the Toronto reference library* by Albert and Ida van Cortland Taverner.

B125. **Van Courtland, Ida.** *Some stage memories.* Address written in 1915 and given to various organizations. Ms. n.d., n.p.

B126. **Webling, Peggy.** *Peggy.* London, Harrap, 1924. 313 p. (Includes account of tours in Canada.)

B127. **Cowan, James A.** Drama according to Marks. *Maclean's Magazine* 39:17-18, 52-58. October 1, 1926.

B128. **(McCrea, Walter Jackson)** *Town hall tonight* by Walter McRaye, pseud. Toronto, Ryerson, 1929. xiv, 256 p. illus.

B129. **Morgan-Powell, Samuel.** *Memories that live.* Toronto, Macmillan, 1929. x, 282 p.

B130. **Hillebrand, Harold Newcomb.** (Montreal and Quebec) In his *Edmund Kean.* N.Y. Columbia University Press, 1933. p. 271-278.

B131. **Martin-Harvey, Sir John.** *The autobiography of Sir John Martin-Harvey.* London, Sampson Low, 1933. xix, 563 p. (Material on his popular tours in Canada.)

B132. **Disher, Maurice Willson** ed. *The Cowells in America: being the diary of Mrs. Sam Cowell, during her husband's concert tour in the years 1860-61.* London, Oxford University Press, 1934. 426 p.

B133. **Hutchison, Percy.** *Masquerade.* London, Harrap, 1936. 286 p. (Includes account of his tours in Canada.)

B134. **Janes, George Nelson.** One night stands. *Saturday Night* 51: 8, January 4, 1936. (Ontario.)

B135. **(McCrea, Walter Jackson)** *Pauline Johnson and her friends* by Walter McRaye, pseud. Toronto, Ryerson (c. 1947). 182 p. illus.

B136. **Ruggles, Eleanor.** *Prince of players: Edwin Booth.* N.Y. Norton, 1953. 401 p. illus. port.

B137. **Walker, Frank Norman.** *Four whistles to wood-up.* Toronto, Upper Canada Railway Society, 1953. 64 p. "Wandering minstrels" p. 35-43.

B138. **Kean, Charles John.** *Emigrant in motley:* the journey of Charles and Ellen Kean in quest of theatrical fortune in Australia and America. London, Rockliff, 1954. xx, 220 p. illus.

B139. **Dunbar, Moira.** The Royal Arctic theatre. *Canadian Art* 15:110-113, spring 1958. illus.

B140. **Marks, Kitty & Croft, Frank.** My life with the original Marks brothers. *Maclean's* 71:16-17, 58-62, June 21, 1958. illus.

B141. **Booth, Michael R.** The actor's eye. Impressions of nineteenth century Canada. *Canadian Literature* no. 13:15-24, summer 1962.

B142. **Booth, Michael R.** Actor in Canada. *A theatrical trip for a wager* in 1859. *Queen's Quarterly* 72:524-532. autumn 1965.

B143. **Trewin, J.C.** ed. *The journal of William Charles Macready 1832-1851.* London, Longman, 1967. 315 p.

B144. **Webster, Margaret.** *The same only different: five generations of a great theatre family.* N.Y. Knopf, 1969. 390 p.

B145. **Power, Tyrone.** *Impressions of America during the years 1833, 1834 and 1835.* N.Y. Blom, 1971 2 v in 1. (Reprint of 1836 ed.)

B146. **Englin, Maureen.** Vaudeville in Canada . . . a veteran's recollections. *Performing Arts* 9: 32-33, winter 1972.

B147. **Isaac, Winifred.** Ben Greet and the Old Vic. London, Published by the author. n.d., p. 95.

An engraving of one of the earliest of the great touring stars, Edmund Kean, dressed in ceremonial costume on the occasion of his investure as an honourary chief of the Huron Indians, October 7, 1826, at his Quebec hotel. (See item B 130).

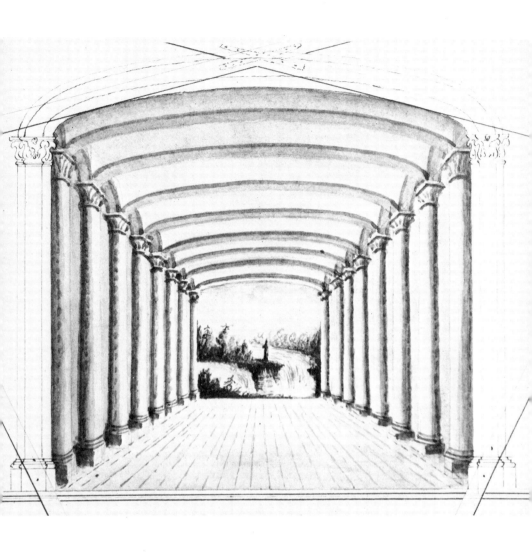

One of a group of pencil and watercolour designs by John Howard of Toronto from the 1850's of a theatre never built. It shows the characteristic deep, narrow stage of the time with a wing and border system and an elaborately painted "view" as scenic background for a play.

The Royal Lyceum

The Royal Lyceum, opened on January 3rd., 1849, was one of Toronto's longest-lived 19th. century theatres. As the following illustrations show, it offers a valuable example of theatrical activity in eastern Canada over the second half of the 19th. century. The floor plan and sketch of the Royal Lyceum interior show a theatre of characteristic structure for its time, and one which corresponds to the following description published prior to its opening: ". . . the interior is fitted up with very great neatness, comprising Stage, Pit, Boxes, and Gallery, and the usual appendages of Dressing Rooms etc. It is arranged to accommodate from 600 to 700 people comfortably, and on extraordinary occasions, from 800 to 900. . . . There are comfortable seatings in the Boxes for upwards of 150 persons, in the Gallery for upwards of 200, and in the Pit for upwards of 300. . . . The Gallery and Boxes . . . in a horseshoe form . . . the ceiling coned and suitably painted and decorated. The stage is very spacious 42 x 32 feet; the front of

ROYAL LYCEUM!
KING STREET WEST

Lessee and Manager, ... Mr. George Holman
Acting Manager, ... Mr. J. R. Spackman
Stage Manager, ... Mr. Geo. H. Barton

POSITIVELY LAST NIGHT BUT ONE
MARIETTA RAVEL!
[L' IMPERATRICE de GRACE.]
"FRENCH SPY."
THURSDAY EVENING, APRIL 4th, 1872,
Positively last time of the military Drama, in 3 Acts, entitled the

FRENCH SPY

Or, the FALL of ALGIERS.

HENRI ST. ALME, \
COL. DESOURCY, \
MATILDE de MIRC. \} . . . . MARIETTA RAVEL \
HAMET,

MOHAMMED, &c. MR. P. SULLIVAN
COL. DESOURCY . . . . MR. E. M. BELLEW
GEN. BEAUMONT . . . . MR. R. J. MASTERS
CAPT. DUBOIS . . . . MR. JOS. BOKER
SERG'T DUBOURG . . . . MR. J. R. SPACKMAN
TONY BAVARD . . . . MR. HARRY LINDLEY

ARABS

ACHMET BEY Dey of Algiers . . . . MR. R. J. MASTERS
MURAD . . . . MR. J. BOKER
GRASSMEN . . . . MR. ALBERT ROBERTS
IBRAHIM . . . . MR. J. EVANS
MAD. DUBOURG . . . . MISS STANLEY
MARIE, her Daughter . . . . MISS FLORENCE WEBSTER

INCIDENTAL TO THE DRAMA,
TERRIFIC SWORD COMBAT,
AND AN EXQUISITE
WILD ARAB DANCE!
THRILLING TABLEAUX, LIFE LIKE BATTLE SCENES, CONCLUDING WITH THE START-
LING DENOUEMENT ENTITLED THE
FALL OF ALGIERS.
To CONCLUDE WITH THE FARCE OF
YOUNG WIDOW

CAPTAIN MANDEVILLE . . . . MR. E. M. BELLEW
SPLASH . . . . MR. HARRY LINDLEY
AURELIA . . . . MISS BLANCHE BRADSHAW
MANDANE . . . . MISS FLORENCE WEBSTER

TO-MORROW, FRIDAY EVENING, APRIL 5th 1872
BENEFIT OF MISS MARIETTA RAVEL
WIZZARD SKIFF.
ALEXIS, \
ACATA, \} . . . . M'LLE MARIETTA RAVEL \
ALERA,

CONCLUDING WITH THE NEW
DUMB BOY OF MANCHESTER.
TOM, ... M'LLE MARIETTA RAVEL

IN PREPARATION THE NEW IRISH SENSATION
"ICHAVOGUE."
MR. DEN THOMPSON APPEARING.

Doors Open at 7.   Curtain Rises at Eight Precisely
Private Boxes $4   Dress Circle 50 cts   Parquette. 25 cts   Family Circle. 25 cts
GOD SAVE THE QUEEN.

THE LEADER STEAM PRINTING HOUSE 52 KING STREET EAST, TORONTO

ROYAL LYCEUM!
KING STREET WEST

Lessee and Manager, ... Mr. George Holman
Acting Manager, ... Mr. J. R. Spackman
Stage Manager, ... Mr. Geo. H. Barton

BENEFIT
AND LAST APPEARANCE BUT ONE, OF THE POPULAR FAVORITE M'LLE
MARIETTA RAVEL!
On which occasion, she will appear in
3 GREAT SPECIALITIES.
FRIDAY EVENING, APRIL the 5th, 1872,
The Musical Sensation, in two Acts, entitled the

WIZZARD SKIFF!
Or, the Massacre of Sico.

ALEXIS, the Dumb Pirate Boy, \
AGATA, the Wild Bohemian, \} . . . . MARIETTA RAVEL \
ALEXA, the Greek Maiden,
CONSTANTINE, ... MR. J. R. SPACKMAN
WO WO, ... MR. P. SULLIVAN
COUNT BRIKINHOFF, ... MR. E. M. BELLEW
PAUL AGNOSTE, ... MR. R. J. MASTERS
WADDLEDORF, ... MR. HARRY LINDLEY
MICHAEL, ... MR. ALBERT ROBERTS
FRITZ, ... MR. JEFFERSON
ANASTASIUS, ... MR. JAMES BOKER
PAULINE, ... MISS BLANCHE BRADSHAW

SYNOPSIS OF SCENERY AND EVENTS.

ACT I.—Scene I.—The Pirates opening chorus, "We have come from the land of the brave, we have stood on the Freeman's Grave." Appearance of the ship of Flame and Coronation with the Comic opera. The determination of the savage. Attempted seduction of Pauline by Brikinhoff, and stolen marriage. Appearance of Agnste. Rescue of Pauline. Grand Bridal Dance. Repulsive appearance of the Burning Skiff. Interruption of Alexis. Encounter with Count Brikinhoff.

DURING THE PIECE, A GRAND
BROAD SWORD COMBAT!
BETWEEN MARIETTA RAVEL AND WOLFO, AND
GREEK BRIDAL DANCE.

To conclude with the celebrated Drama, in two Acts, entitled the
DUMB BOY OF MANCHESTER!
TOM, the Dumb Boy, ... M'LLE MERIETTA RAVEL
Introducing her wonderful Artistic
LIGHTNING MUSKET DRILL,
In which she has no equal.

JANE WILTON . . . . MISS FLORENCE WEBSTER
PATTY . . . . MISS BRADSHAW
MRS. WILTON . . . . MISS BRADSHAW
EDWARD WILTON . . . . MR. P. SULLIVAN
MR. PALMERSTON . . . . MR. E. M. BELLEW
SAM WELTER . . . . MR. HARRY LINDLEY
LORD CHIEF JUSTICE . . . . MR. R. J. MASTERS
JESSE . . . . MR. ALBERT ROBERTS
JAILOR . . . . MR. J. BOKER

TO-MORROW, (SATURDAY), POSITIVELY LAST NIGHT OF
M'LLE MARIETTA RAVEL,
A GREAT BILL.

IN PREPARATION, THE NEW IRISH SENSATION,
"INCHAVOGUE."
MR. DEN THOMPSON APPEARING.

Doors Open at 7.   Curtain Rises at Eight Precisely
SCALE OF PRICES.
Private Boxes, $4 ; Dress Circle, 50 cts Parquette, 25 cts ; Family Circle, 25 cts
GOD SAVE THE QUEEN.

THE LEADER STEAM PRINTING HOUSE, 52 KING STREET EAST, TORONTO

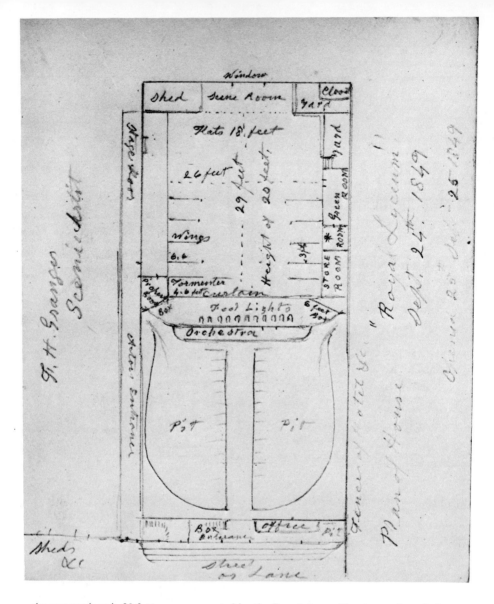

the proscenium is 20 feet . . . surmounted by the Royal Arms. The scenery is entirely new . . . it is lighted with gas." (*British Colonist,* December 29, 1848). The kind of activities which took place within the Royal Lyceum are evident in the two playbills from 1872. Their alluring sketches and promises of excitement in a variety of entertainments, farce, melodrama, spectacle, music, and dance, indicate a theatrical fare with broad popular appeal. Plays for stage Irishmen had a special popularity, and Den Thompson, the stage Irishman on this occasion, was likely the same man who became so famous as author of *The Old Homestead.* The constant day-to-day change of programmes, the practice of touring stars appearing with local resident companies, and "benefit" performances are also evident.

28

THE MILITARY DRAMA AT THE ACADEMY OF MUSIC ON THE EVENING OF FEBRUARY 13.

Military Drama at the Academy of Music

Accounts of the naval spectacles at Sadler's Wells and the equine ones at Astley's in England often inspire awe in a modern reader. But these exotic entertainments were not limited to England. Canada had them too as is shown in this illustration of a "military tableau" at the Academy of Music in Montreal on the visit of the Earl and Countess of Dufferin in 1878. The tableau entitled "the shipping of the troops from Portsmouth to Madras," was an enormous spectacle in which Stevenson's Battery, complete with its horse-drawn field-pieces, such as the one illustrated, the Prince of Wales Regiment, the Royal Fusiliers, and the Montreal Engineers, all with their stores, horses and equipage, were loaded on the steamer evident in the illustration. After all were safely arranged on board, the Earl of Dufferin reviewed the troops. To round out the evening's entertainment in the grandly decorated theatre, Watt Phillip's military drama *Not Guilty* was performed.

Dramatic Representations at St. Mary's College (Montreal)

An illustration of a scene from *Father Isaac Jogues, or the Gospel preached to the Indians* written by the Rev. F. Hamon, S.J., Professor of French Literature and Eloquence at St. Mary's College and performed by students. The play "brings out with remarkable force and fidelity the trials, the sufferings, and the triumphs of the early missionaries among the Indians. The chief characters are: 1st. F. Jogues, type of the Jesuit missionary; 2nd. Oraka, type of the cruel, ferocious Indian, blind enemy of the whites; 3rd. Migisi, a noble warrior representing the chivalrous sentiments of the Indian. . . . In the opening scenes . . . the Missionary is taken prisoner . . . Migisi wishes to save the priest, while Oraka swears to take his life. Migisi finally becomes a Christian and unveils all the intrigues of Oraka . . . who is disarmed and the Missionary seems to be saved; but . . . the priest is basely assassinated by Oraka's accomplice, the juggler. He is brought on stage where he expires. At the moment of his death sounds of angelic music are heard in the distance. In some of the scenes magnificent views are presented, especially the one in which the Missionary is tied to the stake and going to be sacrificed. The stage is filled with warriors and the chorus of little savages sing a canticle of triumph to their God. At the words 'Woe unto him who outrages our God' they stretch forth their hands towards the priest, whilst Oraka brandishes his tomahawk about his head. . . . This is the scene of which an illustration is given."

Canadian Illustrated News, May 28, 1870, p. 469.

The audience in the Peterborough Opera House on Feb. 10, 1908, attending a production of *Why Women Hate* starring May Bell with the Marks Brothers company managed by her husband R.W. Marks. Right, May Bell in *Little Starlight*. See items A22, B127, B140.

C

Twentieth Century
English Canada

GENERAL COMMENT AND SURVEYS AT PARTICULAR PERIODS: THE CULTURAL BACKGROUND.

C1. **Hale, Katherine.** Some prominent players. *Canadian Magazine* 17:35-43, May 1901.

C2. **Sandwell, Bernard Keble.** Hard on judges and audience. *Saturday Night* 67:4, July 5, 1952. (Earl Grey trophy competition 1907-11.)

C3. **Robson, Frederick.** The drama in Canada. *Canadian Magazine* 31:58-61, May 1908.

C4. **Webber, John E.** Plays of the season. *Canadian Magazine* 31: 161-170, 1908.

C5. **(Robson, Frederick).** The romance of the theatre in Canada by Robson Black, pseud. *Canada West Monthly* 6:12-20, May 1909, illus., ports.

C6. **Hardy, Helen Avery.** Successful Canadian players. *Canada West Monthly* 6:169-178, July 1909. ports.

C7. **Hoare, John Edward.** A plea for a Canadian theatre. *University Magazine* 10:239-253, April 1911.

C8. **Sandwell, Bernard Keble.** The annexation of our stage. *Canadian Magazine* 38:22-6, November 1911.

C9. **Webber, John E.** Plays of the season. *Canadian Magazine* 38:277-286, 1911-12.

C10. Canada's theatrical ambitions. *Literary Digest* 45: 622-623, October 12, 1912.

C11. "All-red" theatre. *Literary Digest* 48:493, March 7, 1914.

C12. **Martin-Harvey, Sir John.** Canadian theatres. *University Magazine* 13:212-219, April 1914.

C13. An all English theatre. *Maclean's Magazine* 27:61-62, May 1914.

C14. **Jacob, Fred.** Waiting for a dramatist. *Canadian Magazine* 43:142-146, June 1914.

C15. **Baxter, Arthur Beverly.** Birth of the national theatre. *Maclean's Magazine* 29:27-29, February 1916. illus.

C16. **Farmer, Harcourt.** Play writing in Canada. *Canadian Bookman.* 1:55-56, April 1919.

C17. **Massey, Vincent.** Prospects of a Canadian drama. *Queen's Quarterly* 30:194-212, December 1922.

C18. **Denison, Merrill.** The theatre in Canada. *Canadian Bookman* 5:8, January 1923.

C19. **Logan, John Daniel.** National stage drama. In *Highways of Canadian literature* by John Daniel Logan and Donald G. French. Toronto, McClelland and Stewart, 1924. p. 333-336.

C20. **Stevenson, Lionel.** What about the Canadian drama? In his *Appraisals of Canadian literature.* Toronto, Macmillan, 1926. p. 138-146.

C21. **Lang, Matheson.** Opportunities for a career; Canadian stage progressing. *Canadian Magazine* 67:18, February 1927.

C22. **Morgan-Powell, Samuel.** Stage and film; influence of the United States; school for Canadian actors. *Times (London). Canada Number.* xxii, July 1, 1927.

C23. **Aikins, Carroll.** Canadian plays for Canadian theatres. *Canadian Author and Bookman* 6:30-32, December 1928.

C24. **Voaden, Herman A.** A national drama league. *Canadian Forum* 9:105-106, December 1928.

C25. **Caplan, Rupert.** The ultimate national theatre. *Canadian Forum* 9:143-144, January 1929.

C26. **Denison, Merrill.** Nationalism and drama. In Brooker, Bertram ed. *Yearbook of the arts in Canada 1928-9.* Toronto, Macmillan, 1929. p. 49-55.

C27. **Ayre, Robert.** A national theatre with roots. *Canadian Forum* 10:344-346, June 1930.

C28. **Christie, H.G.F.** A plan for a national theatre. *Canadian Forum* 11:77-78, November 1930.

C29. Our national arts show definite progress. *Curtain Call* 1: 1-2, March 8, 1930.

C30. **Smith, Hilda M.** National drama in Canada. *Canadian Forum* 10:225-226, March 1930.

C31. **Lawton, Roger.** Theatrical situation in Canada. *Saturday Night* 47:3, May 26, 1931.

C32. **Barnard, L.O.** Distinctively Canadian. *Authors' Bulletin.* September 1932. p. 33-37.

C33. **Smith, E. Cecil.** The worker's theatre. *Canadian Forum* 14:39, October 1933.

C34. **Smith, E. Cecil.** The worker's theatre in Canada. *Canadian Forum* 14:68-70, November 1933.

C35. **Christie, H.G.F.** A national theatre? *Maclean's Magazine* 47:46, 49, March 15, 1934.

C36. **Clark, Barrett H.** When is the drama national? *Curtain Call* 6:1-2, December 15, 1934.

C37. **Betts, St. John.** The Canadian heritage. *Curtain Call* 6: 4-5, May 1935.

C38. Canadian playwrights series inaugurated. *Curtain Call* 6: 19, April 1935. (Samuel French Canada Ltd.)

C39. **Morley, Malcolm.** Drama in Canada. *Saturday Night* 50: 12, July 20, 1935.

C40. **Osborne, Rosalynde.** Enter Canadian puppets. *Curtain Call* 6: 8, June 1935.

C41. Canadian national theatre: symposium of views on the form which it shall take. *Curtain Call* 7: 1-2, back cover, June 1936.

C42. **Granville-Barker, Harley.** The Canadian theatre. *Queen's Quarterly* 43:256-267, autumn 1936.

C43. **Morley, Malcolm.** Rise of native drama. *Saturday Night* 51:12, January 4, 1936.

C44. **Sandwell, Bernard Keble.** Better Canadian plays. In Brooker, Bertram ed. *Yearbook of the arts in Canada 1936.* Toronto, Macmillan, 1936. p. 218-221.

C45. **Charlesworth, Hector Willoughby.** *I'm telling you.* Toronto, Macmillan, 1937. xv, 334 p.

C46. **Clark, Barrett H.** As I see the Canadian theatre. *Curtain Call* 9:4-5, April 1938.

C47. **Clark, Barrett H.** Canadian drama. *Saturday Night* 53:6, June 11, 1938.

C48. **Coxwell, Mona.** Resetting the stage. *Saturday Night* 53: 11, April 9, 1938.

C49. **Coulter, John.** The Canadian theatre and the Irish exemplar. *Theatre Arts Monthly* 22:503-509, July 1938.

C50. **McKenzie, Ruth.** Proletarian literature in Canada. *Dalhousie Review* 19: 49-64, 1939.

C51. **Phelps, Arthur L.** Drama. In *Canadian literature today. Canadian Broadcasting Corporation, publications no. 6.* Toronto, University of Toronto Press, 1938. p. 17-23.

C52. **Buchanan, Donald W.** Drama and films. In *Times* (London). Reprinted from the Canada number of the *Times* published on May 15, 1939. London, *Times*, 1939. p. 245-247.

C53. **Phelps, Arthur L.** Canadian drama. *University of Toronto Quarterly* 9:82-94, October 1939.

C54. **Phelps, Arthur L.** Drama in Canada — the audience. *Curtain Call* 11:5-6, September/October 1939.

C55. **Phelps, Arthur L.** Drama in Canada — the stuff for the drama. *Curtain Call* 11:7-8, November 1939.

C56. **Phelps, Arthur L.** Drama in Canada — play making. *Curtain Call* 11:17-18, December 1939.

C57. **Campbell, Loughlin.** War and the theatre. *Curtain Call.* 11:9-10, March 1940.

C58. **Phelps, Arthur L.** Festivals and the national theatre. *Curtain Call.* 11:11-12, May/June 1940.

C59. **Coxwell, Mona.** What the publisher requires of the playwright. *Canadian Author and Bookman* 17:6-7, February 1941.

C60. **Dunn, Murison.** Today and tomorrow in drama. *Canadian Author and Bookman* 17:8-9, February 1941.

C61. **Coulter, John.** Why sabotage the theatre? *Canadian Review of Music and Art* 1:5-6, 18, May 1942.

C62. **Firkins, Yvonne.** Towards a Canadian theatre. *Canadian Author and Bookman* 18:8, December 1942.

C63. **Farquharson, Rica McLean.** Wartime drama in the British Empire: Canada. In *Theatre Annual* (N.Y.) p. 11-18, 1944.

C64. **Watson, Freda.** Reconstruction and the arts; can we have a national theatre? *Saturday Night* 60:38-40, November 25, 1944.

C65. **Charlesworth, Hector.** Horse and buggy theatre. *Civic Theatre Magazine* 1:12-14, October 1945.

C66. **Coulter, John.** Towards a Canadian theatre. *Canadian Review of Music and Art* 4:17, 20, August 1945.

C67. **Rowe-Sleeman, Alice.** National theatre for Canada. *Canadians All* 3:24, 72-73, 77, autumn, 1945.

C68. **Voaden, Herman A.** Theatre record 1945. *Canadian Forum* 25:184-187, November 1945.

C69. Canadian supplement. *Theatre Arts* 30:421-422, July 1946.

C70. **Dickson-Kenwin, G.** The Canadian theatre; the need for training, discipline, and purpose. *Canadian Review of Music and Art* 5:20, 30, October/November 1946.

C71. **Marsh, D.G.** Professional theatre reviving this year. *Saturday Night* 62:24-25, October 26, 1946.

C72. **Voaden, Herman.** The theatre in Canada; a national theatre? *Theatre Arts* 30:389-391, July 1946.

C73. **Angus, William.** Make national theatre fulfil all needs. *Saturday Night* 63:16, November 15, 1947.

C74. **Broderson, George.** Towards a Canadian theatre. *Manitoba Arts Review* 5:18-23, spring 1947.

C75. **Coulter, John.** Some festival visions of a national theatre. *Saturday Night* 62:20-21, May 17, 1947.

C76. **Johnstone, Kenneth.** The season in Canada: Eastern. *Theatre Arts* 31:71-73, July 1947.

C77. **Jones, Emrys Maldwyn.** The season in Canada — Western. *Theatre Arts* 31:73-74, July 1947.

C78. **Tovell, Vincent.** Theatre in Canada. *Here and Now* 1:80-81, December 1947.

C79. **Alford, Walter.** When Canada has theatres, plays will soon follow. *Saturday Night* 64:18-19, October 16, 1948 illus.

C80. **Morley, Malcolm.** Amateurs and actors. *Saturday Night* 64:32-33, October 9, 1948.

C81. **Newton, Norman.** Some dramatic suggestions. *Canadian Forum* 28:110-111, August 1948.

C82. **Novek, Ralph.** Radio drama in Canada. *Northern Review* 2:29-33, July - August 1948.

C83. **Tovell, Vincent.** Native theatre. *Here and Now* 2:81-84, May 1948.

C84. **Galloway, Myron.** Scene: Canada-time: present. *Northern Review* 3:35-37, October/November 1949.

C85. **Galloway, Myron.** The Canadian play and playwright. *Northern Review* 3:38-40, December/January 1949-50.

C86. **King, J. Clifford.** Dominion theatres — Canada. In Campbell, Andrew, ed.

International theatre, ed. by John Andrew, pseud, and Ossia Trilling. London, Sampson Low, 1949. p. 132-133.

C87. **Moore, James Mavor.** Theatre in Canada. *Canadian Life* 1:17, 32, March/April 1949.

C88. **Allen, Ted.** Profile of a bilingual culture. *United Nations World* 4:56-58, July 1950.

C89. **Coburn, John.** *I kept my powder dry.* Toronto, Ryerson, 1950. 185 p. illus.

C90. **Galloway, Myron.** Robert Speaight on Canadian theatre. *Northern Review* 3:48-50, February/March 1950.

C91. **Moore, James Mavor.** The Canadian theatre. *Canadian Forum* 30:108-110, August 1950.

C92. **Skinner, Alan.** Drama. *Food for Thought* 10:25-28, May 1950.

C93. **Coulter, John.** More than a pat on the head. *Saturday Night* 66:12, 28, September 4, 1951. (Estimate of Massey Report.)

C94. **Davies, Robertson.** The theatre: a dialogue on the state of the theatre in Canada. *Royal Commission studies.* Ottawa, King's Printer, 1951. p. 369-392.

C95. Theatre in Canada. Royal Commission on National Development in the Arts, Letters and Sciences 1949-1951. *Report.* Ottawa, King's Printer, 1951. p. 192-200. (Massey Report.)

C96. **Boux, René.** A note on theatre and the Massey Report. *P M Magazine* 1:48-50, December/January 1951-52.

C97. **Whittaker, Herbert.** Our theatre; a youthful bloom. *Saturday Night* 66:8, January 30, 1951. illus.

C98. **Angus, William.** The theatre at Athens — Ontario. *Food for Thought* 12:20-23, April 1952.

C99. **Bennett, Ernest Sterndale.** Canadian theatre. *Canadian Life* 2:11, May/June 1952.

C100. **Ness, Margaret.** Setting the stage. *Saturday Night* 67:14, November 22, 1952.

C101. **Ness, Margaret.** Summer theatre; bumper straw hat crop. *Saturday Night* 67:13, 36, August 16, 1952. illus.

C102. **Pacey, Desmond.** (Drama) In his *Creative writing in Canada.* Toronto, Ryerson, (1952). p. 194-195.

C103. **Whittaker, Herbert.** Canada wants its own theatre. *Theatre Arts* 36:43, 95, August 1952. illus.

C104. **Guthrie, Tyrone.** The development of live drama in Canada. *Saturday Night* 68:7-8, June 6, 1953. illus.

C105. **Whittaker, Herbert.** Canada on stage. *Queen's Quarterly* 60:495-500, winter 1953.

C106. **Arnold, Frank.** Of books, plays and padlocks. *New Frontiers* 4:12, summer 1955.

C107. **Gard, Robert Edward.** Frontier in Canada. In his *Grassroots theatre; a search* *for regional arts in America*. Madison, University of Wisconsin Press, 1955. p. 46-71.

C108. Theatre-going in Canada: a new prospect. *Times* (London) 16, April 27, 1955.

C109. **Beaulne, Guy.** World reviews: Canada. *World Theatre* 5:244-247, summer 1956.

C110. **Cohen, Nathan.** Summer theatre troubles. *Saturday Night* 71:15-16, July 21, 1956 illus.

C111. **Moore, James Mavor.** A theatre for Canada. *University of Toronto Quarterly* 26:1-16, October 1956.

C112. **Speaight, Robert.** The theatre and ballet in Canada. Royal Society of Arts. *Journal*. 104:940-950, October 26, 1956.

C113. **Williams, Norman.** Prospects for the Canadian dramatist. *University of Toronto Quarterly*. 26:273-283, April 1956.

C114. **Birney, Earle.** North American drama today; a popular art? *Transactions of the Royal Society of Canada* 3 ser., v.51, sect. 2:31-42, 1957.

C115. **Cohen, Nathan.** Television and the Canadian theatre; another treadmill to futility. *Queen's Quarterly* 64:1-11, spring 1957.

C116. **Whittaker, Herbert.** The theatre. In Park, Julian ed. *Culture in contemporary Canada*. Ithaca, Cornell University Press, 1957. p. 163-180.

C117. **Moore, James Mavor.** The theatre in English speaking Canada. In Ross, Malcolm, ed. *The arts in Canada; a stocktaking at mid-century*. Toronto, Macmillan, 1958. p. 77-82. illus.

C118. Reviving a theatrical life destroyed by the films: the task before the Canada Council. *Times* (London) January 15, 1958. p. 3.

C119. **Allen, John.** Dominion drama. *Drama* 52:32-35, spring 1959.

C120. **Cohen, Nathan.** Theatre today; English Canada. *Tamarack Review* 13:24-37, autumn 1959.

C121. **Fulford, Robert.** The yearning for professionalism. *Tamarack Review* 13:80-85, autumn 1959.

C122. **Gardner, David.** Canada's theatre; climbing in second gear. *Saturday Night* 74:12-13, 40, May 9, 1959. illus.

C123. **Michener, Wendy.** Popular theatre. *Canadian Forum* 39:146-147, October 1959.

C124. **Michener, Wendy.** Towards a popular theatre. *Tamarack Review* 13:63-79, autumn 1959.

C125. **Moore, James Mavor.** Theatre, some backsliding. *Saturday Night* 74:32-33, August 29, 1959.

C126. *New approach to the problem of theatre art in Canada*. Toronto, Theatre centre, (1959?) 21 p. (mimeographed).

C127. **Tovell, Vincent.** A conversation (on Canadian theatre) by Vincent Tovell and George McGowan. *Tamarack Review* 13:5-23, autumn 1959.

C128. **Whittaker, Herbert.** The audience is there. *Saturday Review* 42:25, October 24, 1959.

C129. **Beaulne, Guy.** World reviews: Canada. *World Theatre.* 8:240-243, autumn 1959.

C130. **Robertson, George.** Drama on the air. *Canadian Literature.* no. 2:59-65, autumn 1959.

C131. **Beckwith, John.** The performing arts. In John T. Saywell ed. *Canadian Annual Review for 1960* Toronto, University of Toronto Press, 1961. p. 328-336.

C132. **Croft, Frank.** When show business was all talk. *Maclean's Magazine.* 73:30-31, 45-47, May 21, 1960. illus.

C133. **Stratford, Philip.** Theatre criticism today. *Canadian Forum.* 39:258-259, February 1960.

C134. **Beaulne, Guy.** World reviews: Canada. *World Theatre.* 10:62-65, spring 1961. illus.

C135. **Evans, J.A.S.** Creative theatre in Canada. *Canadian Commentator.* 5:23, July-August 1961.

C136. **Evans, J.A.S.** Current Canadian theatre. *Canadian Commentator.* 5:20-22, May 1961.

C137. **Evans, J.A.S.** The pocket theatre. *Canadian Commentator.* 5:18-19, February 1961.

C138. **Gardner, David.** Drama: English Canada. In John T. Saywell ed. *The Canadian Annual Review for 1961.* Toronto, University of Toronto Press, 1962. p. 371-386.

C139. **Ross, Mary Lowrey.** Pulling the right strings. *Saturday Night.* 76:32, September 30, 1961.

C140. **Saint-Denis, Michel J.** Drama in Canada. *Canadian Commentator. 5:23-26, June 1961.*

C141. **Shorey, Kenneth.** Canada isn't ready for a National Theatre. *Saturday Night.* 76:36, February 4, 1961.

C142. **Beaulne, Guy.** World reviews: Canada. *World Theatre* 11:370-375, winter 1962-3. illus.

C143. **Friedson, Anthony.** The undemanding audience. *Arts Council News* (Vancouver) 13, no. 8:1-2, May 1962.

C144. **Gardner, David.** Drama: English Canada. In John T. Saywell ed. *The Canadian Annual Review for 1962.* Toronto, University of Toronto Press, 1963. p. 378-390.

C145. **Russel, Robert.** Towards a national theatre. *Canadian Art.* 19:156-157, March-April 1962.

C146. The season's theatre: a report by Robert Russel, Ralph Hicklin, Donald Stainsby and Chester Duncan. *Saturday Night* 77:25-29, June 9, 1962.

C147. **Solly, William.** Nothing sacred: humour in Canadian drama in English. *Canadian Literature.* no. 11:14-27, winter 1962.

C148. Theatre. *Arts Council News* (Vancouver) 14, no. 2:1-3, November 1962.

C149. **Weaver, Robert L.** The role of the Canada Council. *Tamarack Review.* no. 25:76-82, autumn 1962.

C150. **Bruce, Harry.** Theatre: the national movement: talks in Gaspé: ambitions out west, action in Halifax. *Maclean's Magazine* 76:70, September 7, 1963.

C151. **Bryant, Christoper.** Theatre. *Canadian Art* 20:302-303, September-October 1963.

C152. **Cowan, James.** Off stage: on theatre in Canada. *On Stage* 2, no. 1:10, 13. summer 1963.

C153. **Dominion Consultants Associates Ltd.** *A National centre for the performing arts.* A study prepared for the National Capital Arts Alliance. Ottawa, 1963. vii, 105 p. tables, maps, bibl.

C154. **Robertson, Heather.** Culture in Canada. *Manitoba Arts Review* 15:12-15, spring 1963.

C155. **Gardner, David.** Drama: English Canada. In John T. Saywell ed. *The Canadian Annual Review for 1963.* Toronto, University of Toronto Press, 1964. p. 466-482.

C156. **Cohen, Nathan.** In view (regional theatre in Canada). *Saturday Night.* 79:7-8, April 1964.

C157. **Flannery, James.** A lively look at the lively arts in a lively university. *Performing Arts* 3. no. 1:30-32, fall 1964.

C158. **Canadian Conference of the Arts.** *Seminar report 1965.* Toronto, 1965. 36 p. and appendices.

C159. **Rump, Eric S.** Drama: English Canada. In John T. Saywell ed. *Canadian Annual Review for 1964.* Toronto, University of Toronto Press, 1965. p. 453-462.

C160. **Sweeting, Dennis.** Let's stop building theatres that we can't fill. *Maclean's Magazine* 77:56, October 3, 1964.

C161. **Comor, Henry.** Artist's agreement. *Montrealer.* 39:9, August 1965.

C162. **Evans, Ron.** Children's theatre: the empire of dreams. *Performing Arts* 4. no. 2:5-8, winter 1965-6. illus.

C163. **Geller, Vincent.** Yiddish drama (Toronto) in the 30's. In *Candid Canadiana,* Toronto, Morris Graphics Ltd., 1965, p. 36-42.

C164. **Hendry, Thomas B.** Trends in Canadian theatre. *Tulane Drama Review.* 10:62-70, fall 1965. illus.

C165. **Rump, Eric S.** Drama: English Canada. In John T. Saywell ed. *Canadian Annual Review for 1965.* Toronto, University of Toronto Press, 1966. p. 495-502.

C166. *Theatre Yearbook, Un An de Théâtre 1965/6.* Special issue of *The Stage in Canada.* Toronto, Canadian Theatre Centre, 1966. 128 p. illus.

C167. **Whittaker, Herbert.** Stage designer, the theatre's step-child. *Canadian Art.* 22:41-47, May - June 1965. illus.

C168. **Chusid, Harvey.** University theatres in Canada, their influence on future audiences. *Performing Arts* 4 no. 4:22-26, 1966. illus.

C169. **Parker, Gordon.** Theatre and the churches. *Continuous Learning.* 5: xlv - xlvii, March-April 1966.

C170. **Newton, Christopher.** Theatre: the verminous critics criticized. *Saturday Night* 81:54-55, December 1966.

C171. **Rump, Eric S.** Drama: English Canada. In John T. Saywell ed. *Canadian Annual Review for 1966.* Toronto, University of Toronto Press, 1967. p. 438-446.

C172. **Canadian Conference of the Arts.** *Seminar report 1967.* Toronto, 1967. 29 p. and appendices.

C173. **Hendry, Thomas B.** Theatre in Canada. *World Theatre* 16. no. 5-6:412-431, 1967. illus.

C174. **Hendry, Thomas B.** Trends in Canadian theatre. *Tulane Drama Review.* 11:60-65, spring 1967.

C175. **Rump, Eric S.** Drama: English Canada. In John T. Saywell ed. *Canadian Annual Review for 1967.* Toronto, University of Toronto Press, 1968. p. 451-456.

C176. **Bhaneja, B.K.** Theatre in Canada: a perspective. *Performing Arts.* 6 no. 1:46-48, 1968.

C177. **Canadian Conference of the Arts.** *A crisis in the arts.* A brief to the government of Canada. Toronto, Ontario 1968.

C178 **Cappon, Daniel.** Who attends the theatre? *Performing Arts.* 5 no. 3-4:62-64, 1968.

C179. **Edinborough, Arnold.** Theatre, it seems, is alive and well in the west. *Saturday Night* 83:7, 9, December 1968.

C180. **Hunter, Martin.** The roar of the greasepaint — the clash of the cash! *Canadian Banker* 75:24-27. September-October 1968. illus.

C181. **Love, Francis H.** The theatre of revolt. *Stage in Canada* 4, no. 7:6-10, 1968.

C182. **Rump, Eric S.** Drama: English Canada. In John T. Saywell ed. *Canadian Annual Review for 1968.* Toronto, University of Toronto Press, 1969. p. 444-452.

C183. **Calgary Conference on the Visual Arts, 1969.** *The artists - a new power.* Proceedings and recommendations of the Calgary Conference on the visual arts, 1969. Montreal, Canadian Conference of the Arts, 1969. 37, 41 p.

C184. **Moore, James Mavor.** Lively arts. *Maclean's Magazine* 82:116, May 1969.

C185. **Moore, James Mavor.** Lively arts: don't talk of art. If you can act, show me. *Maclean's Magazine* 82:88, December 1969.

C186. **Rump, Eric S.** Drama: English Canada. In John T. Saywell ed. *Canadian Annual Review for 1969.* Toronto, University of Toronto Press, 1970. p. 427-434.

C187. **Twentieth Century Fund.** Task Force on Performing Arts Centres. *Bricks, mortar and the performing arts.* N.Y., 1970. ix, 99 p.

C188. **Association of Canadian Television and Radio Artists.** *Brief to the Advisory Arts Panel and the Canada Council from the Playwrights Circle and the Playwrights committee of ACTRA.* November 1971. 39 p.

C189. **Bladen, Vincent.** *The financing of the performing arts in Canada: an essay in persuasion.* Toronto, Massey College, 1971. 40 p.

C190. **Canadian Theatre Centre.** *Report on a playwright's conference, Niagara-on-the-Lake, August 14, 15, 1971.* Toronto, Canadian Theatre Centre, 1971. n.p.

C191. **Canadian Theatre Centre.** *A strange enterprise — the dilemma of the playwright in Canada:* conclusion and recommendations of a seminar sponsored by the Canada Council at Stanley House, July 19-23, 1971. n.p.

C192. **Canadian Theatre Centre.** *A suggested statement of policy for the Canadian Theatre Centre.* Toronto, July 26, 1971. 21 p.

C193. **Gustafson, David.** Theatre: let's really hear it for Canadian theatre. *Maclean's Magazine.* 84:84, October 1971.

C194. **Gwyn, Sandra.** *Women in the arts in Canada.* Ottawa, Information Centre, 1971. 98 p. (p. 29-40 Women in Canadian theatre).

C195. **Micheli, Carla.** Theatre on campus. Big production or economy style? *Canadian University and College* 6 no. 3:25-27, 30, May/June 1971. illus.

C196. **Peacock, Gordon.** A Plethora of playwrights. *White Pelican* 1:62, winter 1971.

C197. **Watson, Wilfred.** Towards a Canadian theatre. *White Pelican* 1:55-59, winter 1971.

C198. **Champagne, Jane.** Role of music for the theatre. *Canadian Composer* 75:16-23, December 1972. illus.

C199. **Courtney, Richard.** The Canadian child and youth drama association. In Crampton, Esmé ed. *Drama Canada.* Toronto, College of Education Guidance Centre, 1972. p. 13-14.

C200. **Courtney, Richard.** Creativity and theatre for children. *Stage in Canada* 7, no. 2:6-15, 1972.

C201. **Denison, Merrill.** Nationalism and drama. In New, William H. *Dramatists in Canada: selected essays.* Vancouver, University of British Columbia Press, 1972. p. 65-69. (Reprinted from: *Yearbook of the Arts in Canada, 1928-29.*)

C202. **Fulford, Robert.** Reporting back: news of current explorers. *Saturday Night* 87:4, July 1972.

C203. **Gibson, J.** Coming out from under: the new Canadian theatre. *Maclean's* 85:104, November 1972.

C204. **Gray, Jack.** The theatre in Canada. *American Review of Canadian Studies — ACSUS Newsletter* 2:79-84, autumn 1972.

C205. **Hendry, Thomas B.** Theatre in Canada: a reluctant citizen. *American Review of Canadian Studies — ACSUS Newsletter* 2:85-99, autumn 1972.

C206. **Hendry, Thomas B.** Canadian theatre's sudden explosion. *Saturday Night* 87:23-28, January 1972. illus.

C207. **McKay, B.** Theatre for young audiences in Canada. *Stage in Canada* 7 no. 2:20-28, 1972.

C208. **Moore, James Mavor.** The decline of words in drama. In New, William H. ed.

Dramatists in Canada: selected essays. Vancouver, University of British Columbia Press, 1972. p. 97-104 (Reprinted from *Canadian Literature* no. 46. 11-18, autumn, 1970).

C209. **New, William H.** ed. *Dramatists in Canada: selected essays.* Vancouver, University of British Columbia Press, 1972. vii, 204 p.

C210. **Posner, Michael.** Performing arts: a cornerstone of our culture. *Canada and the World* 38:23, December 1972. illus.

C211. **Solly, William.** Nothing sacred: humour in Canadian drama in English. In New, William H. ed. *Dramatists in Canada: selected essays.* Vancouver, University of British Columbia Press, 1972. p. 39-52. (Reprinted from: *Canadian Literature* no. 11:14-27, winter 1962).

C212. **Watson, Wilfred.** The Canadian fact. *White Pelican* 2 no. 1:53-63, 1972.

C213. **Watson, Wilfred.** On radical absurdity. In New, William H. ed. *Dramatists in Canada: selected essays.* Vancouver, University of British Columbia Press, 1972. p. 79-87. (Reprinted from *Canadian Literature* no. 30:36-48, autumn 1966.)

C214 **Woodcock, George.** On the resources of Canadian writing. In Ontario. Royal Commission on Book Publishing. *Background Papers.* Toronto, Queen's Printer and Publisher, 1972. p. 61-85.

C215. **Bladen, Vincent W.** and **Campbell, D.E.** The economics of the performing arts. In *Canadian perspectives in economics.* Toronto, Collier-MacMillan, 1973. Vol. 2, ch. f 11. (8 p.)

C216. **Canadian Conference of the Arts.** *Direction Canada: A declaration of Canadian cultural concern.* Toronto, Canadian Conference of the Arts, 1973. 78 p.

C217. **Canadian Conference of the Arts.** *Direction Canada: supplement containing Direction Atlantic; Direction Ontario; Canada West; Les Rencontres du Québec.* Toronto, Canadian Conference of the Arts, 1973. 360 p.

C218. **Crean, Susan M.** *Who's afraid of Canadian culture:* report of a study of the diffusion of the performing and exhibiting arts in Canada. Toronto, York University, 1973. 98 p. illus.

C219. **Duran, Gillian.** In search of English-Canadian theatre. *Literature and Ideology* 16:19-28, 1973.

C220. **Edinborough, Arnold.** More for the arts: it makes hard-headed sense for business. *Financial Post* 67:11, January 20, 1973. port.

C221. **Edinborough, Arnold.** Why do we run big-business arts as a corner-store project? *Financial Post* 67:27, May 5, 1973. port.

C222. **Frazer, Robbin.** Arts lobby meets officials. (Direction '73) *Performing Arts* 10:29, summer 1973.

C223. **Frazer, Robbin.** Sixty years of memories: the Ottawa little theatre. *Performing Arts* 10:25, summer 1973, port.

C224. **Hendry, Thomas B.** The Canadian conference of the arts: defection '73. *Canadian Forum* 53:2-5, 14, May, 1973.

C225. **Hendry, Thomas B.** Cultural policy. *Canadian Forum* 53:4-5, February, 1973.

C226. **Kossar, L.** Multiculturalism and the arts. *Performing Arts* 10:33-4, 51, winter 1973.

C227. **Mandell, Bernard.** Will an arts lobby work in Canada? *Performing Arts* 10:17-18, spring 1973. illus.

C228. More experimental theatre. *Performing Arts* 10:8, winter 1973.

C229. **New, William H.** Introduction: Canada: annual bibliography of Commonwealth literature. *Journal of Commonwealth Literature* 8:59-64, December, 1973.

C230. **Orr, Carole.** Establishment is a mangy word. *The Last Post* 3:42-43, March 1973.

C231. **Pasquill, Frank T.** *Subsidy patterns for the performing arts in Canada.* Ottawa, Canada Council Information Services, February 1973. 128 p., tables.

C232. **Saddlemyer, Ann.** Serious dramatic criticism needed. *Quill and Quire* 39:2-3, June 1973. illus.

C233. Unions: angels or devils? *Performing Arts* 10:12-13, spring 1973.

C234. Business forms a council to help the arts in Canada. *Financial Post* 68:2, June 22, 1974.

C235. Canadian professional theatres: a checklist. *Canadian Theatre Review* CTR 1:138-144, winter, 1974.

C236. Canadian theatres for the young: a checklist. *Canadian Theatre Review* CTR 2:138-139, spring, 1974.

C237. **Edinborough, Arnold.** Business musters to assist the needy arts. *Financial Post* 68:5, June 1, 1974. illus.

C238. **Edinborough, Arnold.** Good is okay — but the best is what we now want in the arts. *Financial Post* 68:16, March, 1974. port.

C239. **Edinborough, Arnold.** Here's an innovative shot-in-the-arm that's helping our theatre. *Financial Post* 68:13, January 26, 1974. Reprinted as "How the Chalmer's foundation makes a little go a long way", *Performing Arts* 11:11-13, spring, 1974. illus.

C240. **Edinborough, Arnold.** Money worries still plague it — but art scene looks bright. *Financial Post* 68:9, January 5, 1974. port.

C241. **Edinborough, Arnold.** White-faces the new white hope for young actors and young audiences? (Benson and Hedges Street Theatre). *Performing Arts* 11:48-9, fall, 1974. illus.

C242. **Faulkner, Hugh.** The Liberal Program. *Canadian Theatre Review* CTR 3:31-33, summer 1974.

C243. **Faulkner, Hugh.** View from the top. *Canadian Theatre Review* CTR 3:17-28, summer 1974.

C244. Grants by du Maurier council. *Performing Arts* 11:12, winter 1974.

C245. **Hay, Peter.** Cultural politics. *Canadian Theatre Reivew* CTR 2:7-15, spring 1974.

C246. **Hay, Peter.** Cultural politics: a provincial approach. *Canadian Theatre Review* CTR 3:11-16, summer 1974.

C247. **Hay, Peter.** Standing room only on the prairie circuit. *Maclean's* 87:94, April, 1974. port.

C248. **Hendry, Thomas B.** The Masseys and the masses. *Canadian Theatre Review* CTR 3:6-10, summer 1974.

C249. **Lane, William.** The collective writer. *Motion* 3:18-19, November-December, 1974.

C250. **Leggatt, Alexander.** Drama (Letters in Canada: 1973) *University of Toronto Quarterly.* 43:371-377, summer, 1974.

C251. **Mullaly, Edward J.** Canadian drama: Canadian theatre review. *Fiddlehead* 101:74-5, spring 1974.

C252. One-third income from commercials. *Marketing* 79:16, August 19, 1974.

C253. **Pasquill, Frank T.** Cultural senility: funding patterns. *Canadian Theatre Review* CTR 2:16-23, spring 1974.

C254. Puppets on tour. *Performing Arts* 11:9, spring, 1974. illus.

C255. **Rubin, Don.** Aside: changing times. *Canadian Theatre Review* CTR 3:4-5, summer 1974.

C256. **Rubin, Don.** Aside: creating the impossible. *Canadian Theatre Review* CTR 2:4-6, spring 1974.

C257. **Rubin, Don.** Aside: the regional system. *Canadian Theatre Review* CTR 4:4-5, fall 1974.

C258. **Rubin, Don.** *Creeping toward a culture: the theatre in Canada since 1945.* Guelph, Alive Press, 1974. 30 p. Previously published in *York Theatre Journal,* fall 1972; *Alive Magazine,* no. 29, June 1973; *Canadian Theatre Review,* winter 1974.

C259. **Rubin, Don, Mezei, Stephen and Stuart, Euan Ross.** Aside: an editorial viewpoint. *Canadian Theatre Review.* CTR 1:4-5, winter 1974.

C260. **Ryga, George.** Theatre in Canada: a viewpoint on its development and future. *Canadian Theatre Review.* CTR 1:28, winter 1974.

C261. **Treacher, G.J.P.** Theatre Canada festival. *Atlantic Advocate* 64:36-9, August 1974. illus.

C262. **Wylie, Betty Jane.** Don't let the audience cough. *Motion* 2:14-15, July-August, 1974. illus.

C263. **Zaharia, Andrei.** In comparison: a European trained director looks at the Canadian actor. *Motion* 2:21, July-August, 1974.

C264. **Cameron, Duncan.** ed. *The arts in Canada 1975: viewpoint/Les arts au Canada en 1975-aperçus.* Ottawa, Canada Council, 1975. 41 p.

C265. **Canadian Conference of the Arts.** *The arts and education* (prepared by Joan Horsman) Toronto, Canadian Conference of the Arts, 1975. 16 p.

C266. **Canadian Conference of the Arts.** *The arts and the media.* (prepared by Joan Horsman) Toronto, Canadian Conference of the Arts, 1975. 16 p.

C267. **Canadian Conference of the Arts.** *The arts and the municipalities.* (prepared by Joan Horsman and Paul Schafer) Toronto, Canadian Conference of the Arts, 1975. 27 p.

C268. **Davies, Robertson.** A dialogue on the state of theatre in Canada. *Canadian Theatre Review* CTR 5:16-36, winter, 1975. Originally printed in *A Selection of Essays Prepared for the Royal Commission on National Development in the Arts, Letters and Sciences.* Ottawa, 1951.

C269. duMaurier awards theatres across Canada. *Performing Arts* 12:7-8, spring 1975.

C270. **Leggatt, Alexander.** Drama (Letters in Canada: 1974) *University of Toronto Quarterly* 44: 343-355, summer 1975.

C271. **McCaughna, David.** Behind the scenes, dramaturges shape the future of the theatre. *Performing Arts* 12:33-34, spring 1975.

C272. **Maulucci, Anthony S.** The Canadian theatre conference: report. *Motion* Vol. 4, no. 2:29-30, 1975.

C273. **Nelson, Keith D.** The plight of the Canadian dramatist. *Canadian Drama/ L'Art Dramatique Canadien* 1:7-11, spring 1975.

C274. **Rubin, Don.** Aside: Canada and the I.T.I. *Canadian Theatre Review* CTR 7:4-5, summer 1975.

C275. **Rubin, Don.** Aside: looking back and ahead. *Canadian Theatre Review* CTR 5:4-5, winter 1975.

C276. **Rubin, Don.** Aside: winding up the CTC. *Canadian Theatre Review* CTR 6:4-6, spring 1975.

C277. **Slotkin, Lynn.** A better fate. *Motion* 4:48, January-March 1975.

C278. **Souchotte, Sandra.** Workers theatre in the thirties part I. *This Magazine* 9:3-5, May-June 1975. illus.

C279. **Souchotte, Sandra.** Workers theatre in the thirties part II. *This Magazine* 9:3-6, July-August 1975. illus.

C280. **Swann, Peter.** Ancillary thoughts on the council for business and the arts in Canada. *Performing Arts* 12:43, spring 1975.

C281. **White, C.A.** Arts: a window on our identity. *Canada and the World* 40:18-19, April 1975.

ATLANTIC PROVINCES

C282. **Crosby, Laurel.** Atlantic tour of the Canadian players. *Atlantic Advocate* 47: 43-46, January 1957. illus.

C283. **Warrington, Irma.** Magic at Tatamagouche. *Food for Thought* 17:182-185, January 1957.

C284. **Golding, Jack.** The story of the Imperial Capitol Theatre (Saint John, N.B.). *Atlantic Advocate* 48: 25-31, March 1958.

C285. **Fergusson, C. Bruce.** *The Arts in Nova Scotia.* Paper read at the Nova Scotia Arts Council Annual Meeting, 21, October 1961. Wolfville, N.S. Halifax, Dept. of Education, Adult Education Division. (1961).

C286. **Halifax Board of Trade.** *Professsional repertory theatre in Halifax.* Report of the Feasibility Committee: report for the establishment of a theatre centre in Canada: Maritimes Theatre Project, preliminary budget. Halifax, 1962.

C287. **Golding, Helen.** The Neptune Theatre. *Atlantic Advocate* 53: 17-24, August 1963. illus.

C288. **Michener, Wendy.** Theatre '63: Halifax: the Neptune Theatre. *Tamarack Review* no. 28: 78-86, spring 1963.

C289. **Robinson, Cyril.** Neptune's brave new venture. *Weekend Magazine* no. 37:7, 1963.

C290. **Robinson, Cyril.** Kids get in the act: Halifax has a successful theatre for and by children. *Weekend Magazine* no. 16: 24-25, 1965.

C291. **Silcox, Peter.** Summer at the Neptune. *Canadian Forum* 45: 136-137, September 1965.

C292. **Archibald, Genevieve.** Maritimes are getting ideas! *Performing Arts* 4 no. 2: 52-54, winter 1965-66.

C293. **Galloway, David.** Drama, historical and contemporary. In *Arts in New Brunswick.* Fredericton, University of New Brunswick Press, 1967. p. 45-72.

C294. Neptune Theatre. *Commercial News* 48: 37, March 1968.

C295. **Swarbrick, Brian.** The Playhouse. In *Arts in New Brunswick.* Fredericton, University of New Brunswick Press, 1967. p. 73-74.

C296. **Halpert, Herbert** ed. *Christmas mumming in Newfoundland.* Toronto, University of Toronto Press for Memorial University of Newfoundland, 1969. 246 p.

C297. **Bruce, Harry.** The Neptune theatre is, at last, a beloved institution. *Saturday Night* 86: 18-22, 1972.

C298. Mermaid theatre (Wolfville, N.S.) *Atlantic Advocate* 62: 42-44, August 1972.

C299. **Mullaly, Edward J.** The rebirth of theatre in New Brunswick. In Crampton, Esmé. ed. *Drama Canada.* Toronto, College of Education Guidance Centre, 1972. p. 34-38.

C300. **Perkyns, Dorothy.** Neptune theatre's Robert Sherrin. *Atlantic Advocate* 63: 38-39, December 1972. port.

C301. **White, Harvey.** In the Maritimes, a first class repertory theatre. *Commentator* 13: 27-29, March 1969. illus.

C302. **Bruce, Harry.** *Happy birthday, dear Neptune: a tenth anniversary historical sketch.* Rothmans of Pall Mall, Canada. 1973. 48 p. illus.

C303. **Callbeck, L.C.** Charlottetown's confederation centre. *Atlantic Advocate* 63:39-40, April 1973.

C304. **Callbeck, L.C.** Charlottetown summer festival. *Atlantic Advocate* 63:52, 54, May 1973.

C305. **Callbeck, L.C.** Neptune theatre's outreach program. *Atlantic Advocate* 63:38-39, April 1973.

C306. **Callbeck, L.C.** Queen will attend P.E.I. summer festival opener. *Atlantic Advocate* 63:31, March 1973.

C307. **Callbeck, L.C.** Theatre and the arts (Moncton district drama council festival of one-act plays). *Atlantic Advocate* 63: 38, April 1973. illus.

C308. **Callbeck, L.C.** Theatre and the arts: semi-professional winter theatre company formed by Ron Irving. *Atlantic Advocate* 63:51, February 1973.

C309. **Claus, Joanne.** Greasepaint gossip: another Maritime export. (Theatre New Brunswick) *Atlantic Advocate* 64: 31, 38-39, October 1973. port.

C310. Culture, controversy and codfish: St. John's summer festival. *Performing Arts* 10:26, fall 1973.

C311. Festivities galore for Prince Edward Island. *Atlantic Advocate* 63:61, February 1973.

C312. **Gottraux, C.** Theatre New Brunswick. *Atlantic Advocate* 63:54,62, May 1973.

C313. **Gottraux, C.** Theatre New Brunswick is well into its most successful season. *Atlantic Advocate* 63:32, March 1973. illus.

C314. In Halifax: Keith Turnbull at 2nd. stage. *Motion* 1:40-41, March-April 1973. illus.

C315. **Kneebone, S.** Theatre New Brunswick. *Atlantic Advocate* 63:22-24, February 1973. illus., port.

C316. The Maritimes move west. (Charlottetown tour) *Performing Arts* 11:5, summer 1973. illus.

C317. **Mullaly, Edward J.** Arts (New Brunswick drama festival) *Atlantic Advocate* 63:47, 51-52, May 1973.

C318. **Mullaly, Edward J.** Have play, will travel: Theatre New Brunswick. *Performing Arts* 10:17-18, fall 1973. illus.

C319. **Mullaly, Edward J.** Maritime refreshment: Theatre New Brunswick. *Performing Arts* 10:23, spring 1973.

C320. **Perkyns, Dorothy.** Experimenting in Halifax: Pier 1 theatre. *Performing Arts* 10:24-25, summer 1973. illus.

C321. Small town setting: theatre arts festival international. *Performing Arts* 190:19, fall 1973.

C322. Theatre. (Neptune theatre). *Atlantic Advocate* 64:26, December 1973.

C323. Theatre and the arts. *Atlantic Advocate* 63:57, June 1973.

C324. (Theatre New Brunswick first of Canada's theatres to go into year 'round production). *Atlantic Advocate* 63:49, January 1973.

C325. **Rubin, Don.** The pushy players down east. *Maclean's* 86:102, May 1973. port.

C326. Youth season for the Neptune. *Performing Arts* 10:7, winter 1973.

C327. **Arlett, Ian.** What really happened in Halifax pier one. *Motion* 2:49, May-June 1974.

C328. **Brookes, Christopher.** Useful theatre. *This Magazine* 8:3-7, June 1974. illus.

C329. **Callbeck, L.C.** Eliza and the argonauts. *Atlantic Advocate* 65:22,25 September 1974. illus.

C330. **Callbeck, L.C.** New stars rising. *Atlantic Advocate* 64:20, August 1974. port.

C331. **Claus, Joanne.** Atlantic theatre: drama's focus on youth. *Atlantic Advocate* 65:22, 24-26, October 1974. illus.

C332. **Claus, Joanne.** Atlantic version of Frankenstein story: this fellow's no monster. *Atlantic Advocate* 64:32-34, August 1974. port.

C333. **Claus, Joanne.** Profile: Robert Percival: a man of mixed media. *Atlantic Advocate* 64:22, 24-25, February 1974. port.

C334. **Claus, Joanne.** TNB has coast-to-coast winner. *Atlantic Advocate* 64:42-44, 46, July 1974. illus.

C335. Doris Baillie Phillips wins playwrighting competition. *Atlantic Advocate* 65:53, October 1974. port.

C336. Help for the mummers. *Atlantic Advocate* 64:52, February 1974.

C337. **Lamberton, Debbie Kaetz.** Mermaid theatre sets lofty goal. *Atlantic Advocate* 64:40-43, May 1974. illus.

C338. **Losier, M.J.** Theatre thriving. Tidnish, Nova Scotia. *Atlantic Advocate* 65:59, November 1974. illus.

C339. **MacAndrew, Barbara.** What's up down east. (Charlottetown). *Motion* 2:43-44, July-August 1974.

C340. **Perkyns, Dorothy.** Neptune's 11th season in review. *Performing Arts* 11:39-41, summer 1974. illus.

C341. Religious rock musical for Nova Scotia. *Performing Arts* 11:12, fall 1974. illus.

C342. Revival of mummery. *Performing Arts* 11:10, spring 1974.

C343. Ten-year-old Anne tours across Canada. *Performing Arts* 11:7, winter 1974.

C344. **Warrick, Paddy.** Theatre date with Joey. *Atlantic Advocate* 65:45, October 1974. port.

C345. **Webster, J.** Another stage triumph for Sharon (Pollock). *Atlantic Advocate* 64:50, August 1974. port.

C346. Neptune theatre gets face lift. *Performing Arts* 12:7, spring 1975.

C347. **Pratt, Martha.** Anne of green gables optimism needed for Charlottetown summer festival. *Performing Arts* 12:20-21, summer 1975. port.

C348. **Pratt, Martha.** Galleries and performing arts: 2 innovations from P.E.I. turn tradition on its ear. *Performing Arts* 12:42, summer 1975. port.

C349. Theatre dramatizes Micmac Indian heritage. *Performing Arts* 12:5, spring 1975.

C350. Theatricals for children. *Atlantic Advocate* 65:58, April 1975.

ONTARIO

C351. *Theatre Nights* (Souvenir programmes from Toronto Press Club "Theatre Nights") 1905-1909 Annually. 5 numbers. Contain cast lists of annual play: articles.

C352. Eight men speak. *Varsity* (Toronto). Friday, January 19, 1934. p. 2.

C353. Worker's theatre: Ontario in the 1930's. *New Frontiers* 3: 28-30, summer 1954.

C354. **Johnston, Forrest.** All Canadian drama plan makes hit at Kingston. *Saturday Night* 63: 19, September 25, 1947.

C355. **(Sandwell, Bernard Keble)** A new quality on the Canadian stage. By Lucy van Gogh, pseud. *Saturday Night* 64: 2-3, March 22, 1948. illus. (New Play Society).

C356. **Lucow, Maurice.** $75,000 gamble pays off for Toronto angels. *Financial Post* (Toronto) 46: 7, August 9, 1952. (Melody Fair.)

C357. Shakespeare festivals in Canada; the Earle Grey players. *Food for Thought* 13: 8-12, May/June 1953.

C358. **(Lyle-Smith, Alan)** *The Shakespeare festival; a short history of the initial five years of Canada's first Shakespeare festival, 1949-1954* by Alan Caillou pseud., Arnold M. Walter and Frank Chappell. Toronto, Ryerson, 1954. 46 p. illus.

C359. **Campbell, Douglas.** Canadian players on the snowplough circuit. *Theatre Arts* 39: 71-73, 88, April 1955. illus.

C360. Persona grata man of many parts. *Saturday Night* 70: 12, 14 July 23, 1955. (Douglas Campbell - Canadian Players).

C361. **Moon, Barbara.** Canadian theatre's fiery godmother. *Maclean's* 71: 18-19, 52-55, February 15, 1958. illus. (Dora Mavor Moore and New Play Society.)

C362. **Evans, J.A.S.** Theatre in Toronto. *Canadian Commentator* 4: 12-14, December 1960.

C363. **Winter, Jack.** The theatre season. Toronto. *Canadian Forum* 40: 178-179, November 1960.

C364. **Cohen, Nathan.** Tryouts and triumphs in Toronto. *Theatre Arts* 45: 22-24, 77-78, October 1961. illus.

C365. **Gardner, David.** Canadian players Artic "Lear". *Saturday Night* 76: 46-47, November 11, 1961.

C366. **Gardner, David.** The Crest: cause for appraisal and celebration. *Saturday Night.* 76: 19-21, March 18, 1961. illus.

C367. Exit muttering by Donald Jack: Grenville St. playhouse. *Alphabet* no.4:6 June 1962.

C368. **Hicklin, Ralph.** The theatre season in Toronto 1961-62: a survey. *Tamarack Review* no. 25: 60-68, autumn 1962.

C369. **Hood, Hugh.** The ingenue I should have kissed but didn't. *Tamarack Review* no. 25: 3-17, autumn 1962.

C370. **Panzica, Norman.** The Crest: quo vadis? *Performing Arts* 1: 5-6, 63, spring-summer 1962.

C371. **Terry, Pamela.** Six days and a dream by John Volinska: Drao Players *Alphabet* no. 4: 6-7, June 1962.

C372. **Fulford, Robert.** On satire: the country changed but Spring Thaw didn't. *Maclean's Magazine* 76: 57-58, May 4, 1963.

C373. Hungary's loss, Toronto's gain, a theatre in the Budapest manner. *Maclean's Magazine* 76: 63, June 1, 1963.

C374. **Russel, Robert.** Crest theatre . . . . *Canadian Art* 20: 60-61, January-February 1963.

C375. **Russel, Robert.** Theatre a way of creating an ideal theatre company in Toronto. *Canadian Art* 20: 184-185, May-June 1963.

C376. **Allan, Andrew.** Drama in the Court House. *Performing Arts* 2 no. 4: 5-8, winter-spring 1964. illus.

C377. **Fulford, Robert.** On Canadian drama. *Maclean's Magazine* 77: 45, January 25, 1964.

C378. **Evans, Ron.** Nineteen sixty-seven minus one. *Performing Arts* 4 no. 1: 29-31, fall 1965.

C379. *Royal Alexandra Theatre:* a collection of newspaper clippings with reviews of stage performances at this theatre. March 1911 - October 1965. Toronto (7 reels of microfilm).

C380. **Allen, Robert Thomas.** Voilà! The lion growled in French! *Maclean's Magazine* 79: 33-37, January 1, 1966. illus. (Museum Children's Theatre.)

C381. Contrasts: three professional theatres at the crossroads. *Performing Arts* 4 no. 2: 42-45, winter 1965-66.

C382. **Kalman, Rolf.** Rolf Kalman interviews Barry Morse. *Performing Arts* 4 no. 4: 16-20, 1966. illus.

C383. **Kalman, Rolf.** Toronto: a name or a community. *Performing Arts* 4 no. 4: 52-55, 1966. illus.

C384. **Brown, Mary.** Experiment in Canadian drama. *Canadian Literature* no. 31: 54-58, winter 1967.

C385. Historic Niagara-on-the-Lake makes history again. *Performing Arts* 6 no. 1: 25-27, 1968. illus.

C386. **Wood, Ted.** Theatre Toronto: filling a cavity left by the Crest. *Montrealer* 42: 18-20, February 1968. illus.

C387. **Carson, Neil.** Toronto opens its 1968 theatre season. *Commentator* 13: 23-25, February 1969. illus.

C388. **Carson, Neil.** Toronto workshop productions. *Commentator* 13:22-23, April 1969.

C389. Theatre Toronto: a strong hand needed. *Performing Arts* 6 no. 2:4-8, 11-12, 1969. illus.

C390. **Carson, Neil.** Chicago 70: more than a stage trial of a trial. *Commentator* 14: 19-20, June 1970. illus.

C391. **Carson, Neil.** Dance of Life: "Hair" in Toronto. *Commentator:* 14: 19-20, February 1970.

C392. **Carson, Neil.** Generation gaps:two plays at Toronto's Hart House. *Commentator* 14:19-20, January 1970.

C393. **Carson, Neil.** St. Lawrence Centre for the arts brings out the best and the worst. *Commentator* 14: 12-13, May 1970.

C394. **Carson, Neil.** Vintage Shaw at the Shaw Festival 1970. *Commentator* 14: 19-20, September 1970.

C395. **Dzeguze, Kaspers.** "Hair" et sa tribu de jeunes comédiens canadiens ordinaires (ou presque) *Magazine Maclean* 10:30-32, April 1970. illus.

C396. **Dzeguze, Kaspers.** What "Hair" is doing to a bunch of otherwise ordinary Canadian kids. *Maclean's Magazine* 83:48-51, April 1970. illus.

C397. **Kroll, J.** America hurrah! improvisation of Chicago 70 by the Toronto Workshop company. *Newsweek* 75:90, June 8, 1970.

C398. **Levine, Paul.** Theatre chronicle: Chicago 70 produced by the Toronto Workshop. *Canadian Forum* 50:174-176, July-August 1970.

C399. **Novick, Julius.** Theatre: Toronto workshop's production of Chicago 70 in New York. *Nation* 210: 734, June 15, 1970.

C400. **Oliver, E.** Off Broadway: Chicago 70 - improvisation by the Toronto workshop company. *New Yorker* 46: 51, June 6, 1970.

C401. **Price, C.** At the Shaw festival: the sentimental coward. *Commentator* 15: 19-20, September 1971.

C402. **Batten, Jack.***Honest Ed's story.* Toronto, Doubleday, 1972. 237 p.

C403. **Brissenden, L. Constance.** Collective creativity: Toronto Workshop Productions. *White Pelican* 2 no. 1, 35-52, 1972.

C404. **Frazer, Robbin.** A dark historic epic: National Arts Centre. *Performing Arts* 9: 26, winter 1972.

C405. A good year for theatre at N.A.C. *Performing Arts* 9: 7, winter 1972.

C406. **Hewes, Henry.** Shavian cream; Shaw revivals. *Saturday Review - World* 55: 60, August 12, 1972.

C407. Irish arts theatre. *Performing Arts* 9:4, winter 1972. port.

C408. Light and funny: Theatre in the Dell. *Performing Arts* 9: 27, winter 1972.

C409. **Mezei, Stephen.** New company at the Colonnade. *Performing Arts* 9: 26, winter 1972.

C410. A mixed beginning: Royal Alexandra. *Performing Arts* 9: 27, winter 1972.

C411. N.A.C. tours schools. *Performing Arts* 9: 9, winter 1972.

C412. **Raeburn, Alan.** Entertainment in variety: Theatre Passe Muraille. *Performing Arts* 9: 28, winter 1972.

C413. **Rubin, Don.** Evolving to professionalism: theatre London. *Performing Arts* 9: 25, winter 1972.

C414. **Schwarz, Ernest J.** The Studio lab theatre foundation. In Crampton, Esmé. ed. *Drama Canada.* Toronto, College of Education Guidance Centre, 1972. p. 18-20.

C415. Tarragon celebrates its first birthday. *Performing Arts* 9:4, winter 1972.

C416. The trial of Kafka. *Performing Arts* 9:27-28. winter 1972.

C417. **Whittaker, Herbert.** The alternate theatre in Toronto. *Stage in Canada* 7:6-9, September 1972.

C418. The workingman. *Canadian Labour* 17:19, October 1972. illus.

C419. Anyone for one-act plays? Tarragon theatre. *Performing Arts* 10:28, summer 1973. port.

C420. **Berger, J.** Week of festivals: theatre Ontario festival. *Performing Arts* 10:19, spring 1973. port.

C421. Best kind of encouragement. (Theatre London). *Performing Arts* 10:7, fall 1973. illus.

C422. Blood without gore: theatre in camera. *Performing Arts* 10:21-22, spring 1973.

C423. **Book, Sam.** *Economic aspects of the arts in Ontario.* A study by Sam Book for the Ontario Arts Council. Toronto, Ontario Arts Council, 1973. 56 p.

C424. Branch plant with a difference. (Second City). *Performing Arts* 10:4, fall 1973. illus.

C425. **Card, R.** Drama in Toronto: the forgotten years 1919-1939. *English Quarterly* 6:67-81, spring 1973. illus.

C426. **Constantinidi, Mela.** Toronto: marionettes à l'honneur. *Vie des Arts* 73:73, hiver 1973-4. illus.

C427. **Crean, Susan M.** Up front with the artists: the AGO affair. *Canadian Forum* 53:63-67, November-December 1973. bibl.

C428. **Dorrell, Robin.** Ottawa gamble. *Motion* 2:63, November-December 1973.

C429. **Dorrell, Robin.** Ottawa: the power of positive thinking. *Motion* 1:62-63, September-October 1973.

C430. **Edinborough, Arnold.** First you find an audience — then you build the theatre. (Sarnia) *Financial Post* 67:10, July 7, 1973. illus., port.

C431. **Edinborough, Arnold.** Home at last: Shaw festival settles cosily into a jewel. *Financial Post* 67:10, June 23, 1973. illus., port.

C432. **Edinborough, Arnold.** Logic, perhaps, one doesn't expect, but why no passion? *Financial Post* 67:31, February 3, 1973. illus., port.

C433. **Erdelyi, Joseph.** And reap they did: Lindsay little theatre. *Performing Arts* 10:25-26, summer 1973.

C434. **Erdelyi, Joseph.** Another good year: Kawartha summer theatre. *Performing Arts* 10:23, fall 1973. port.

C435. **Erdelyi, Joseph.** A big plus for Toronto: theatre plus. *Performing Arts* 10:22-23, fall 1973. illus., port.

C436. **Erdelyi, Joseph.** Play of its very own: Lindsay little theatre. *Performing Arts* 10:22, spring 1973.

C437. **Evanchuk, Peter M.** Thunder Bay goes gay . . . 90's that is. *Motion* 1:43, January-February 1973. illus.

C438. Experimental troupe head for Europe. (Théâtre de l'homme). *Performing Arts* 10:5, fall 1973. illus.

C439. Festival Ontario started with a $250.00 grant. *Ontario Library Review* 57: 191-192, September 1973.

C440. Filling the void: classical stage production. *Performing Arts* 10:20, spring 1973. illus.

C441. **Frazer, Robbin.** Audience of the future. (Youth section NAC). *Performing Arts* 10:29, spring 1973.

C442. **Frazer, Robbin.** Oh what a lovely war! national arts centre. *Performing Arts* 10:23, spring 1973. illus.

C443. **Frazer, Robbin.** Sixty years of memories: the Ottawa little theatre. *Performing Arts* 10:25, summer 1973. illus.

C444. **Frazer, Robbin.** Strange story of Gaspard: national arts centre. *Performing Arts* 10:22, spring 1973.

C445. Freeman wins Chalmers award. *Performing Arts* 10:5, spring 1973.

C446. From the people, for the people. (Open Circle Theatre). *Performing Arts* 10:4-5, summer 1973. illus.

C447. Hamilton Place opens. *Performing Arts* 10:7, winter, 1973. illus.

C448. Irish are coming: Irish arts theatre. *Performing Arts* 10:21, spring 1973. port.

C449. **Keil, Martha, McLarty, James** and **Wittgens, Claudia.** Toronto - theatre scene. *Motion* 1:37-39, March-April 1973. illus.

C450. **McLarty, James.** A dilemma no longer. *Motion* 1:43-45, July-August 1973. port.

C451. **Mezei, Stephen.** Change of address: Shaw festival. *Performing Arts* 10:19, fall 1973. illus.

C452. **Mezei, Stephen.** Cultural farming: Huron county playhouse. *Performing Arts* 10:22, fall 1973.

C453. **Mezei, Stephen.** Fighting the size: O'Keefe centre. *Performing Arts* 10:19-20, spring 1973. illus., port.

C454. **Mezei, Stephen.** To be or not to be: factory theatre lab. *Performing Arts* 10:24, summer 1973. illus.

C455. **Mortimer, P.J.** A look at the first theatre Ontario festival. *Performing Arts* 10:35-36, summer 1973. illus., port.

C456. Rise of the alternative. *Time* (Canada) 102:14, 15, November 12, 1973.

C457. **Rubin, Don.** Theatre: moving toward a sense of community. *Maclean's* 86:92, February 1973. port.

C458. Safe, but not sure: Toronto workshop productions. *Performing Arts* 10:26-27, summer 1973.

C459. **Salutin, Rick.** 1837 - diary of a Canadian play. *This Magazine* 7:11-15, May-June 1973. illus.

C460. Senior citizens form theatre company and orchestra. *Performing Arts* 10:4, spring 1973.

C461. **Theatre Ontario.** Dialog. *Performing Arts* 10:35-36, winter 1973. illus.

C462. **Theatre Ontario.** Dialog. (Direction '73). *Performing Arts* 10:43-45, fall 1973. illus.

C463. 3-D television anyone? (Theatre-in-the-home). *Performing Arts* 10:7, fall 1973. illus.

C464. To Gogol with love: Toronto workshop productions. *Performing Arts* 10:22-23, spring 1973.

C465. Toronto dance theatre premieres new work. *Performing Arts* 10:5, winter 1973. illus.

C466. Toronto theatre scene. *Motion* 1:39-41, January-February 1973. illus.

C467. **Traucht, H.** Mirror of life: Toronto free theatre. *Performing Arts* 10:27-28, summer 1973. illus.

C468. Tremblay's Toronto success. *Performing Arts* 10:26, summer 1973. illus.

C469. Visual delight Tarragon theatre. (Stag King). *Performing Arts* 10:20-21, spring 1973. illus.

C470. What now at the centre? (St. Lawrence Centre). *Performing Arts* 10:20, spring 1973.

C471. Actors can think. (Performing theatre company). *Performing Arts* 11:8, fall 1974. illus.

C472. Arts: export wry. (Second City). *Time* (Canada). 104:10, September 9, 1974. illus.

C473. **Baker, R.** County assembly: Petrolia. *Ontario Library Review* 58:220-222, December 1974. illus.

C474. **Doherty, Brian.** *Not bloody likely: the Shaw Festival 1962-1973.* Toronto, J.M. Dent, 1974. 160 p. illus.

C475. **Dorrell, Robin.** Dollars and sense. *Motion* 2:15-16, July-August 1974.

C476. **Dorrell, Robin.** Ottawa experiment. *Motion* 2:55, January-February 1974. illus.

C477. **Dorrell, Robin.** Ottawa writers. *Motion* 3:36, November-December 1974.

C478. Drama and comedy for Toronto. (St. Lawrence Centre). *Performing Arts* 11:10, fall 1974.

C479. Drama : how to bake a gopher pie. (TWP Ten Lost Years). *Time* (Canada). 103:15, May 13, 1974. illus.

C480. **Edinborough, Arnold.** After five years the national arts centre has finally made it. *Performing Arts* 11:21-24, summer 1974. illus., port.

C481. **Edinborough, Arnold.** Summer theatre: it's still fun but not straw hat. *Financial Post* 68:21, August 1974.

C482. Factory theatre lab is still growing. *Performing Arts* 11:12, summer 1974. port.

C483. From London to Bucharest in silence. *Performing Arts* 11:8, summer 1974. illus.

C484. **James, Geoffrey.** Arts: uneasy laughter (You're gonna be alright, Jamie Boy). *Time* (Canada) 103:10, January 28, 1974. illus.

C485. **James, Geoffrey.** Drama: slight Shaw. *Time* (Canada) 103:10, June 24, 1974. illus.

C486. **Kohl, Helen.** Clowns. *Performing Arts* 11:27-30, winter 1974. illus.

C487. **McCaughna, David.** Summer and Shaw. *Motion* 2:45, July-August 1974.

C488. **McLarty, James.** Fighting back with the NAC. *Motion* 2:44-45, September-October 1974. port.

C489. **Major, Leon.** The St. Lawrence centre: Leon Major replies. (See: Thomas, D. High cost of a cultural white elephant. *Performing Arts* 11:22-24, spring 1974.) *Performing Arts* 12:14-16, summer 1974. illus., port.

C490. **Miller, M.J.** Theatre: the documentary drama of Paul Thompson. *Saturday Night* 89:35-37, July 1974. illus.

C491. Multi-cultural theatre. *Performing Arts* 11:11, fall 1974.

C492. Music and theatre at Niagara-on-the-lake. *Performing Arts* 11:10, summer 1974.

C493. Muskoka summer theatre — past and present and future growth. *Performing Arts* 11:6, fall 1974. illus.

C494. National theatre school. *Performing Arts* 11:7, spring 1974. illus.

C495. New school of theatre opens. *Performing Arts* 11:12, fall 1974.

C496. Ontario (Festival) lends support to community festivals. *Ontario Library Review* 58:267, December 1974.

C497. Ontario straw hat circuit. *Performing Arts* 11:7-8, summer 1974. illus.

C498. Ontario theatre festival 1974. *Performing Arts* 11:9, summer 1974.

C499. Plays and politics. (Toronto Workshop Productions). *Performing Arts* 11:11-12, summer 1974. port.

C500. Plus for Toronto. (Theatre Plus). *Performing Arts* 11:10, summer 1974. illus.

C501. Sean Mulcahy moves to Press theatre. *Performing Arts* 11:11, winter 1974.

C502. Second season for women's theatre group. (Red Light Theatre). *Performing Arts* 11:6, fall 1974. illus.

C503. Shaw festival travels. *Performing Arts* 11:7, spring 1974.

C504. **Shoveller, Brock** and **Shoveller, John.** *Toronto, we love you: our theatres.* Toronto, Simon and Pierre, 1974. n.p. illus.

C505. Teaching the quiet art. (mime). *Performing Arts* 11:11, fall 1974.

C506. **Theatre Ontario.** Dialogue. (Ontario theatre festival). *Performing Arts* 11: 34-35, spring 1974. illus., port.

C507. Toronto dance theatre's new season. *Performing Arts* 11:12-13, winter 1974.

C508. TWP to complete season then tour Europe. *Performing Arts* 11:9-10, winter 1974.

C509. **Thomas, Dorothy.** High cost of a cultural white elephant. (St. Lawrence Centre). *Performing Arts* 11:22-24, spring 1974. illus.

C510. **Wallace, Bob.** Paul Thompson at theatre passe muraille: bits and pieces. *Open Letter* Series 2, no. 7:49-71, winter 1974.

C511. **Wylie, Betty Jane.** Autumn arts in the Soo. *Performing Arts* 11:33, winter 1974.

C512. Youth's summer act. (Ontario youtheatre). *Performing Arts* 11:12, summer 1974. illus.

C513. **Balay, Billyann.** Niagara-on-the-Lake concocts a summer theatre cocktail. *Performing Arts* 12:18-19, summer 1975. port.

C514. **Book, Sam H., Globerman, S.** and **National Research Centre of the Arts.** *The audience for the performing arts.* Toronto, Ontario Arts Council, 1975. 220 p. tables.

C515. **Book, Sam H., Globerman, S.** and **National Research Centre of the Arts.** *The audience for the performing arts: highlights of a study of attendance patterns in Ontario.* Toronto, Ontario Arts Council, 1975. 24 p., tables.

C516. **Canadian Theatre Review.** A chronological commentary. (The Crest theatre) *Canadian Theatre Review* CTR 7:17-23, summer 1975.

C517. **Canadian Theatre Review.** Crest chronology. *Canadian Theatre Review* CTR 7:45-51, summer 1975.

C518. **Canadian Theatre Review.** The Crest: a photographic view. *Canadian Theatre Review* CTR 7:24-33, summer 1975.

C519. Children's theatre at your finger tips. *Performing Arts* 12:8, spring 1975.

C520. **Davis, Donald.** Interview: the Davis view. (Crest Theatre). *Canadian Theatre Review* CTR 7:34-44, summer 1975.

C521. **Edinborough, Arnold.** For theatre success may not be enough — cities must help too. (Theatre London). *Financial Post* 69:30, March 22, 1975. port.

C522. **Evans, Chad.** Herman Voaden and the Symphonic theatre. *Canadian Theatre Review* CTR 5:37-43, winter 1975.

C523. **Grant, Diane.** Nellie McLung and the Redlight theatre. *This Magazine* 8:16-19, January-February 1975. illus.

C524. It's a good year for mime. (Canadian Mime Theatre). *Performing Arts* 12:9, spring 1975.

C525. **James, Geoffrey.** Arts: Riel revived. *Time* (Canada) 105:8-9, February 3, 1975. port.

C526. **James, Geoffrey.** Drama: native Shaw. (Robertson Davies' Question Time). *Time* (Canada) 105:10-11, March 10, 1975. port.

C527. **McFadgen, Lynn.** The play's the thing. (Playwrights Co-op). *Quill and Quire* 41:9, 20, February 1975.

C528. Ontario straw hat circuit makes a holiday memorable. *Performing Arts* 12:6, summer 1975.

C529. Redlight theatre tours western Canada for I.W.Y. *Performing Arts* 12:5, summer 1975. illus.

C530. **Schulman, M.** Galleries and performing arts, part 1: lyric theatre — communion of the arts. *Performing Arts* 12:42, spring 1975. illus.

C531. **Stuart, Euan Ross.** The Crest controversy. *Canadian Theatre Review* CTR 7:8-11, summer 1975.

C532. Tarragon theatre closes its doors for a year. *Performing Arts* 12:5, summer 1975.

C533. **Theatre Passe Muraille.** Collective conversation: the space show. *Canadian Theatre Review* CTR 6:14-27, spring 1975.

C534. **Van Bridge, Tony.** Running the show at Shaw: interview by Arnold Edinborough. *Performing Arts* 12:cover, 15-17, spring 1975. port.

C535. What? a big city summer festival. (Theatre Plus). *Performing Arts* 12:6, summer 1975.

C536. **Whittaker, Herbert.** Recollections of achievement. (Crest Theatre). *Canadian Theatre Review* CTR 7:12-16, summer 1975.

MANITOBA

C537. **Carr, Judith.** Manitoba Theatre Centre. The first in a national chain of professional theatres? *Performing Arts* 1 no. 2: 44-45, October 1961. illus.

C538. **Dafoe, Christopher.** The Winnipeg story. *Tamarack Review* no. 25: 41-47, autumn 1962.

C539. **Hendry, Thomas B.** Manitoba Theatre Centre. *Canadian Art* 19:155, March-April 1962.

C540. **Winters, Kenneth.** Look ahead by Len Peterson: Manitoba Theatre Centre. *Alphabet* no. 4: 7-8, June 1962.

C541. **Henry, Ann.** A tale of two theatres. *Performing Arts* 4 no. 1: 32-35, fall 1965. illus.

C542. **Henry, Ann.** Stratford comes to Winnipeg. *Performing Arts* 4 no. 3: 32-37, spring 1966. illus.

C543. MTC avant-garde theatre. *Performing Arts* 9: 5, winter 1972.

C544. **Page, Malcolm.** The humane fanatics of the living theatre. *West Coast Review* 6:20-26, January 1972.

C545. **Evanchuk, Peter M.** Actor's showcase — Winnipeg. *Motion* 1:46-47, May-June 1973. illus.

C546. New season at Manitoba theatre centre. *Performing Arts* 10:5, winter 1973. port.

C547. **Runnells, Rory.** Notes from Winnipeg on a sisyphus. *Motion* 1:46-49, July-August 1973. illus.

C548. **Runnells, Rory.** Winnipeg season. *Motion* 1:64, September-October 1973.

C549. Arts groups got duMaurier council grants (MTC). *Financial Post* 68:23, November 23, 1974.

C550. **Dafoe, Christopher.** MTC: past and present. *Canadian Theatre Review* CTR 4: 6-10, fall 1974.

C551. **Hendry, Thomas B.** 1974 financial report. (MTC) *Canadian Theatre Review* CTR 4:20-21, fall 1974.

C552. **Hendry, Thomas B.** A view from the beginning. (MTC) *Canadian Theatre Review* CTR 4:13-19, fall 1974.

C553. **Hirsch, John.** Healthy disengagement. (MTC) *Canadian Theatre Review* CTR 4:26-31, fall 1974.

C554. How is Winnipeg's rainbow theatre still growing? *Performing Arts* 11:10, fall 1974. illus.

C555. **Manitoba Theatre Centre.** *Manitoba theatre centre to 1974.* Winnipeg, Manitoba Theatre Centre, 1974. 25 p.

C556. **Cansino, B.** What's in store for Winnipeg's warehouse? (MTC). *Performing Arts* 12:30-31, spring 1975. illus.

C557. New artistic director at Manitoba theatre centre. *Performing Arts* 12:9, spring 1975.

C558. Rainbow stage produces two summer favourites. *Performing Arts* 12:5, summer 1975.

SASKATCHEWAN ━━━━━━━━━━━━━━━━━━━━━━━━━━━━━━━━━━━━

C559. **Bourne, Alan.** Creating a theatrical oasis. *Performing Arts* 9:34-35, winter 1972.

C560. **Howard, Rhena.** The Globe theatre. In Crampton, Esmé. ed. *Drama Canada.* Toronto, College of Education Guidance Centre, 1972. p. 20-21.

C561. Globe company moves to its own theatre. *Performing Arts* 10:7, winter 1973.

C562. Not just a theatre company. (Twenty-fifth Street House). *Performing Arts* 10:4, fall 1973. illus.

C563. **Edinborough, Arnold.** Legend finds life on stage — but the theatre could die. *Financial Post* 68:13, November 23, 1974. port.

C564. More Canadian plays premiere in Saskatoon. (Twenty-fifty Street House). *Performing Arts* 11:8, fall 1974. illus.

C565. **O'Neill, Patrick B.** (compiler) *The History of theatre in Saskatoon from 1897 to 1955.* (prepared by students at Dept. of Drama, University of Saskatchewan, under the direction of P.B. O'Neill). unpublished, held at Saskatoon Public Library, Local History Department, 1974?

C566. **Edinborough, Arnold.** Suddenly a windfall for theatre: one firm shows the way. *Financial Post* 69:12, March 29, 1975.

C567. Church is new home for Saskatoon theatre. (Twenty-fifth Street House). *Performing Arts* 12:7, spring 1975.

C568. **O'Neill, Patrick B.** Regina's golden age of theatre: her playhouses and players. (1903-1918). *Saskatchewan History* 28: 29-37, winter 1975. illus., bibl. f.

C569. **Portman, Jamie.** Regina's globe theatre toughs it out. *Performing Arts* 12:33-34, summer 1975. port.

ALBERTA

C570. **Bilsland, John W.** Edmonton's Studio Theatre. *Tamarack Review* no. 25: 26-32, autumn 1962.

C571. **Sowton, Ian.** Cockcrow and the Gulls by Wilfred Watson: Studio Theatre, Edmonton. *Alphabet* no. 4: 4-5, June 1962.

C572. **Orrell, John.** Theatre activities in Alberta. *Culture* 26: 191-194, June 1965.

C573. **Davis, Montgomery.** Edmonton-Citadel Theatre, Studio Theatre. *Performing Arts* 5 no. 1:36-38, 40-41, 1967. illus.

C574. **Newhouse, M.** Citadel theatre for young audiences. *Fine* 20-23, summer 1969. (Fine Arts Council of Alberta Teachers' Association, University of Alberta).

C575. **Edinborough, Arnold.** Support Canadian plays but we deserve better than the "V.P"." *Financial Post* 66: 18, December 2, 1972. (Citadel Theatre). illus.

C576. **Finland, Olive.** Citadel-on-wheels. In Crampton, Esmé. ed. *Drama Canada.* Toronto, College of Education Guidance Centre, 1972. p. 24-26.

C577. Banff extends festival. *Performing Arts* 10:7, spring 1973.

C578. Children pack Citadel over holiday season. *Performing Arts* 10:4-5, spring 1973. illus.

C579. **Edinborough, Arnold.** Museum, theatre, gallery — Edmonton has really struck oil. *Financial Post* 67:14, March 24, 1973. port.

C580. Great music and dance: Banff festival of the arts. *Performing Arts* 10:20-21, fall 1973. illus., port.

C581. **Mezei, Stephen.** Ryga's play bombs. *Performing Arts* 10:21, fall 1973.

C582. **Portman, Jamie.** Cattle, oil, and art. *Performing Arts* 10:32-33, spring 1973. illus., port.

C583. **Rivard, Y.** Banff festival of the arts, Eric Harvie theatre. *Dance Magazine* 47:82-83, October 1973.

C584. University post for winner. (University of Alberta - Clifford Lee award, national playwrighting competition). *Performing Arts* 10:5, fall 1973.

C585. **White, Joy Roberts.** What's going on in Edmonton? *Performing Arts* 10:29, winter 1973. illus.

C586. **White, Joy Roberts.** Arts in Edmonton: under a new roof. *Performing Arts* 10: 27-28, spring 1973. illus.

C587. Alberta shows "Sticks and Stones". *Performing Arts* 11:13, winter 1974.

C588. Alberta theatres exchange plays. (Citadel and Theatre Calgary). *Performing Arts* 11: 6-7, fall 1974. port.

C589. Alberta theatre project brings history to life. *Performing Arts* 11:11, winter 1974.

C590. **Edinborough, Arnold.** Alberta's gasping arts make a gutsy last try for survival. *Financial Post* 68:16, June 15, 1974. port.

C591. **Edinborough, Arnold.** Opera, symphony, the stage: Calgary's where the excitement is. *Financial Post* 68:14, February 23, 1974. port.

C592. Edmonton theatre expands. (Waterdale Associates). *Performing Arts* 11:15, winter 1974.

C593. Edmonton theatre scene expands. (Waterdale Associates, Theatre 3, Citadel). *Performing Arts* 11:7, spring 1974. illus.

C594. Edmonton's theatre 3 expands. *Performing Arts* 11:11, fall 1974.

C595. **Keeley, M.** Cultural sodbusting by the travelling citadel. *Performing Arts.* 11: 38-39, winter 1974. illus.

C596. New face and lunch at the citadel. *Performing Arts* 11: 11-12, winter 1974.

C597. **Portman, Jamie.** Calgary expands its theatre horizons. *Performing Arts* 11: 25-27,spring 1974. port., illus.

C598. Prairie story at theatre 3. *Performing Arts* 11:7, winter 1974.

C599. Summer comedies in Alberta. *Performing Arts* 11:8, summer 1974.

C600. Waterdale associates continue at Christmas in playhouse. *Performing Arts* 11:8, fall 1974. illus.

C601. Banff summer school makes improvements. *Performing Arts* 12:8, spring 1975.

C602. Citadel spells success in western Canada. *Performing Arts* 12:6, summer 1975. illus.

C603. duMaurier awards theatres across Canada. *Performing Arts* 12: 7-8, spring 1975.

C604. **Edinborough, Arnold.** Edmonton pipes new blood into our vital regional theatre. *Financial Post* 69:24, April 5, 1975.

C605. **Edinborough, Arnold.** The magic of Banff inspires excellence in its students. *Performing Arts* 12: 21-22, summer 1975.

C606. Edmonton's theatre 3 plans tour of Alberta. *Performing Arts* 12:5-6, summer 1975.

C607. Frances Hyland stars in Tremblay play. *Performing Arts* 12:9, spring 1975. port.

C608. **Oman, Mary M.** Calgary round-up. *Motion* 4: 44-45, January-March 1975.

C609. Studio theatre mounts competition winner. (University of Alberta - Clifford Lee competition, Tom Grainger's "The Injured"). *Performing Arts* 12:9, spring 1975.

C610. Theatre restaurant opens in Edmonton. *Performing Arts* 12:8, spring 1975.

BRITISH COLUMBIA

C611. **Community Arts Survey Committee, Vancouver.** *The arts and our town; Vancouver, Canada.* Vancouver, Junior League of Vancouver, 1946. 201 p.

C612. **Crighton, Dorothy V.** U.S. actors lead in Victoria festival. *Saturday Night* 62:12, September 28, 1946.

C613. **Francis, Margaret.** Bernhardts of the West Coast in Vancouver spotlight. (by Margaret and Robert Francis). *Saturday Night* 63:18, September 11, 1948.

C614. **Agazarian, Yvonne.** Everyman theatre. *P.M. Magazine* 1: 13-15, November 1951. (Vancouver repertory theatre).

C615. **Gardner, Ray.** Vancouver's enchanted evenings under the stars. *Maclean's* 70: 18-19, 40-41, August 3, 1957. illus.

C616. **Goldschmidt, Nicholas.** A Salzburg for Canada? *Food for Thought* 17: 189, 192-194, January 1957.

C617. **Closingchild, Thomas D.** Between festivals: a letter from Vancouver. *Tamarack Review* no. 10: 64-72, winter 1959.

C618. **Haworth, Peter.** Playwrights in Vancouver. *Canadian Literature* no. 8:47-50, spring 1961.

C619. **Kenyon, W.A.** Kwakiutl masks. *World Theatre* 10:1, spring 1961.

C620. **Haworth, Peter.** Theatre in Vancouver. *Tamarack Review* no. 25:18-25, autumn 1962.

C621. **Hesse, Jurgen.** Experimental theatre a lost effort? *Performing Arts* 2 no. 2: 24-25, spring 1963.

C622. **Windsor, John Best.** *Nowhere else to go.* Sidney, B.C., Gray's Publishing, 1964. v, 139 p. illus. (Victoria B,C,).

C623. **Middleton, Gilbert.** Theatre at Vancouver. *Saturday Night* 79:27-28, July 1964.

C624. **Juliani, John.** Vancouver. Pro hockey - no, pro-theatre - yes. *Performing Arts* 4 no. 3: 42-47, spring 1966. illus.

C625. **Howard, Irene.** Vancouver theatre diary: two companies and their audience. *Canadian Forum* 47: 252-254, February 1968.

C626. **Russell, Lawrence.** Theatre of the invisible. *B.C. Library Quarterly* 33: 28-36, July-October 1969. (Chilliwack, B.C.)

C627. **Roberts, Sheila.** *Shakespeare in Vancouver 1889-1918.* Vancouver, Vancouver Historical Society, 1971. 31 p. illus.

C628. **Lazarus, John.** *Backyard theatre.* Vancouver, B.C. Cedar House, 1972.

C629. Battling the stereotype. (Women's Theatre Cooperative). *Performing Arts* 10:5, fall 1973. port.

C630. **Edinborough, Arnold.** Victoria's bastion theatre: dedication that can't be denied. *Financial Post* 67:15, September 8, 1973. port.

C631. **Hay, Peter.** Theatre: a conflict of dramatic interest. *Maclean's* 86:94, June 1973. port.

C632. **Heald, Joseph.** And now let's hear from the N.D.P. in B.C. *Motion* 2:33, November-December 1973.

C633. **Long, Kenneth.** Preview: an interview with John Juliani. *West Coast Review* 7:87-88, January 1973.

C634. **Stemo, L. Johanne.** *Theatre under the stars.* Vancouver, B.C. Cedar House, 1973.

C635. **Wyman, Max.** Vancouver's recipe for making the audience feel good. *Performing Arts* 10:20-21, winter 1973. illus.

C636. West Coast playwrights organize. *Performing Arts* 10:5, spring 1973.

C637. **Edinborough, Arnold.** Fighting risk-taker sets new course for Vancouver. (Playhouse theatre). *Financial Post* 68:2, October 26, 1974.

C638. **Farevaag, Marta.** Vancouver. *Motion* 2:7, September-October 1974.

C639. Full season for Vancouver's playhouse. *Performing Arts* 11:10, fall 1974.

C640. **Lane, William.** Working solidarity: west coast playwrights. *Motion* 3:34-35, November-December 1974.

C641 Puppet theatre lovers: Vancouver's where it's at. *Performing Arts* 11:10, winter 1974.

C642. What goes into making an actor? (Camosun College, Victoria). *Performing Arts* 11:9, fall 1974.

C643. **Wyman, Max.** Cost low, quality high in east Vancouver. (Vancouver east cultural centre). *Performing Arts* 11:28, spring 1974. illus.

C644. **Wyman, Max.** Take a little theatre with your lunch. (City Stage). *Performing Arts* 11:20-21, winter 1974.

C645. Black history show reconstructs the present. (Free t'be). *Performing Arts* 12:7, spring 1975. illus.

C646. **Edinborough, Arnold.** Nothing new in entertainment? Here's dinner theatre. (Stage West). *Financial Post* 69:24, February 1, 1975. port.

C647. **Farevaag, Marta.** Vancouver scene. *Motion* 4:32, January-March 1975.

C648. **Juliani, John.** Savage space. *Canadian Theatre Review* CTR 6:50-55, spring 1975.

C649. Playhouse theatre plans changes. *Performing Arts* 12:7, spring 1975.

C650. Tamahnous experiments with Indian myths. *Performing Arts* 12:6, summer 1975.

C651. Talent-rich but facilities poor. (Notre Dame University Theatre, Nelson, B.C.). *Performing Arts* 12:8, spring 1975.

C652. Theatre grants total $160,000. (Bastion Theatre). *Financial Post* 69:14, March 29, 1975.

The Tamahnous Theatre Workshop production of *The Tempest* at the Vancouver East Cultural Centre February 1974, directed by John Gray. Tamahnous, (a Chilcotin Indian word meaning magic), is one of Canada's most innovative and experimental acting companies focusing on the actor as an instrument of sound and emotion in the tradition of Grotowski's 'poor theatre.' From the *Canadian Theatre Review Yearbook 1974* (published Fall 1975). See item C650.

D

Twentieth Century
French Canada

D1. **Jéhin-Prume, Mariel.** Nos théâtres: causerie artistique. *Le Monde Illustré,* 17éme année, no. 884: 829, 13 avril, 1901.

D2. La saison théâtrale à Montréal en pleine activité. *Le Monde Illustré,* 19ème année no. 24: 564-565, 11 octobre, 1902.

D3. **Charbonneau, Jean.** Causerie théâtrale: le conservatoire d'art dramatique. *Le Terroir,* janvier-septembre 1909: 60-64.

D4. **Charbonneau, Jean.** Causerie théâtrale. *Le Terroir,* janvier-septembre 1909: 24-26.

D5. **Robert, George H.** ed. *L'annuaire théâtrale, 1908-9.* Montreal. 1909. (no more published) 260 p. illus.

D6. **Dugas, Marcel Henry** *Le théâtre à Montréal. Propos d'un huron canadien,* par Marcel Henry (pseud.). Paris, Henri Falque, 1911. 247 p.

D7. Parisian scorn of the French theatre in Canada. *Literary Digest* 80: 34, February 23,1924. illus.

D8. **Shaw, R.L.** Un spectacle immense. *Maclean's Magazine* 40: 14-15, 77, October 1, 1927.

D9. **Guthrie, Tyrone.** From the theatrical notebooks of Tyrone Guthrie. *Maclean's* 72: 20-21, 76-82, December 5, 1959. illus. (Montreal 1929.)

D10. **Guthrie, Tyrone.** Montreal. In his *A life in the theatre.* N.Y., McGraw-Hill, 1959. p. 71-79. (Visit in 1929).

D11. **Montigny, Louvigny De.** Théâtre canadien. In his *Les boules de neige; comédie en trois actes, précedé d'un lever de rideau: "Je vous aime".* Montreal, Déom Frère, 1935. vii-xxiv.

D12. **Béraud, Jean.** Pour un théâtre national. In his *Initiation à l'art dramatique.* Montréal, Dussault and Peladeau, 1936. p. 183-227.

D13. **Houle, Léopold.** Notre théâtre et la critique. *Transactions of the Royal Society of Canada* 3 ser., v. 35, sect. 1: 77-90, 1941.

D14. **Houle, Léopold.** Retour aux classiques. *Transactions of the Royal Society of Canada* 3 ser., v. 36, sect. 1: 59-69, 1942.

D15. **Légault, Emile.** Le théâtre qu'il nous faut. *Amérique français* 2: 27-35, juin 1943.

D16. **Duhamel, Roger.** Notre grand Fridolin. *Relations* 5: 137-138, mai 1945.

D17. **Houle, Léopold.** *L'histoire du théâtre au Canada; pour un retour aux classiques.* Montréal, Fides, 1945. 170 p. bibl.

D18. **Houle, Jean Pierre.** Les compagnons. *Action Universitaire* 12:20-22, décembre 1945.

D19 **Laurent Edouard.** Reflexions sur le théâtre. *Culture* 6: 39-54, janvier 1945.

D20. **Légault, Emile.** Perspectives sur les compagnons. *Relations* 5: 272-273, octobre 1945.

D21. **Béraud, Jean.** Le théâtre. In *Variations sur trois thèmes* par Jean Béraud. Leon Franque, Marcel Valois. Montréal, Editions Fernand Pilon, 1946. p. 9-183.

D22. **Coleman, Francis A.** The theatre in Canada; Les Compagnons. *Theatre Arts* 30: 391-392, July 1946.

D23. **Duhamel, Roger.** Le feuilleton des spectacles. *Relations* 6:311, octobre 1946.

D24. **Mulligan, Louis.** Shakespeare and l'entente cordiale. *Canadian Review of Music and Art* 5: 17-18, February 1946.

D25. **Rittenhouse, Charles B.** Montreal experiences theatre renaissance. *Saturday Night* 62:23, September 14, 1946.

D26. Troupe from Canada. *Newsweek* 28: 84, December 23, 1946. illus. (Les Compagnons).

D27. **Whittaker, Herbert.** Fridolin our star. *Canadian Review of Music and Art* 5: 11-13, February 1946. illus.

D28. **Ampleman, Jean.** L'aventure des Compagnons. *Nouvelle Relève* 5: 844-848, août/septembre 1947.

D29. **Ampleman, Jean.** Le théâtre: théâtre canadien. *Nouvelle Relève* 6: 273-276, février 1948.

D30. **Laurent, Edouard.** Tit-coq, un conscrit qui passera à l'histoire. *Culture* 9: 378-383, décembre 1948.

D31. **Pellascio-Morin, Ernest.** Théâtre canadien. *Revue Dominicaine* 54: 230-234, novembre 1948.

D32. **Gélinas, Gratien.** Un théâtre national et populaire. *L'Action Universitaire* 15: 30-39, avril 1949.

D33. **Jasmin, Judith.** Problèmes du spectacle au Canada. *Nouvelle Revue Canadienne* 1: 77-80, février/mars 1951. 1:72-76, avril/mai, 1951.

D34. **Boucher, Pierre.** Nos publics de théâtre. *Revue de l'Université Laval* 8: 351-357, décembre 1953.

D35. **Légault, Emile.** *Confidences.* Montréal, Fides, 1955 illus. (Autobiography of founder of Compagnons.)

D36. **D'Auteuil, Georges Henri.** Situation de notre théâtre. *Relations* 16: 290-293, octobre 1956.

D37. Auditoria, professional theatre, civic theatre. In *The arts in Montreal. Report of a survey of Montreal's artistic resources.* Montreal, Junior League of Montreal. (c. 1956) p. 27-44.

D38. **Dussault, J.-C.** Essai pour un vrai théâtre. *Vie des Arts* 6:25, 1956.

D39. **Roux, Jean Louis.** Le théâtre du nouveau monde. *Theatre Canada* no. 36: 2-3, September/October 1957.

D40. **Beaulne, Guy.** Le théâtre de langue française au Canada; son évolution depuis la fin de la deuxième grande guerre. *Vie française* 12: 223-238, mars/avril 1958.

D41. **Béraud, Jean.** Le théâtre au Canada français. In Ross, Malcolm ed. *The arts in Canada: a stocktaking at mid-century.* Toronto, Macmillan, 1958. p. 67-76. illus.

D42. **D'Auteuil, Georges Henri.** A l'enseigne du théâtre national populaire. *Relations* 215: 287-298, novembre 1958.

D43. **Hoos, Peter.** A multilingual theatre for Montreal. *Theatre Arts* 42: 58-59, December 1958. illus.

D44. **Moon, Barbara.** Why the world wants more of the "Théâtre du nouveau monde". *Maclean's* 71: 19, 62-66, May 24, 1958. illus.

D45. **Trueman, Albert William.** Le théâtre du nouveau monde. *Food for Thought* 19: 76-78, November 1958.

D46. **Whittaker, Herbert.** French Canada's success story. *Theatre Arts* 42: 22-23, 72-75, March 1958. illus.

D47. **Baxter, C.** Théâtre du nouveau monde; Montreal players truly international. *Financial Post* (Toronto) 53: 51-52, February 7, 1959.

D48. **D'Auteuil, Georges Henri.** Une affiche bien garnie. *Relations* no. 228: 321-322, décembre 1959.

D49. **Gélinas, Gratien.** Credo of the Comédie-Canadienne; the faith behind the little miracle. *Queen's Quarterly* 66: 18-25, spring 1959.

D50. **Hamelin, Jean.** Theatre today: French Canada. *Tamarack Review* 13: 38-47, autumn 1959.

D51. **Sabbath, Lawrence.** Comédie-Canadienne's first year. *Saturday Night* 74: 19-21, September 26, 1959. illus.

D52. **Sabbath, Lawrence.** French theatre in Quebec (province). *Canadian Commentator* 3: 10-12, October 1959.

D53. **Sabbath, Lawrence.** Théâtre du nouveau monde's ninth season. *Saturday Night* 74: 20-22, December 5, 1959. illus.

D54. **D'Auteuil, Georges Henri.** Crise du théâtre. *Relations* no. 230: 36-37, February 1960.

D55. **Beaulne, Guy.** Notre théâtre, image de notre milieu. *Revue Domincaine* 66: 25-37, juillet-août 1960.

D56. **Bobet, Jacques.** Le héros, l'anti-héros et le dramaturge. *Liberté* 2: 301-306, octobre 1960.

D57. **Bobet, Jacques.** Le cahier de doléances. *Liberté* 2: 213-215, mai-août 1960.

D58. **Kempf, Yerri.** Le théâtre et les justes. *Cité Libre* 11: 28-29, janvier-février 1960.

D59. **Marsolais, Gilles.** Eclairages sur le problème du théâtre. *Revue Dominicaine* 66: 156-161, avril 1960.

D60. **Primeau, Marguerite.** Gratien Gélinas et le théâtre populaire au Canada français. *Canadian Literature* 4: 31-39, spring 1960.

D61. **Winter, Jack.** Theatre season: Montreal. *Canadian Forum* 40: 201-205, December 1960.

D62. **Winter, Jack.** Theatre in Quebec. In John T. Saywell ed. *Canadian Annual Review for 1960.* Toronto, University of Toronto Press, 1961. p. 337-342.

D63. **Beaulne, Guy.** Le théâtre de langue française. In John T. Saywell ed. *Canadian Annual Review for 1961.* Toronto, University of Toronto Press, 1962. p. 387-395.

D64. **D'Auteuil, Georges Henri.** Reprise d'automne. *Relations* no. 251:309-311, novembre 1961.

D65. **D'Auteuil, Georges Henri.** Théâtre de Carnaval. *Relations* no. 243:67-68, mars 1961.

D66. **D'Auteuil, Georges Henri.** Théâtre de printemps. *Relations* no. 245:126-127, mai 1961.

D67. **D'Auteuil, Georges Henri.** Triple jeu. *Relations* no. 247:184-185, juillet 1961.

D68. **D'Auteuil, Georges Henri.** Trois époques de théâtre. *Relations* no. 246:161-162, juin 1961.

D69. **Darcy, J.** Triomphe de Bousille au festival de Vancouver. *Magazine Maclean* 1:85, octobre 1961.

D70. **Grandmont, Eloi de.** *Dix ans de théâtre au Nouveau Monde.* Montréal, Leméac, 1961. 159 p. illus.

D71. **Hamelin, Jean.** Des amateurs au sens pur. *Magazine Maclean* 1:53, août 1961.

D72. **Hamelin, Jean.** Québec n'occupe pas la place qui lui revient. *Magazine Maclean.* 1:79, novembre 1961.

D73. **Hamelin, Jean.** Plus de relâche pour le théâtre. *Magazine Maclean.* 1:65, septembre 1961.

D74. **Kempf, Yerri.** Chacun sa verité et M. Jean Gascon son erreur. *Cité Libre* 12:29-30, juin/juillet 1961.

D75. **Kempf, Yerri.** Des bons mots de Guitry. *Cité Libre* 12:32, octobre 1961.

D76. **Kempf, Yerri.** Esprit parisien et esprit de commis-voyageur. *Cité Libre* 12:30-31, août/septembre 1961.

D77. **Kempf, Yerri.** Musset dans l'Ile Sainte-Hélène. *Cité Libre* 12:30-32, novembre 1961.

D78. **Lamarche, Antonin.** Le théâtre dans le mouvement ouvrier. *Revue Dominicaine* 67:50-51, janvier/février 1961.

D79. **Robert, Guy.** Le théâtre du Québec. *Revue Dominicaine* 67:19-36, juillet/août 1961.

D80. **Savard, Félix-Antoine.** La pressante necessité d'un grand théâtre chez nous. *Lectures* 7:155-156, janvier 1961.

D81. **Savard, Félix-Antoine.** Le théâtre que je rève. *Revue de l'Université Laval* 15:427-429, janvier 1961.

D82. **D'Auteuil, Georges Henri.** Les classiques à l'honneur. *Relations* 22:78-79, mars 1962.

D83. **Beaulne, Guy.** Le théâtre de langue française. In John T. Saywell ed. *Canadian Annual Review for 1962.* Toronto, University of Toronto Press, 1963. p. 391-399.

D84. **Bosco, Monique.** Les apprentis-sorciers. *Magazine Maclean* 2:26-28, 63, avril 1962. illus.

D85. **Ferry, Anthony.** French Canada's famous but tired TNM finds its second youth. *Maclean's Magazine.* 75:70-71, December 15, 1962.

D86. **Hamelin, Jean.** Montreal: the French theatre. *Tamarack Review* no. 25:69-75, autumn 1962.

D87. **Hénault, Gilles.** Vous voulez jouer du Racine? Cher jeune ami fondez une troupe! *Magazine Maclean* 2:81, décembre 1962.

D88. **Johnstone, Ken.** Première à la Poudrière. *Magazine Maclean* 2:29-31, 40, juin 1962. illus.

D89. **Kempf, Yerri.** A l'Egregore et au Stella. *Cité Libre* 13:31, mai 1962.

D90. **Kempf, Yerri.** Un festival de bienfaisance. *Cité Libre* 13:31-32, juin/juillet 1962.

D91. **Kempf, Yerri.** Visitation poétique à la boulangerie. *Cité Libre* 13:30-32, février 1962.

D92. **Kempf, Yerri.** Des lauriers pour le T.N.M. *Cité Libre* 13:31-32, janvier 1962.

D93. **Moon, Barbara.** Woman who stages plays in five languages. *Maclean's Magazine* 75:19-21, June 16, 1962. illus. (La Poudrière, Montreal).

D94. **Patry, Pierre.** Le paradoxe du succès. *Liberté* 4:286-288, avril 1962.

D95. **Russel, Robert.** Camus double bill at the Comédie Canadienne, Montreal. *Canadian Art* 19:185, May-June 1962.

D96. **Russel, Robert.** Théâtre du Nouveau Monde, a climate of urgency. *Canadian Art* 19:235-237, May-June 1962.

D97. **Sabbath, Lawrence.** Invasion of French theatre. *Performing Arts* 1:34-36, spring-summer 1962.

D98. **D'Auteuil, Georges Henri.** Les festivals d'art dramatique. *Relations* 23:138-139, mai 1963.

D99. **Beaulne, Guy.** Le théâtre de langue française. In John T. Saywell ed. *Canadian Annual Review for 1963.* Toronto, University of Toronto Press, 1964. p. 483-493.

D100. **Bobet, Jacques.** La semaine poids-plumes. *Liberté* 5:154-157, mars/avril 1963.

D101. **Constantineau, Gilles.** Notre théâtre est figé, désuet et nuisible . . . vive le cinéma. *Magazine Maclean* 3:10, 47, août 1963.

D102. **Hénault, Gilles.** A ceux qui s'engagent dans le théâtre, il faut crier: casse-cou. *Magazine Maclean* 3:77-78, mai 1963.

D103. **Hénault, Gilles.** La critique fait de son mieux dans des conditions difficiles. *Magazine Maclean* 3:61, mars 1963.

D104. **Hénault, Gilles.** Notre théâtre est dans le noir: une enquête est-elle souhaitable? *Magazine Maclean* 3:47, janvier 1963.

D105. **Hénault, Gilles.** Poésie et peinture ont leur passeport, notre théâtre, non! *Magazine Maclean* 3:81, juin 1963.

D106. **Jasmin, Claude.** Le théâtre descend dans la rue. (Paul Buissoneau). *Magazine Maclean* 3:19-21, 37-38, août 1963. illus. (Children's theatre).

D107. **Rochette, Gilles.** C'est vrai que *notre* théâtre est figé, désuet et nuisible; *le* théâtre, non! *Magazine Maclean* 3:89-90, novembre 1963.

D108. **Sabbath, Lawrence.** French Canadian theatre as an art form. *Canadian Art* 20:356-357, November-December 1963.

D109. **Sabourin, Jean-Guy.** Apprentis-sorciers. *Maintenant* 16:139, avril 1963.

D110. **D'Auteuil, Georges Henri.** Le théâtre. *Relations* no. 281:152-153, mai 1964.

D111. **Bosco, Monique.** Festival au Gésu: Sartre est interdit. *Magazine Maclean* 4:70-71, avril 1964.

D112. **Kempf, Yerri.** Art is money. *Cité Libre* 15:30-31, octobre 1964.

D113. **Kempf, Yerri.** La fiesta des dieux aztèques. *Cité Libre* 15:31-32, janvier 1964.

D114. **Kempf, Yerri.** Miracle au Rideau Vert. *Cité Libre* 15:31-32, août-septembre 1964.

D115. **Kempf, Yerri.** *Les trois coups a Montréal: chroniques dramatiques 1959-1964.* Montréal, Déom, 1965. 383 p.

D116. **Sabbath, Lawrence.** French theatre in Quebec. In John T. Saywell ed. *Canadian Annual Review for 1964.* Toronto, University of Toronto Press, 1965. p. 463-469.

D117. **Berthiaume, André.** L'homme et la parole. *La Barre du Jour* 1:60-61, juillet/décembre, 1965.

D118. **Brierly, John.** Montreal English theatre. *Montrealer* 39:9, July 1965.

D119. **Cunningham, Jack.** Instant theatre. *Montrealer* 39:9, March 1965.

D120. **Desrochiers, Pierre.** Le 60 jours du théâtre d'été. *Magazine Maclean* 5:27-29, 47-49, novembre 1965.

D121. **Fahmy-Eid, Nadia.** Le théâtre de langue française. In John T. Saywell ed. *Canadian Annual Review for 1965.* Toronto, University of Toronto Press, 1966. p. 503-511.

D122. **Ferron, Jacques.** Le permis de dramaturge. *La Barre du Jour* 1:65-70, juillet/décembre, 1965.

D123. **Fox, Colin.** Montreal, land of the too frequent phoenix. *Performing Arts* 4:2-7, fall 1965. illus.

D124. **Hénault, Gilles.** L'optimisme est-il permis? *Magazine Maclean* 5:47, janvier 1965.

D125. **Jasmin, Claude.** "Faire parler les autres" un métier difficile! *La Barre du Jour* 1:80-84, juillet/décembre, 1965.

D126. **Kattan, Naim.** Montreal letter: French Canadian plays. *Tamarack Review* no. 37:60-64, autumn 1965.

D127. **Kempf, Yerri.** Comment peut-on être auteur dramatique? *La Barre du Jour* 1:21-22, juillet/décembre, 1965.

D128. **Kempf, Yerri.** Théâtre et société à Montréal. *Cité Libre* 16:27-29, juillet 1965.

D129. **Laurendeau, André.** Ça a commencé dans un théâtre de l'est de Montréal. *Magazine Maclean* 5:48, août 1965.

D130. **Maître, Manuel.** Experimental theatre in Old Montreal (Les Saltimbanques) *C.I.L. Oval* 34:8-10, fall 1965. illus.

D131. **Piazza, François.** Le critique dans le théâtre. *La Barre du Jour* 1:26-32, juillet/décembre, 1965.

D132. **Rémillard, Jean-Robert.** Théâtre et revolution québecoise. *La Barre du Jour* 1:91-93, juillet/décembre, 1965.

D133. **Sabourin, Jean-Guy.** Des hommes et du théâtre. *La Barre du Jour* 1:23-35, juillet/décembre, 1965.

D134. **Saint-Denis, Denys.** Amérique 1965 . . . *La Barre du Jour* 1:94-95, juillet/décembre, 1965.

D135. **Stafford, Jan.** Théâtre et société. *La Barre du Jour* 1:8-15, juillet/décembre, 1965.

D136. Théâtre Québec. *La Barre du Jour* (numéro spécial.) vol.1, no. 3-4-5, juillet/décembre, 1965. 172 p.

D137. **D'Auteuil, Georges Henri.** Le théâtre. *Relations* no. 306:181-184, juin 1966.

D138. **Bosco, Monique.** Un public de théâtre dont on se moque. *Magazine Maclean* 6:46-47, juillet 1966.

D139. **Guay, Jacques.** Un théâtre, un quartier. *Magazine Maclean* 6:59, septembre 1966.

D140. **Sabourin, Jean-Guy.** Quelques reflexions sur notre théâtre. *Cahiers de Sainte-Marie* 1:81-83, mai 1966.

D141. **Thiboutot, Yvon.** Théâtre populaire: maison de la culture. *Culture vivante* 4:21-25, 1966.

D142. **Vigneault, Jacques.** Le théâtre de langue française. In John T. Saywell ed. *Canadian Annual Review for 1966.* Toronto, University of Toronto Press, 1967. p. 447-456.

D143. **Dansereau, Jeanne.** Le Monument National: Ah! la belle époque. *Magazine Maclean* 7:20-21, 43-45, février 1967. illus.

D144. **Desrosiers, Pierre.** La nouvelle dramaturgie québecoise. *Culture Vivante* 5:71-77, 1967.

D145. **Doré, Fernand.** C'est la saison des abonnés. *Magazine Maclean* 7:82, novembre 1967.

D146. **Doré, Fernand.** Les jeunes au théâtre (Nouvelle compagnie théâtrale L'Egregore) *Magazine Maclean* 7:66, juin 1967.

D147. **Doré, Fernand.** Pourquoi pas des auteurs canadiens? *Magazine Maclean* 7:82-83, avril 1967.

D148. **Doré, Fernand.** Recruter le public qui est là. *Magazine Maclean* 7:78, décembre, 1967.

D149. **Doré, Fernand.** Roux relance le T.N.M. *Magazine Maclean* 7:54, juillet 1967.

D150. **Doré, Fernand.** Le théâtre ne paie pas. *Magazine Maclean* 7:82-83, mai 1967.

D151. **Dubé, Marcel.** Problem of language for the French-Canadian playwright. *World Theatre* 16:432-434, 1967.

D152. Footlight footnote. *Montrealer* 41:9, 42-44, January 1967.

D153. **Gouin, Ollivier-Mercier.** *Comédiens de notre temps: enquête.* Montreal, Editions du Jour, 1967. 139 p.

D154. **Hénaut, Dorothea Todd.** Montreal: artistic freedom on trial. *Arts Canada* 24:1-2, December 1967 supplement. illus.

D155. **Piazza, François.** Présence du théâtre québecois. *Théâtre Vivant* 3:3-8, juin 1967. illus.

D156. **Sabourin, Jean-Guy.** Le théâtre. *Culture Vivante* 5:24-27, 1967.

D157. **Vallon, Claude.** *Le dossier canadien du théâtre romand.* Lausanne, La Cité Editeur, 1967. 125 p. illus., bibl.

D158. **Vigneault, Jacques.** Le théâtre de langue française. In John T. Saywell ed. *Canadian Annual Review for 1967.* Toronto, University of Toronto Press, 1968. p. 457-464.

D159. **Béliard, Bernard.** Image d'un public de théâtre. *Culture Vivante* 9:22-26, 1968.

D160. **Doré, Fernand.** Les comédiens sont au vert. *Magazine Maclean* 8:46-7, juillet 1968.

D161. **Doré, Fernand.** Même les cinéastes y viennent. *Magazine Maclean* 8:46, janvier 1968.

D162. **Doré, Fernand.** Les "petits créateurs" en pleine effervescence. *Magazine Maclean* 8:62, décembre 1968.

D163. **Doré, Fernand.** 3 compagnies en quête de subventions. *Magazine Maclean* 8:75, octobre 1968.

D164. **Dubé, Marcel.** *Textes et documents.* Ottawa, Leméac, 1968. 80 p.

D165. **Gélinas, Marc F.** Orientations de la dramaturgie nouvelle. *Culture Vivante* 9:11-16, 1968.

D166. **Godin, Gérald.** Québec au stade du théâtre engagé. *Magazine Maclean* 8:78, novembre 1968.

D167. **Hamelin, Jean.** *The theatre in French Canada, 1936-66.* Quebec. Dept. of Cultural Affairs, 1968. 86 p. illus.

D168. **O'Rourke, Pat.** Backstage at the Revue. *Montrealer* 42:6-8, 29-30, December 1968. illus.

D169. **Roux, Jean-Louis.** Préface In: Grandmont, Eloi de. *Théâtre.* Montréal, Maisonneuve, (1968) Vol. 1.

D170. **Vigneault, Jacques.** Le théâtre de langue française. In John T. Saywell ed. *Canadian Annual Review for 1968.* Toronto, University of Toronto Press, 1969. p. 453-463.

D171. **Boutet, Edgar.** *85 ans de théâtre à Hull.* Hull, Société historique de l'ouest de Québec, 1969. 60 p. illus.

D172. *Le centre d'essai des auteurs dramatiques. Trois ans aprés sa fondation.* Montréal, Le Centre d'Essai des Auteurs Dramatiques, 1969, 16 p. mimeographed.

D173. **Doré, Fernand.** Le dernier mot appartient aux auteurs audacieux. *Magazine Maclean* 9:91, 93, novembre 1969.

D174. **Doré, Fernand.** Levac cherche le théâtre intégrale. *Magazine Maclean* 9:38, 40, août, 1969.

D175. **Gagnon, Gilles.** Le théâtre des Compagnons de Saint-Laurent. *Culture* 30:129-145, 1969.

D176. **Greffard, Madeleine.** Les lettres québecoises en 1968: le théâtre. *Etudes Littéraires* 2:221-237, août 1969.

D177. **Kattan, Naim.** Le théâtre et les dramaturges a Montréal. *Canadian Literature* 40:43-48, 1969.

D178. **Landriault, Bernard.** Dürrenmatt au Théâtre du Capricorne. *Vie des Arts* 57:58, hiver, 1969-70. illus.

D179. *Répértoire 1965-1968.* Montréal, Le Centre d'Essai des Auteurs Dramatiques, 1969. 30 p.

D180. **Roux, Jean-Louis.** Le théâtre québecois. *Europe* 47 no. 478-479:222-228. February-March, 1969.

D181. **Temkine, Raymonde.** L'activité théâtral au Québec. *Europe* 47 no. 478-479:228-238, February-March 1969.

D182. **Vigneault, Jacques.** Le théâtre de langue française. In John T. Saywell ed. *Canadian Annual Review for 1969.* Toronto, University of Toronto Press, 1970. p. 435-444.

D183. **Brunet, Yves-Gabriel.** Au théâtre populaire du Québec, une chevauchée fantastique. *Vie des Arts* no. 59:44-5, English text 80-81, summer 1970. illus.

D184. **Gélinas, Marc F.** "A l'Ensyme Boum Boum". *Magazine Maclean* 10:48, juillet 1970. illus. (Children's theatre)

D185. **Gélinas, Marc F.** Théâtre du Même Nom. *Magazine Maclean* 10:56, mai 1970. illus.

D186. **Gélinas, Marc F.** T'es pas tanné Réjean Ducharme? *Magazine Maclean* 10:68, avril 1970.

D187. **Gélinas, Marc F.** Notre théâtre nous ressemble. *Magazine Maclean* 10:42, 44, mars 1970.

D188. **Gélinas, Marc F.** On ne choisit pas ses compagnons de voyage. *Magazine Maclean* 10: 44, 46, février 1970.

D189. **Gélinas, Marc F.** Le théâtre, le cinéma et la messe. *Magazine Maclean* 10:42, 44, janvier 1970.

D190. **Godin, Jean Cléo.** Chroniques: le théâtre. *Etudes françaises* 6:504-511, novembre 1970.

D191. **Hamblet, Edwin C.** *Marcel Dubé and French Canadian drama.* N.Y. Exposition Press, 1970. 112 p.

D192. **Brunet, Yves Gabriel.** Derrière le Rideau Vert. *Vie des Arts* 62:54-55, printemps, 1971. illus.

D193. **Gélinas, Marc F.** Un théâtre populaire du Québec? *Magazine Maclean* 11:37, août 1971.

D194. **Tard, Louis Martin.** *Vingt ans de théâtre au Nouveau Monde.* Montreal, Editions du Jour, 1971. 175 p. illus.

D195. **Wojciechowska, Cécile Cloutier.** L'avant-garde dans la littérature québecoise. *Présence Francophone* no. 3:60-68, automne, 1971.

D196. **Dorsinville, Max.** The changing landscape of drama in Quebec. In New, William H. ed. *Dramatists in Canada: selected essays.* Vancouver, University of British Columbia Press, 1972. p. 179-195.

D197. Experiment in Montreal. *Performing Arts* 9:7, winter 1972. (Théâtre du Rideau Vert).

D198. **Gélinas, Marc F.** Théâtre: nous sommes de plus en plus chez nous, chez nous. *Magazine Maclean* 12:46, janvier 1972.

D199. **Germain, Jean Claude.** Ite, missa est. *Magazine Maclean* 12:80, décembre 1972.

D200. **Hamblet, Edwin.** Le monde clos: Dubé et Anouilh. In New, William H. ed. *Dramatists in Canada: selected essays.* Vancouver, University of British Columbia Press, 1972. p. 151-154. (Reprinted from: *Canadian Literature* no. 45:52-55, summer 1970.)

D201. **Kattan, Naim.** Le théâtre et les dramaturges à Montréal. In New, William H. ed. *Dramatists in Canada: selected essays.* Vancouver, University of British Columbia Press, 1972. p. 145-150. (Reprinted from: *Canadian Literature* no. 40:43-48, spring 1969.)

D202. Théâtre au Québec. 1950-1972. *Nord* no. 4 and 5, fall 1972-winter 1973. (special issue), Sillery, Editions de l'Hôte, 1973. 228 p. bibl.

D203. **Bélair, Michel.** *Le nouveau théâtre québecois.* Montréal, Leméac, 1973. 205 p.

D204. **Dubé, Marcel.** *Textes et documents,* part 2: la tragédie est un acte de foi. Montréal, Leméac, 1973.

D205. French theatre at the national arts centre. *Performing Arts* 10:7, winter 1973. illus.

D206. **Godin, Jean Cléo,** et **Mailhot, Laurent.** *Le théâtre québecois contemporain.* Montréal, Université de Montréal, 1973. 275 p.

D207. **Germain, Jean Claude.** Docteur Jekyll, Mister Hyde. *Le Maclean* 13:60, mai 1973. port.

D208. **Germain, Jean Claude.** Le mal anglais. *Le Maclean* 13:64, avril 1973.

D209. **Germain, Jean Claude.** Ne pas confondre tréteaux et tribunes. *Le Maclean* 13:52, septembre 1973. illus.

D210. **Germain, Jean Claude.** Le théâtre: le revolver sur l'eunuque. Le Maclean 13:58-59, mars 1973. illus.

D211. **Germain, Jean Claude.** Le théâtre: un theatre qui crève de santé. *Le Maclean* 13:31, 33, janvier 1973.

D212. **Germain, Jean Claude.** Un échec réussi. *Le Maclean* 13:60, juin 1973. illus.

D213. **Germain, Jean Claude.** Un homme qui sait ou il va. (Théâtre du rideau vert). *Le Maclean* 13:44, juillet 1973, port.

D214. **Hausvater, Alexander.** Lennoxville — 2. *Motion* 1:60-61, September-October 1973.

D215. **Hausvater, Alexander.** Montreal one more season. *Motion 1:38-40, July-August 1973. illus.*

D216. **Hausvater, Alexander.** Montreal season. *Motion* 1:58, September-October 1973.

D217. **Lamarche, Gustave.** *Le théâtre québecois dans notre littérature.* Trois Rivières, Université du Québec à Trois Rivières, Centre de théâtre québecois, 1973. 35 p. bibl.

D218. **Laurendeau, André.** It all began in a theatre in the east of Montreal. In *Witness for Quebec.* Toronto, MacMillan, 1973, p. 255-259. (previously published as Ça a commencé dans un théâtre de l'est de Montréal. *Le Maclean* 5:48, août 1965).

D219. **Mailhot, Laurent.** Théâtre: letters in Canada. *University of Toronto Quarterly* 42:363-366, summer 1973.

D220. **Robb, Edith.** Women on the go: Viola Légér, Acadian actress. *Chatelaine* 46:10, 14, May 1973. port.

D221. **Shek, Ben.** En français le grand cirque ordinaire. *Performing Arts* 10:16-19, winter 1973. illus.

D222. **Shek, Ben.** Quebec letter: la sagouine. *Performing Arts* 10:32-33, fall 1973. port., tab.

D223. **Shek, Ben.** Quebec letter: ça et là. *Performing Arts* 10:33-34, fall 1973. illus.

D224. **Spensley, Philip.** Anglophone theatre scene: ah, Montreal is Montreal! *Performing Arts* 10:20-23, summer 1973. illus., port.

D225. **Spensley, Philip.** Formula for success: festival Lennoxville. *Performing Arts.* 10:11-17, fall 1973. illus.

D226. Théâtre midi T.N.M. — duMaurier. *Commerce* 73:79, avril 1973. illus.

D227. **Anderson, Christopher.** Drama: chamber pots and wigs. (Festival Lennoxville). *Time* (Canada) 104:11, July 15, 1974.

D228. **Billington, Dave.** Festival Lennoxville: festival where? *Performing Arts* 11:28-31, summer 1974. illus., port.

D229. **Booth, Amy.** Montreal operation: English theatre to end dramatic drought. (Centaur Theatre). *Financial Post* 68:19, April 13, 1974.

D230. **Genest, Jean.** Jean Tetreau au théâtre. *L'Action Nationale* 63:781, avril-mai 1974.

D231. **Hausvater, Alexander.** The commercial play. *Motion* 2:51, May-June 1974.

D232. **Kapica, J.** Jeanine Beaubien sits on a multi-cultural powderkeg. (La Poudrière). *Performing Arts* 11:25-26, fall 1974. illus., port.

D233. **Mailhot, Laurent.** Théâtre: letters in Canada. *University of Toronto Quarterly* 43:377-380, summer 1974.

D234. **Maulucci, Anthony.** To be. (The actor's school and the French-Canadian actor). *Motion* 2:19-20, July-August 1974.

D235. New for Montreal audiences. (Centaur Theatre). *Performing Arts* 11:8, spring 1974.

D236. **Saint-Jacques, Denis.** Des Canadiens, des Québecois, une Acadienne ou l'invisibilité du théâtre au théâtre. *Etudes Françaises* 10:151-159, mai 1974.

D237. **Shek, Ben.** Quebec's new playwrights go national with a bit of help from C.E.A.D. *Performing Arts* 11:19-20, summer 1974. illus., port.

D238. **Treacher, G.J.P.** Theatre Canada festival. *Atlantic Advocate* 64:36-39, August 1974. illus.

D239. **Balay, Billyann.** Lennoxville is a showcase of Canadian talents each year. *Performing Arts* 12:24, summer 1975, port.

D240. **Cotnam, Jacques.** Du théâtre québecois actuel. *La Dryade* (Belgique) 81:51-59, printemps 1975.

D241. du Maurier awards theatres across Canada. *Performing Arts* 12:7-8, spring 1975.

D242. **Mailhot, Laurent.** Théâtre (Letters in Canada: 1974) *University of Toronto Quarterly* 44:355-359, summer 1975.

D243. **Théâtre du Rideau Vert.** *Théâtre du Rideau Vert: 25 ans, 1949-1974.* Montréal, Théâtre du Rideau Vert, 1975. n.p., illus., port.

A photograph of *Les Belles-Soeurs* by Michel Tremblay as performed at Le Théâtre du Rideau Vert in their 1968-9 season.

See items listed in Index under Théâtre du Rideau Vert and Michel Tremblay.

E

Little Theatre Movement

E1. **Aikins, Carroll** ed. Survey of Canadian amateur stage. *Canadian Forum* 9:51-62, November 1928.

E2. **Burton, Jean.** The little theatre in the country. *Canadian Forum* 7:211-212, April 1928.

E3. Canadian little theatre. *Canadian Forum* 9:41, November 1928.

E4. **Taylor, Dorothy G.** What about the little theatres? *Canadian Forum* 9:42-43, November 1928.

E5. **Aikins, Carroll.** The amateur theatre in Canada. In Brooker, Bertram ed. *Yearbook of the arts in Canada* 1928-29. Toronto, Macmillan 1929. p. 43-48.

E6. **Bishop, George Walter** ed. Some prominent societies in Canada. In *Amateur dramatic yearbook and community theatre handbook* 1928-29. London, Black, 1929. p. 183-193.

E7. The little theatre. *Curtain Call* 1:7, December 21, 1929.

E8. **Bridle, Augustus.** Creative theatre reviewed. *Curtain Call* 1:3, April 12, 1930.

E9. The little theatre movement. *Curtain Call* 1:3, February 8, 1930.

E10. Our acting amateurs. *Curtain Call* 2:6-7, December 1, 1930.

E11. The season's work in review. *Curtain Call* 1:1-2, May 10, 1930.

E12. The theatre of the future. *Curtain Call* 1:7, April 12, 1930.

E13. **Lerner, Gertrude.** Footlights in Canada; an estimate of the little theatre movement in Canada. *Drama Magazine* 21:17-18, 24, June 1931.

E14. **Key, Archibald.** The theatre on wheels. *Canadian Forum* 13:462-463, September 1933.

E15. Little theatre should be a community project. *Canadian Bookman* 15:13, January 1933.

E16. **Allan, Martha.** The future of the Canadian little theatre. *Curtain Call* 6:1-2, 13-14, November 17, 1934.

E17. **Brighouse, Harold.** What do they act? *Curtain Call* 6:1-2, October 17, 1934.

E18. **Bessborough, Vere Brabazon Ponsonby, 9th Earl of.** Community drama sweeps Canada. *Curtain Call* 7:3, 14, December 1935.

E19. **Morley, Malcolm.** Canada's kitchen drama. *Saturday Night* 50:12, August 10, 1935.

E20. **Ramsay, Alexander.** The one-act play and the little theatre. *Curtain Call* 6:2-3, April 1935.

E21. **Pyper, Nancy.** Among the amateurs. *Saturday Night* 53:11, March 5, 1938.

E22. **Campbell, Loughlin.** Reflections on the decline of the little theatre. *Curtain Call* 11:19-20, November 1939.

E23. **Hoare, John Edward.** Community theatre to Canadian theatre. *Saturday Night* 59:14, February 5, 1944.

E24. **Morley, Malcolm.** Amateurs and actors. *Saturday Night* 64:32-33, October 9, 1948.

E25. **Somerset, Dorothy.** The amateur theatre takes stock; how does the emergence of professional theatre in Canada affect amateur groups? *Food for Thought* 8:20-25, May 1948. illus.

E26. **Ness, Margaret.** The theatre tips a new straw hat. *Saturday Night* 65:8-9, July 4, 1950. illus.

E27. Canada's lively "little theatre". *Food for Thought* 17:175-181, January 1957.

E28. **Tyrwhitt, Janice.** Amateur theatre's cast of thousands. *Maclean's Magazine* 75:22-23, 54, January 6, 1962. illus.

E29. **Chadwick, Stella.** "So you want to start an amateur theatre . . . " *Performing Arts* 4 no. 2:16-20, winter 1965-6.

ATLANTIC PROVINCES

E30. **Soper, P. Lloyd.** St. John's players. *Atlantic Guardian* 1:19-20, 31, September 1945.

E31. **Robertson, J.L.** The little theatre movement in Nova Scotia. *Canadian Review of Music and Art* 5:14-16, February 1946. illus.

E32. **Wetmore, Donald.** Nova Scotians enjoy learning drama. *Food for Thought* 13:27-29, March 1953.

E33. **Wich, Sylvia.** Theatre in Newfoundland. *Atlantic Advocate* 48:55-59, May 1958. illus.

E34. **Loomer, L.S.** Chocolate cove playhouse. *Atlantic Advocate* 50:95-99, September 1959. illus.

QUEBEC

E35. **Denison, Merrill.** The little theatres — the community players of Montreal. *Canadian Bookman* 6:32, February 1923.

E36. M.R.T. Season begins. *Curtain Call* 6:15, October 17, 1934. (Montreal Repertory Theatre).

E37. Students on stage. *Canadian Stage, Screen and Studio* 1:4-6, March 1936. illus.

E38. Meet Mr. Atterbury. *Canadian Stage, Screen and Studio* 1:4-5, January 1937. (Corona Barn Theatre, Montreal).

E39. **Bolton, Mada Gage.** The Lakeshore summer theatre (Montreal). *Curtain Call* 12:5-6, October 1940.

E40. Brae Manor Theatre (Montreal); success story. *Curtain Call* 12:6, April 1941.

E41. The Work of Hart House Theatre. *Canadian Bookman* 2:30-31, December 1920.

E42. **Coventry, Alan Freeth.** The technical work of a little theatre. *Canadian Forum* 1:108-109, January 1921. (Players Club, Toronto.)

E43. **Forsythe, Bertram.** Hart House Theatre and Canadian drama by Bertram Forsythe and E.A. Dale. *Acta Victoriana* 46:212-213, February 1922.

E44. **Denison, Merrill.** The Arts and letters players (Toronto) *Canadian Bookman* 5:31-32, February 1923.

E45. **Denison, Merrill.** Hart House theatre. *Canadian Bookman* 5:61-63, March 1923.

E46. **Denison, Merrill.** The little theatres; Ottawa drama league. *Canadian Bookman* 5:32, February 1923.

E47. **Smillie, Eleanor Anna.** Ottawa drama league. *Canadian Bookman* 5:151-152, June 1923.

E48. **Denison, Merrill.** A backwoods commedia dell'arte. *Theatre Arts Monthly* 12:682-685, September 1928. illus.

E49. *Hart House theatre, Toronto.* A description of the theatre and the record of its first nine seasons, 1919-1928. Toronto. n.d. 22 p. illus. plan.

E50. The curtain ascends at Hart House theatre. *Curtain Call* 1:1-2, November 9, 1929.

E51. English drama at Hart House. *Curtain Call* 1:1-2, November 23, 1929.

E52. Settlement children see dress rehearsal. *Curtain Call* 1:1-3, December 21, 1929.

E53. Wizard of Oz next play. *Curtain Call* 1:1, December 7, 1929. (Hart House).

E54. Analysis of "The Show-Off" by American critic. *Curtain Call* 1:1-2, April 12, 1930.

E55. Drama class gives Shakespeare production. *Curtain Call* 1:1-2, January 25, 1930. (Hart House).

E56. Hart House: a community theatre. *Curtain Call* 1:1-2, January 11, 1930.

E57. Romantic comedy for ninety-seventh production. *Curtain Call* 1:1-2, February 8, 1930.

E58. Spring speeds activities at Toronto's little theatre. *Curtain Call* 1:1-2, February 22, 1930.

E59. Typical American comedy next Hart House production. *Curtain Call* 1:1-2, March 22, 1930.

E60. **Patton, G.E.** Drama in the country. *Echoes* no. 129:15, December 1932.

E61. Gala season begins at Hart House. *Curtain Call* 6:3-4, October 17, 1934.

E62. **Margetson, Mary.** Hart House theatre. *Saturday Night* 50:12-13, September 14, 1935.

E63. **Gibbons, Kay.** The Actors' Colony theatre. *Curtain Call* 7:7, March 1936. (Bala, Muskoka).

E64. **Herity, J.O.** Dramatic history made with rural comedy. *Curtain Call* 7:10, May 1936. (Markham Drama Club 1906).

E65. Play contest. *New Frontier* 1 no. 3:25, June 1936.

E66. **Moore, Jocelyn.** The Canadian contest plays. *New Frontier* 1:13-14, March 1937. (Toronto).

E67. Play contest. *New Frontier* 1 no. 10:6, February 1937.

E68. Second play contest. *New Frontier* 2 no. 3:21, July-August 1937.

E69. **Smith, Hilda M.** Town Hall tonight. *Curtain Call* 9:17-18, October 1937. (Port Stanley, Ont.)

E70. Toronto masquers' club; a pictorial history. *Canadian Stage, Screen and Studio.* 2:7-12, December 1937.

E71. Trinity players (Toronto). *Canadian Stage, Screen and Studio* 1:18-19, March 1937. 2:13, 16, December 1937.

E72. **Skinner, Alan.** The London little theatres — past and present. *Curtain Call* 12:5-6, December 1940.

E73. **Farquharson, Rica McLean.** International seasoning of Ottawa little theatre. *Curtain Call* 12:3-4, May-June 1941.

E74. **Hardy, Alison Taylor.** The Ottawa little theatre — past and present. *Curtain Call* 12:3-4, January 1941.

E75. **Skinner, Alan.** A theatre grows in London. *Canadian Review of Music and Art* 5:31, 33-34, February 1946.

E76. **Bridle, Augustus.** *The story of the club.* Toronto, Arts and Letters Club, 1945 vi, 83 p. illus.

E77. **Kelly, Donald G.** Once-upon-a-time there was a Canadian theatre. *Canadians All* 3:28, 48, 60, spring 1945. (University College Players' Guild, Toronto.)

E78. Next rehearsal Tuesday. *Varsity Graduate* (Toronto) 1:11-13, June 1948. illus.

E79. **Fleming, Helen M.** The player's guild of Hamilton. *Canadian Forum* 29:87-88, July 1949.

E80. Play season at Hart House. *Varsity Graduate* 3:2-5, December 1949. illus.

E81. Tryout Town. *Time* 55:22-23, February 6, 1950. (London Little Theatre).

E82. Player's guild of Hamilton. *Canadian Life* 1:31, 39, winter 1951. illus.

E83. Up with the big ones. *Saturday Night* 66:19, January 23, 1951. (Woodstock Little Theatre).

E84. **Richards, Stanley.** Black ink — and no black magic. *Theatre Arts* 37:64-65, June 1953. illus.

E85. Ottawa little theatre. *Theatre Canada* no. 37:2-4, November/December 1957.

E86. **Miller, J.E.** *The history of the Sudbury Little Theatre Guild 1948-1962.* 1963. 75 p.

E87. **Brown, Mary.** Chronicle. *Canadian Literature* no. 31:54-58, winter 1967. (University of Western Ontario Summer Theatre 1966).

E88. **Halpenny, Francess.** Shall we join the ladies? (Women's Alumni Theatre). *University of Toronto Graduate* 2:48-51, 102-109, December 1968.

E89. **Montagnes, Ian.** *An uncommon fellowship: the story of Hart House.* Toronto, University of Toronto Press, 1969. viii, 204 p.

E90. **Mullock, A.C.** *The Player's Guild of Hamilton.* Centennial booklet, compiled and edited by A.C. Mullock, H. Waldick, G. Smith, D. Penrose, S. Peters, R. Siles. Hamilton 1975.

PRAIRIE PROVINCES

E91. **Hesson, Hilda.** The community players of Winnipeg. *Canadian Bookman* 5:121, May 1923. 5:152, June 1923.

E92. **Young, Landon.** The little theatre of Winnipeg. *Canadian Forum* 7:370-372, September 1927.

E93. Little theatre in Manitoba; dramatic festivals organized. *Canadian Bookman* 14:60, May 1932.

E94. **McGurk, John.** Nights without end. *Commonwealth* 20:150-151, June 8, 1934. (North-West Canada.)

E95. Manitoba's stage. *Canadian Stage, Screen and Studio* 1:4-5, October 1936.

E96. **Hesson, Hilda.** John Craig and the little theatre. *Curtain Call* 8:11-12, April 1937. (Winnipeg Little Theatre).

E97. **Gowan, Elsie Park.** The Edmonton little theatre — past and present. *Curtain Call* 2:7, March 1941.

E98. **Douglas, Francis.** Some notes on Masquers' overseas tour. *Canadian Review of Music and Art* 5:39-42, February 1946. illus. (Winnipeg Masquers' Club with Toronto and Montreal Masquers' Clubs).

E99. **Henderson, Roy D.** The theatre in Saskatchewan. *Canadian Review of Music and Art* 5:32-33, February 1946.

E100. Workshop 14. *Saturday Night* 65:25, February 7, 1950. illus. (Calgary).

E101. Theatre golden rule days. *Saturday Night* 66:11, May 1, 1951. (Workshop 14. Betty Mitchell).

E102. **Craig, Irene.** *The first quarter of a century of the Manitoba drama league* by Irene Craig and A.G. Smith. (Winnipeg, Manitoba Drama League, 1956). (mimeographed).

E103. **Prendergast, Tannis.** "WLT" origins and influence. *Food for Thought* 18:267-274, March 1958. (Winnipeg Little Theatre).

E104. **Craig, Irene.** *An informal record covering activities to December 1959 of the Manitoba drama league.* (Winnipeg) 1961. 46 p.

E105. New amateur theatre organization. *Performing Arts* 9:7, winter 1972. (Manitoba).

E106. **Alexander, Mary H.T.** Little theatres of the West. *Maclean's Magazine* 34:52, 54. October 1, 1921.

E107. **Cash, Gwen.** A community theatre in the wilds. (Naramata, B.C.) *Maclean's Magazine* 34:52-53, January 1, 1921.

E108. **Kerr, Ruth H.** The Home theatre of the Canadian players. *Theatre Arts Magazine* 6:67-72, January 1922.

E109. **Beaufort, Aileen.** Carroll Aikins: Home producer. *Canadian Magazine* 60:557-562, April 1923. illus.

E110. Theatre in the wilderness. *Living Age* 316:549-550, March 3, 1923. (Home Theatre.)

E111. **Bullock-Webster, Llewelyn.** The Canadian drama award. *Curtain Call* 7:3, October 1935. (B.C. drama).

E112. **Crighton, Dorothy V.** Command performance. *Curtain Call* 6:20, April 1935. (B.C. drama).

E113. **Morley, Malcolm.** Drama at the coast. *Saturday Night* 50:12, 15, August 24, 1935.

E114. **Crighton, Dorothy V.** The fifth annual B.C. drama festival. *Curtain Call* 7:5, 17, May 1936.

E115. **Crighton, Dorothy V.** The Pacific coast drama conference. *Curtain Call* 7:4-5, May 1936.

E116. **Firkins, Yvonne.** Community drama in British Columbia. *Curtain Call* 12:7-8, October 1940.

E117. **MacCorkindale, Archie.** Drama goes north. *Curtain Call* 11:5-6, January 1940. (B.C. Little theatre).

E118. **MacCorkindale, Archie.** Victoria letter. *Curtain Call* 12:10, October 1940.

E119. **Firkins, Yvonne.** A Canadian theatre comes of age. *Curtain Call* 13:8, November 1941. (Vancouver Little Theatre.)

E120. **Bullock-Webster, Llewelyn.** *A series of informal talks on community drama in British Columbia.* Victoria, B.C. Dept. of Education, School and Community Drama Branch. (1940-1943). Pamphlets held in Metropolitan Toronto Central Library.

E121. **Parkes, J. Delisle.** The little theatre movement in British Columbia. *Canadian Review of Music and Art* 5:25-26, 34, February 1946. illus.

E122. **Perrault, Ernest.** Dorothy Somerset curtain call. *P.M. Magazine* 1:9-13, December/January 1951-52.

Hart House Theatre

The photo above is of Carroll Aikins' *God of Gods,* performed in the 1921-22 season, and the first full-length Canadian play at Hart House. The play had previously been given a more elaborate production by the Birmingham Repertory Theatre, England, and was subsequently published in 1926 in *Canadian Plays from Hart House,* Volume II. The scene shown here occurs toward the end of the play were the newly initiated Indian priestess, Suiva, is performing a death rite on a man who has transgressed the sanctity of the sacred precinct. Unknown to Suiva, the victim is her lover. The rather rough setting shown is worth viewing in light of the author's grand stage directions:

"The scene represents a rocky canyon and is divided from left to right by a deep chasm at the bottom of which is a swift stream. The chasm is spanned by a huge, hideous stone image of the God of Gods. . . . The altar is approached by three stone steps; . . . To the left, well forward, is a high, flat-topped rock . . . To the right is a sheer cliff pierced by a cavern with a door-like opening. The background shows only the scarred face of a cliff tufted with ferns and stunted pine trees." (p.30).

Above is a scene from Merrill Denison's one act play, *The Prize Winner*, done at Hart House in the 1927-28 season. The scene takes place in the backstage area of a circus tent. The photo below offers a strong contrast to the previous ones in its minutely detailed realistic setting. The play is Noel Coward's *I'll Leave It to You*, done during the 1925-26 season.

See items listed in Index under Hart House Theatre.

F

Dominion Drama Festival

F1. Dominion drama festival; little theatre news from the different Canadian cities. *Canadian Bookman* 14: 126, November 1932.

F2. Drama league festivals; news of the little theatres. *Canadian Bookman* 15: 39-40, March 1933.

F3. **Bruce, Herbert A.** The national drama league of Canada. Address at the conclusion of the performance in the dominion drama festival finals at Hart House theatre, March 26, 1934. In his *Our heritage and other addresses*. Toronto, Macmillan, 1934: 200-202.

F4. New regulation governing festival of 1935. *Curtain Call* 6: 5-6, October 17, 1934.

F5. **Alexander, Henry.** The drama festival and the little theatre. *Curtain Call* 6: 1-2, 15, February 1935.

F6. All roads lead to Ottawa. *Curtain Call* 6: 1, April 1935. (D.D.F.)

F7. **Crighton, Dorothy V.** Festival honours to Victoria playwright. *Curtain Call* 6: 9, June 1935.

F8. **Morley, Malcolm.** *D.D.F. adjudicators trip.* Press clippings, programmes, articles on microfilm. (Metropolitan Toronto Central Library).

F9.**Morley, Malcolm.** Dominion festival. *Saturday Night* 51:11, December 28, 1935.

F10. **Morley, Malcolm.** Drama in Canada's Winnipeg drama judging. *Saturday Night* 50: 11, August 3, 1935.

F11. **Morley, Malcolm.** Drama in Eastern Ontario. *Saturday Night* 50:12, September 21, 1935.

F12. **Morley, Malcolm.** Festivalia. *Curtain Call* 7: 1-2, 7-8, November 1935.

F13. **Morley, Malcolm.** *Theatre journey: ramblings of an adjudicator.* Ms. on microfilm, 1935 n.p. (Metropolitan Toronto Central Library).

F14. **Morley, Malcolm.** Toronto festival. *Saturday Night* 51: 30-31, December 7, 1935.

F15. **Bernhardt, Clara.** The play's the thing. *Curtain Call* 8: 1, December 1936. (D.D.F.)

F16. **(Grein, Alice Augusta Greeven).** Dominion drama festival. In her *J. T. Grein, the story of a pioneer 1862-1935* by his wife, Michael Orme, *pseud.* London, Murray, 1936. p. 329-339. illus.

F17. **Eayrs, Hugh.** Correspondence (concerning D.D.F.) *New Frontier* 2: 20, July-August, 1937.

F18. Fiesta the fifth. *Curtain Call* 8: 1-2, 13-16, May-June 1937. (D.D.F.)

F19. **Gould, Mona.** On to Ottawa. *Curtain Call* 8: 1-2, March 1937. (D.D.F.)

F20. **Grant, Alexander.** Romeo and Juliet at Winnipeg pleases critics. *Curtain Call* 8: 11, January 1937.

F21. **Gullan, Marjorie** and **Kerby, Gertrude.** Ukrainian play praised. *Curtain Call* 8: 3, January 1937. (Winnipeg).

F22. **Pressman, David.** The drama festival. *New Frontier* 2: 26, June 1937.

F23. **Pyper, Nancy.** A director's critique: This mad world. *Curtain Call* 8: 4, January 1937.

F24. **McGinley, Alfred.** Winnipeg prepares for the festival. *Curtain Call* 9: 6, January 1938.

F25. **Morley, Malcolm.** An adjudicator's log. *Curtain Call* 9: 1-2, March 1938.

F26. **Morley, Malcolm.** Highlights in Toronto. *Curtain Call* 9: 4-6, May 1938. (D.D.F.)

F27. **Morley, Malcolm.** Victoria to Windsor. *Curtain Call* 9: 5, 15, April 1938. (D.D.F.)

F28. **Pyper, Nancy.** Drama festival. *Saturday Night* 53: 19, April 9, 1938.

F29. **Osborne, H.C.** Status of the Dominion Drama Festival defined. *Curtain Call* 12: 1-2, February 1941.

F30. **Coulter, John.** Time for dusting off the drama festival. *Saturday Night* 62: 20, March 22, 1947.

F31. **Coulter, John.** A festival adjudicator should wear two masks. *Saturday Night* 62: 18-19, April 26, 1947.

F32. **Tovell, Vincent.** Festival postscript. *Canadian Forum* 27: 64, June 1947.

F33. **(Sandwell, Bernard Keble).** Drama festival exhibits many fine offerings. By Lucy Van Gogh, pseud. *Saturday Night* 63: 2-3, 28, May 15, 1948. illus.

F34. Dominion drama festival. Illustrations. *Saturday Night* 64: 2-3, May 24, 1949.

F35. **Milne, William S.** Drama festival afterthoughts. *Canadian Forum* 30: 82-83, July 1950.

F36. **Cowan, John.** *Canada's Governor Generals, 1867-1952.* Toronto, York Publishing, 1952. p. 142. 2nd ed. 1965, p. 154.

F37. Drama festival, Saint John. Illustrations. *Saturday Night* 67: 12, April 26, 1952.

F38. Whiskey angel. *Newsweek* 39: 45, April 28, 1952. (Dominion Drama Festival - Calvert Trophy).

F39. **Whittaker, Herbert.** Drama festival enters new era. *Saturday Night* 67: 16, June 7, 1952.

F40. Dominion drama festival. *New Frontiers* 4: 1, summer 1955.

F41. **Colby, Mel.** The Dionysian drama festival. *New Frontiers* 5: 36, summer 1956.

F42. **Dominion Drama Festival.** *The procedure and organization of the Dominion Drama Festival, 1956.* (Ottawa 1956) 1, 10, 25 leaves.

F43. **Fowke, Helen Shirley.** A national occasion; A report of the dominion drama festival in Halifax. *Atlantic Advocate* 48: 55-59, June 1958. illus.

F44. **Hatfield, G.H.D.** The dominion drama festival comes to Nova Scotia. *Nova Scotia Teachers' Bulletin* 34: 28-9, April 1958.

F45. **West, Richard.** Maritime adventure; a report on the regional drama festivals. *Atlantic Advocate* 48: 79-81, March 1958. illus.

F46. **McKay, A.G.** Western Ontario drama. *Waterloo Review* 2, no. 1: 13-16, summer 1959.

F47. **McKay, A.G.** Western Ontario drama. *Waterloo Review* 2, no. 5: 15-19, summer 1960.

F48. **Smith, Marion B.** What is the role of the D.D.F.? *Saturday Night* 75: 54, June 10, 1961.

F49. **Sabbath, Lawrence.** Let's abolish the D.D.F. — almost! *Saturday Night* 76: 54, June 10, 1961.

F50. Broadcasters group back Canada drama festival. *Arts Management* no. 19: 2, August 1963.

F51. **Ljungh, Esse W.** Curtain going up! Dominion Drama Festival. *Performing Arts* 2, no. 3: 28-30, summer 1963.

F52. **Hesse, Jurgen.** The D.D.F. awards. *Performing Arts* 3, no. 1:48-53, fall 1964. illus.

F53. **Stewart, Mrs. Carl.** D.D.F. report. (Mrs. Carl Stewart interviewing Kate Reid, William Hutt, Gratien Gélinas, Jean Gascon, John Colicos). *Performing Arts* 2, no. 4: 36-44, spring 1964.

F54. **Daley, Frank.** Dominion Drama Festival 1966, triumph or travesty? *Performing Arts* 4, no. 4:44-48, 1966. illus.

F55. New challenge for the Dominion Drama Festival. *Performing Arts* 5, no. 1: 41-47, 1967. illus.

F56. **Wilson, Marian M.** Essential bridge: the Dominion Drama Festival. *Performing Arts* 5, no. 3-4: 32-35, 1968.

F57. **Frazer, Robbin.** First forty years. *Performing Arts* 9: 10-13, winter 1972. illus., port.

F58. **Edinborough, Arnold.** It was agony, it was joy — theatre when we needed it most. *Financial Post* 67:10, July 14, 1973. port.

F59. **Lee, Betty.** *Love and whiskey: the story of the Dominion Drama Festival.* Toronto, McClelland and Stewart, 1973. 335 p.

F60. Newfoundland hosts D.D.F. *Performing Arts* 11:11, summer 1974.

F61. **Hendry, Thomas B.** Colonial theatre, the history of a dinosaur. *Canadian Forum* 54: 32-33, March 1975. (Review of *Love and Whiskey*).

ogressive "EIGHT MEN SPEAK" Workers'
rts Club — December 4th, 1933 — Theatre

Workers' Theatre

The workers' theatre in Canada has an exciting history which includes such events as those surrounding the play *Eight Men Speak*. In December, 1933, and again in 1934, the Toronto Progressive Arts Club, as part of its campaign to force authorities to investigate an alleged attempt to murder Tim Buck in his cell at Kingston Penitentiary, performed this controversial play. The performance was banned by governmental order and the Walker Theatre in Winnipeg temporarily lost its licence when the Winnipeg Progressive Arts Club tried to stage the play there. See items listed in Index under Workers' Theatre.

The film version of Sophocles' *Oedipus Rex* featuring members of the distinguished 1955 Stratford Festival cast: Douglas Campbell as Oedipus, Eric House as the Priest and Old Shepherd, Robert Goodier as Creon, Donald Davis as Tiresias, Eleanor Stuart as Jocasta, Tony van Bridge as the Man from Corinth, William Hutt as the Chorus Leader, Gertrude Tyas as the Nurse, Nomi Cameron and Barbara Franklin as Ismene and Antigone and Douglas Rain as the Messenger. Members of the chorus, attendants on Creon and suppliants included Robert Christie, Ted Follows, David Gardner, Bruno Gerussi, William Shatner, John Horton, William Cole and Robin Gammell.

G

Stratford Festival

GENERAL

G1. **Marquis, Leonard.** *The Stratford story* by Leonard Marquis and Margaret Rowe. Stratford, Shakespeare Festival Foundation of Canada, 1954. 48 p. illus.

G2. *Stratford festival 1953-1957; a record in pictures and text of the Shakespearean festival in Canada* with a foreword by the Rt. Hon. Vincent Massey and an introduction by Herbert Whittaker. Toronto, Clarke Irwin, 1958. xxxii, 72 p. illus.

G3. **Guthrie, Tyrone.** My part in the Stratford adventure. *Maclean's* 72: 13-15, 84-94, November 21, 1959. illus.

G4. **Stratford, Philip.** Stratford after six years; a miracle reconsidered. *Queen's Quarterly* 66: 2-17, spring 1959.

G5. **Stratford Shakespearean Festival Foundation of Canada.** *The Stratford Shakespearean festival of Canada* 1953-1959. Stratford, 1959. 28 p. illus.

G6. **Shakespeare Seminar**, Stratford, Ont. *Stratford Papers on Shakespeare.* Toronto, Gage, 1960-64. 5 v.

G7. **Ganong, Joan.** *Backstage at Stratford.* Toronto, Longmans, 1962. 198 p. illus.

G8. **Monsarrat, Nicholas.** *To Stratford with love.* Toronto, McClelland and Stewart, 1963. 128 p.

G9. **Knight, George Wilson.** *Shakespearian production.* Evanston, Ill., Northwestern University Press, 1964. 323 p. (Postscript pages 291-300 deal with Stratford, Ont.)

G10. **Raby, Peter.** comp. *The Stratford scene 1958-1968.* Toronto, Clarke Irwin, 1968. 256 p. illus.

G11. **Jackson, B.W.** ed. *Stratford papers 1965-67.* Hamilton, McMaster University 1969. 232 p.

G12. **Jackson, B.W.** ed. *Stratford papers 1968-69.* Hamilton, McMaster University, 1972, 161 p.

G13. **Smith, Robert Dennis Hilton.** Stratford Shakespearean festival. In *Encyclopedia Canadiana.* Ottawa, Grolier Society of Canada (c. 1972) v. 9, p. 420-421. illus.

G14. **Aikens, James.** *Stratford,* Jackdaw 33, Clarke Irwin, 1973.

1953

G15. Annual affair. *Time* 62: 28, August 31, 1953.

G16. **Davies, Robertson.** Through ritual to romance. *Saturday Night* 68: 7-8, August 1, 1953. illus.

G17. First Shakespeare festival in Canada. *Vogue* 121: 80-81, May 15, 1953. illus.

G18. **Guthrie, Tyrone.** Problems of the next Stratford festival. *Saturday Night* 69: 7-8, December 12, 1953. illus.

G19. **Guthrie, Tyrone.** *Renown at Stratford; a record of the Shakespeare festival in Canada 1953* by Tyrone Guthrie, Robertson Davies and Grant Macdonald. Toronto, Clarke Irwin, 1953. viii, 128 p. illus.

G20. **Guthrie, Tyrone.** Shakespeare finds a new Stratford. *Theatre Arts* 37: 76-77, September 1953. illus.

G21. **House, A.W.** The miracle of Stratford. *Industrial Canada* 54: 60-65, September 1953. illus.

G22. **Johnston, James.** "Sea of troubles" ended for Stratford? *Financial Post* (Toronto) 47: 15, May 30, 1953.

G23. **MacLeod, Virginia.** Shakespeare festival. *New Frontiers* 2: 22, fall 1953.

G24. **Pilditch, James.** The Stratford Shakespearean festival. *Canadian Geographical Journal.* 47: 242-247, December 1953. illus.

G25. **Reaney, James.** The Stratford festival. *Canadian Forum* 33: 112-113, August 1953.

G26. **Scheff, Aimée.** Shakespeare arrives in Canada. *Theatre Arts* 37: 83, July 1953.

G27. **Scott, Margerie.** Theatre adventure; second thoughts after first nights at Stratford, Ontario. *Theatre World* 49: 24-26, October 1953. illus.

G28. Shakespeare at Stratford, Ontario. *Food for Thought* 13: 12, May/June 1953.

G29. **Stratford Shakespearean Festival Foundation of Canada.** *The Stratford festival 1953.* Stratford, 1953. 26 p.

G30. **Thistle, Lauretta.** Stratford, Ontario. *Saturday Review* 36: 25-26, August 1, 1953.

1954

G31. **Barkway, Michael.** The bard will be back again. *Financial Post* (Toronto) 48: 7, August 14, 1954.

G32. **Brady, Lloyd.** Three miracles at Stratford. *Rotarian* 85: 24-25, 50-52, October 1954. illus.

G33. **Davies, Robertson.** Simplicity and artifice combine at Stratford. *Saturday Night* 69: 5, 9-10, July 31, 1954. illus.

G34. **Davies, Robertson.** Stratford: second year. An air of certainty. *Saturday Night* 69: 5, 7-9, July 17, 1954. illus.

G35. **Guthrie, Tyrone.** *Twice have the trumpets sounded; a record of the Stratford Shakespearean festival in Canada 1954* by Tyrone Guthrie, Robertson Davies and Grant Macdonald. Toronto, Clarke Irwin, 1954. xiv, 193 p. front. illus.

G36. **Hewes, Henry.** Triple "en tente". *Saturday Review* 37: 33-34, July 31, 1954.

G37. "The Merchant of Venice". *New Frontiers* 3: 2, winter 1954.

G38. Stratford '54. *New Frontiers.* 3: 38-39, autumn 1954.

G39. **Stratford Shakespearean Festival Foundation of Canada.** *The Stratford festival, 1954.* Stratford, 1954. 24 p.

G40. **Thomas, Eugenie.** Shakespeare and Sophocles in a tent. *Saskatchewan Bulletin* 20: 22-24, October 1954.

G41. **Borth, Christy.** Will Shakespeare comes to Canada. *Montrealer* 29: 24-25, September 1955. illus.

G42. **Borth, Christy.** Will Shakespeare come to Canada. *Reader's Digest* 67: 41-44, September 1955. (Condensed from the *Montrealer*, September 1955.)

G43. **Clarke, Cecil.** Stratford, Ontario. (Canada). *World Theatre* 5: 42-50, winter 1955/1956. illus.

G44. **Cohen, Nathan.** Tyrone Guthrie, a minority report. *Queen's Quarterly* 62: 423-426, autumn 1955.

G45. **Davies, Robertson.** Stratford: firm and permanent growth. *Saturday Night* 70: 7-8, July 23, 1955. illus.

G46. **Davies, Robertson.** *Thrice the brinded cat hath mew'd; a record of the Stratford Shakespearean festival in Canada 1955* by Robertson Davies, Tyrone Guthrie, Boyd Neel and Tanya Moiseiwitsch. Toronto, Clarke Irwin, 1955. xii. 179 p. illus.

G47. **Edinborough, Arnold.** Shakespeare confirmed at Canadian Stratford. *Shakespeare Quarterly* 6: 435-440, fall 1955.

G48. **Fulford, Robert.** The backstage star of Stratford. *Mayfair* 29: 25-32, July 1955. illus.

G49. **Hewes, Henry.** Astringency in Ontario. *Saturday Review* 38: 26, June 4, 1955.

G50. **McVicar, Leonard H.** From little acorns .... Stratford's Shakespeare festival. *Recreation* 48: 110-111, March 1955. illus.

G51. **Moon, Barbara.** Why Guthrie outdraws Shakespeare. *Maclean's* 6: 18-19, 50-52, August 6, 1955. illus.

G52. **Osman, Mary.** Other adventures at Stratford. *Food for Thought* 15: 27-30, May/June 1955.

G53. **Stone, Martin.** Stratford '55. *New Frontiers* 4:8, fall 1955.

G54. Stratford festival. *Canadian Geographical Journal* 50: ix-xi, April 1955. illus.

G55. **Stratford Shakespearean Festival Foundation of Canada.** *The annual Stratford Shakespearean festival of drama and music 1955.* Stratford, 1955. 48 p. illus.

G56. **Valk, Diana Quirk.** *Shylock for a summer; the story of one year (1954-55) in the life of Frederick Valk,* with notes by Tyrone Guthrie and Donald Davis. London, Cassell, 1958. xix, 134p. front. illus.

G57. Architect's plan for proposed permanent Stratford, Ontario Shakespearean festival theatre. *Shakespeare Quarterly* 7:frontispiece, fall 1956.

G58. **Baxter, Sir Arthur Beverley.** Canada showed the Old Vic how. *Maclean's* 69:4, 66-67, March 17, 1956.

G59. Bickell fund aids theatre. *Financial Post* (Toronto) 50:5, January 28, 1956.

G60. **Callwood, June.** How Stratford went to Broadway. *Maclean's* 69:8-11, 50-53, March 3, 1956. illus.

G61. **Cohen, Nathan.** Tamburlaine: shadow over Stratford. *Saturday Night* 71:9-10, March 17, 1956.

G62. **Davies, Robertson.** Stratford revisited: amazing festival. *Saturday Night 71:14-* 15, September 1, 1956.

G63. **Edinborough, Arnold.** Consolidation at Stratford, Ontario. *Shakespeare Quarterly* 7:403-406, fall 1956.

G64. **Guthrie, Tyrone.** Shakespeare comes to Stratford, Ontario. *New York Times Magazine* 26-27, June 10, 1956. illus.

G65. **McGeachy, J.B.** Fourth Stratford festival ready to go; Shakespeare, Molière, music and swans. *Financial Post* (Toronto) 50:7, June 16, 1956.

G66. Molière at Stratford. *Time* 68:12, July 16, 1956. illus.

G67. Start permanent theatre at Stratford next week. *Financial Post* (Toronto) 50:4 August 18, 1956.

G68. **Stone, Martin.** Have you been to Stratford. *New Frontiers* 5:26, summer 1956.

G69. **Stratford Shakespearean Festival Foundation of Canada.** *The 1956 Stratford Shakespearean festival.* Stratford, 1956. 40 p. illus.

──────────────────── **1957** ────────────────────

G70. **Allen, Robert Thomas.** How a teenager's dream came true at Stratford. *Maclean's* 70:28-29, 75-79, October 12, 1957. illus.

G71. Canada's Shakespeare capital: *Theatre Arts* 41:78, July 1957. illus.

G72. **Davies, Robertson.** Stratford 1957: magnificent, masterful. *Saturday Night* 72:8-9, 35. July 20, 1957. illus.

G73. Doing Shakespeare proud: fine new theatre instead of tent at Stratford, Ontario. *Times* (London) 6, August 19, 1957.

G74. **Driver, Tom F.** Shakespeare in Ontario. *Christian Century* 74:1138-1139, September 1957.

G75. **Edinborough, Arnold.** Canada's permanent Elizabethan house. *Shakespeare Quarterly* 8:511-514, fall 1957.

G76. **Fairfield, Robert.** The new theatre at Stratford. *Food for Thought* 17:173-174, 188, January 1957. illus.

G77. **Kirstein, Lincoln.** Letter from Canada. *The Nation* 185:288-290, October 1957.

G78. **Moore, James Mavor.** Snobs at Stratford. *Canadian Commentator* 1:7-8, September 1957.

G79. **Phillips, Alan.** What Shakespeare's doing to Stratford. *Maclean's* 70:28-29, 71-72, June 22, 1957. illus.

G80. **Sangster, Dorothy.** The designing woman of Stratford. *Maclean's* 70:16-19, 54-56, July 20, 1957. illus. (Tanya Moiseiwitsch).

G81. **Stratford Shakespearean Festival Foundation of Canada.** *The 1957 Stratford Festival of Canada.* Stratford, 1957. 48 p.

G82. **Stratford Shakespearean Festival Foundation of Canada.** *Stratford festival permanent theatre; general information.* Stratford, 1957. 12 p. illus.

1958

G83. Audiences biggest ever; Stratford bonds a hit, too. *Financial Post* (Toronto) 52:4, October 4, 1958.

G84. **Barkway, Michael.** Stratford magic is still strong. *Financial Post* (Toronto) 58:14, July 19, 1958.

G85. **Davies, Robertson.** The Stratford season; a great poetic theatre. *Saturday Night* 73:14-15, 36-37, July 19, 1958.

G86. Drama, music and mime for you at our Stratford. *Financial Post* (Toronto) 52:12, July 19, 1958.

G87. **Edinborough, Arnold.** A lively season at Canada's Stratford. *Shakespeare Quarterly* 9:535-538, fall 1958. illus.

G88. **Plunkett, Patrick Mary.** Shakespeare in Ontario. *America* 100:44-45, October 11, 1958.

G89. **Stratford Shakespearean Festival Foundation of Canada.** *The Stratford festival Canada 1958.* Stratford, 1958. 56 p. illus.

G90. Theatre is world first. *Financial Post* (Toronto) 58:68, February 22, 1958. diagr.

G91. **Weales, Gerald.** The bard in Ontario. *The Reporter* 19:42-43, September 4, 1958.

G92. **Whittaker, Herbert.** Handsome drama prize. *Canadian Commentator* 2:8, June 1958.

G93. **Wyatt, Euphemia Van Rensselaer.** The Stratford Shakespearean festival. *Catholic World* 188:156-158, November 1958.

1959

G94. **Edinborough, Arnold.** Shakespeare fights for recognition. *Saturday Night* 74:7-9, July 18, 1959.

G95. **Oklopkov, Nikolai P.** I was in Stratford. *U.S.S.R. Illustrated News* no. 8 (54): 22-24, August 1959. illus.

G96. Sales higher for Stratford. *Financial Post* (Toronto) 53:21, June 20, 1959.

G97. **Stratford, Philip.** Shakespearean festival: a pre-season inventory. *Canadian Forum* 39:81, July 1959.

G98. **Stratford, Philip.** Stratford 1959. *Canadian Forum* 39:105-107, August 1959.

G99. Stratford sets record as 1959 festival ends. *Financial Post* (Toronto) 53:11, September 26, 1959.

G100. **Stratford Shakespearean Festival Foundation of Canada.** *The Stratford festival 1959.* Stratford, 1959. 48 p. illus.

— 1960 —

G101. **Edinborough, Arnold.** Artistic success in Canada. *Shakespeare Quarterly* 11:455-459, fall 1960.

G102. **Edinborough, Arnold.** Stratford's slow but solid start. *Saturday Night* 75:12-14, July 23, 1960.

G103. **Ferry, Anthony.** The tyranny of the Stratford stage. *Canadian Forum* 40:106-109, August 1960.

G104. **Stratford, Philip.** New Canadian plays presented. *Canadian Literature* no. 6:49-52, autumn 1960.

G105. **Stratford, Philip.** Orchestrating the arts: Stratford Festival 1960. *Canadian Forum* 40:185-188, November 1960.

— 1961 —

G106. **Cummings, L.** The Stratford, Ontario, Shakespeare festival, 1961. *Drama Survey* 1:238-241, October 1961.

G107. **Edinborough, Arnold.** Power, glory and froth at Stratford. *Saturday Night* 76:7-10, July 22, 1961. illus.

G108. **Evans, J.A.S.** Stratford — maturity brings misgivings. *Canadian Commentator* 5:18, 23, September 1961.

G109. **John, Michael.** An international face for Canada — the Stratford festival. *Performing Arts* 1, no. 1:18-19, March 1961.

G110. **Smith, Peter D.** Sharp wit and noble scenes: a review of the 1961 season of the Stratford, Ontario festival. *Shakespeare Quarterly* 13:71-77, winter 1962.

G111. **Winter, Jack.** "Canvas barricade." *Canadian Commentator* 5:2, 16, October 1961.

G112. **Winter, Jack.** Stratford 1961. *Canadian Forum* 41:137-140, September 1961.

— 1962 —

G113. **Balk, Wes.** Stratford, Ontario. *Drama Survey* 2:195-200, October, 1962.

G114. **Dobbs, Kildare.** Shakespeare game. *Saturday Night* 77:11-13, July 7, 1962. illus.

G115. **Lamb, Sidney.** Stratford: university tour. *Canadian Art* 19:184-185, May-June 1962.

G116. **Pettigrew, John.** Stratford's tenth season: a director's year. *Queen's Quarterly* 69:442-454, autumn 1962.

G117. **Reaney, James.** Letter from Stratford. *Canadian Art* 19:371-372, September-October 1962.

G118. **Russel, Robert.** On interpreting Shakespeare: four dimensions of reality. *Canadian Art* 19:311-313, July/August 1962.

G119. **Smith, Peter D.** Toil and trouble: a review of the 1962 season of the Stratford, Ontario festival. *Shakespeare Quarterly* 13:521-527, autumn 1962.

G120. **Stratford, Philip.** Ten birthday wishes to Stratford. *Canadian Forum* 42:174-176, November 1962.

G121. **Tovell, Vincent.** The Stratford Festival: the tenth year. *Tamarack Review* no. 25:49-59, autumn 1962.

G122. **Winter, Jack.** Stratford 1962. *Canadian Forum* 42:124-125, September 1962.

--- **1963** ---

G123. **Cohen, Nathan.** Stratford so far. *Saturday Night* 78:7-9, August 1963.

G124. **Davies, Robertson.** Tyrone Power and Dr. Thomas Guthrie in Canada. *Drama Survey* 3, no. 1:91-96, May 1963.

G125. **Edinborough, Arnold.** Stratford Shakespearean festival (Ontario). *Shakespeare Quarterly* 14:433-436, autumn 1963.

G126. **Guthrie, Tyrone.** If a theatre is to prosper. . . . *New York Times Magazine* July 28, 1963. p. 7, 27, 30, 32. illus.

G127. **Jones, David E.** Shakespeare festival 1963: Stratford, Ontario. *Drama Survey* 3:301-304, fall 1963.

G128. **Keith, W.J.** In defence of Stratford. *Canadian Forum* 43:193-195, December 1963.

G129. **Pettigrew, John.** Stratford 1963. *Queen's Quarterly* 70:441-448, autumn 1963.

G130. **Russel, Robert.** Theatre '63. Stratford: the taming of the bard. *Tamarack Review* no. 28:72-77, summer 1963.

--- **1964** ---

G131. **André, Marion.** Richard and Lear at Stratford. *Montrealer* 38:33-36, September 1964.

G132. **Davies, Robertson.** Stratford's festival of man. *Saturday Night* 79:21-23, August 1964.

G133. **Edinborough, Arnold.** Canada's credible Lear and moving Richard. *Shakespeare Quarterly* 15:391-395, autumn 1964.

G134. **Hatch, Robert.** Tyrone Guthrie: the artist as a man of the theatre. *Performing Arts* 2 no. 4:55-59, winter/spring 1964.

G135. **Pettigrew, John.** Stratford, 1964. *Queen's Quarterly* 71:434-443, autumn 1964.

G136. **Richards, Stanley.** "A cygnet for Shakespeare" (Stratford festival, Canada) *Players Magazine* 40:211-213, April 1964.

G137. **Sidnell, Michael J.** A moniment without a tombe: the Stratford Shakespearean Festival Theatre: Ontario. In English Association. *Essays and Studies* n.s. 17:41-54, 1964. illus.

G138. **Stratford, Philip.** Every inch a king? *Canadian Forum* 44:100-101, August 1964.

G139. **Stratford, Philip.** Innovations and reservations. *Canadian Forum* 44:132-133, September 1964.

1965

G140. **Edinborough, Arnold.** Canadian Shakespeare festival. *Shakespeare Quarterly* 16:325-327, autumn 1965.

G141. **Edinborough, Arnold.** Stratford, theirs and ours. *Saturday Night* 80:15-17, August 1965.

G142. **Gascon, Jean.** Dessous à Stratford: le théâtre vit! *Magazine Maclean* 5:59-60, septembre 1965.

G143. **Jones, David E.** The three Stratfords, 1964. *Drama Survey* 4:76-82, spring 1965.

G144. **Morris, Royden.** How mail and record system helps to make Festival tick. *Office Administration* 11:47-49, February 1965. illus.

G145. **Pettigrew, John.** Stratford's festival theatre, 1965. *Queen's Quarterly* 72:563-575, autumn 1965.

1966

G146. **Dobbs, Kildare.** Oooo! that Shakespearean rag, it's so elegant, so intelligent. *Saturday Night* 81:17-19, August 1966. illus.

G147. **Edinborough, Arnold.** Canadian Shakespeare festival. *Shakespeare Quarterly* 17:399-402, autumn 1966.

G148. **Evans, Ron.** The changing face of Stratford. (Ron Evans interviews Michael Langham) *Performing Arts* 4, no. 4:6-13, 1966. illus.

G149. **Keith, W.J.** Shakespeare at Stratford: doves, hawks, revisers. *Canadian Forum* 46:135-136. September 1966.

G150. **Pettigrew, John.** Drama at the Avon. *Canadian Forum* 46:138, September 1966.

G151. **Pettigrew, John.** Stratford's Festival theatre: 1966. *Queen's Quarterly* 73: 384-397, autumn 1966.

G152. **Edinborough, Arnold.** Centennial Stratford. *Saturday Night* 82:20-23, August 1967.

G153. **Edinborough, Arnold.** Stratford, Ontario, 1967. *Shakespeare Quarterly* 18:399-403, autumn 1967.

G154. **Keith, W.J.** Comments on Stratford at the crossroads. *Canadian Forum* 47:133-134, September 1967.

G155. **Pettigrew, John.** Stratford 1967. *Queen's Quarterly* 74:509-521, autumn 1967.

G156. **Cohen, Nathan.** Stratford after fifteen years. *Queen's Quarterly* 75:35-61, spring 1968.

G157. **Edinborough, Arnold.** Stratford's summer season is full of fun and frolic. *Saturday Night* 83:29-31, August 1968. illus.

G158. **Edinborough, Arnold.** Director's role at Canada's Stratford. *Shakespeare Quarterly* 20:443-446, autumn 1969.

G159. **Pettigrew, John.** Stratford plays, 1969. *Journal of Canadian Studies* 4:3-9, November 1969.

G160. **Carson, Neil.** European plays at Stratford. *Commentator* 14:18-19, October 1970.

G161. **Carson, Neil.** 1970 Stratford season. *Commentator* 14:14-15, July/August 1970. illus.

G162. **Edinborough, Arnold.** Gallic romp through Shakespeare: an account of the 1970 season at Ontario's Stratford festival. *Shakespeare Quarterly* 21:457-459, autumn 1970.

G163. **Jackson, B.W.** Contemporary theatre at the Avon. *Journal of Canadian Studies* 5:18-22, November 1970.

G164. **Pettigrew, John.** Stratford's festival theatre, 1970. *Journal of Canadian Studies* 5:11-18, November 1970.

G165. **Carson, Neil.** 1971 Stratford season: grandeur and horror in the Duchess. *Commentator* 15:19-20, July/August 1971. illus.

G166. **Jackson, B.W.** At the Avon. *Journal of Canadian Studies* 6:24-30, November 1971.

G167. **Jackson, B.W.** Shakespeare at Stratford, Ontario 1971. *Shakespeare Quarterly* 22:365-370, autumn 1971.

G168. **McEnaney, F.** Theatre: a star danced and under that was Stratford born. *Maclean's Magazine* 84:69, July 1971. illus.

G169. **Pettigrew, John.** The festival theatre. *Journal of Canadian Studies* 6:15-23, November 1971.

1972

G170. **Jackson, B.W.** Shakespeare at Stratford, Ontario 1972. *Shakespeare Quarterly* 23:388-394, fall 1972.

G171. **Jackson, B.W.** Stratford's Avon Theatre and Third Stage, 1972. *Journal of Canadian Studies* 7:56-61, November 1972.

G172. **McCracken, M.** Theatre: coming to that place you share with everyone. *Maclean's Magazine* 85:80, July 1972.

G173. **Pettigrew, John.** Stratford's Festival Theatre, 1972. *Journal of Canadian Studies* 7:48-55, November 1972.

1973

G174. **Davis, Donald.** Theatrically speaking, where are we? *Financial Post* 67:6, November 17, 1973. port.

G175. **Edinborough, Arnold.** Stratford gets on with creation of a national theatre. *Financial Post* 68:10, April 27, 1973. port.

G176. **Edinborough, Arnold.** Stratford's glorious summer created new artistic climate. *Financial Post* 67:28, June 16, 1973. port.

G177. **Rubin, Don.** Buy Canadian or by Canadian: Stratford festival. *Performing Arts* 10:24-25, fall 1973. illus.

G178. **Rubin, Don.** Stratford's cultural exports to be (Canadian) or not to be. *Performing Arts* 10:12-15, summer 1973, illus., port.

G179. **Wylie, Betty Jane.** Theatre: why Stratford looks abroad for direction. *Maclean's* 86:95, December 1973. port.

1974

G180. Arts: fountain of youth. *Time* (Canada) 103:8-13, April 29, 1974. port.

G181. **Edinborough, Arnold.** Editorial (on Robin Phillips at Stratford). *Performing Arts* 11:13, summer 1974.

G182. **Hendry, Thomas B.** Terrific idea for the Stratford festival. *Saturday Night* 89:19-22, February 1974. illus.

G183. **Jackson, B.W.** Stratford's Avon theatre and Third stage, 1973. *Journal of Canadian Studies* 9:9-13, February 1974.

G184. **Maddocks, M.** Stratford solution. *Time* (Canada) 103:42, June 17, 1974.

G185. **Nau, T.** Stratford's experimental theatre moves into the main stream. *Performing Arts* 11:19-21, fall 1974. illus., port.

G186. **Pettigrew, John.** Stratford's festival theatre, 1973. *Journal of Canadian Studies* 9:3-9, February 1974.

G187. **Phillips, Robin.** On being invited to Canada. *Canadian Theatre Review* CTR 1:60-64, winter 1974.

G188. **Phillips, Robin.** (et. al.). Whither Stratford? *Canadian Theatre Review* CTR 3:34-41, summer 1974. (Article contains: text of letter from several Canadian directors to Board of Governors of Stratford Festival; letter to CTR from Stratford Governors; text of Robin Phillips announced plans for Stratford.)

G189. Shaw to headline at Stratford festival. *Performing Arts* 11:12, winter 1974.

G190. Stratford festival tours with par excellence cast. *Performing Arts* 11:10-11, winter 1974.

G191. Stratford success down under. *Performing Arts* 11:8, spring 1974. illus.

G192. **Wylie, Betty Jane.** Lights, action, camera! (Stratford festival television "She Stoops to Conquer"). *Motion* 2:9, May-June 1974.

1975

G193. **Edinborough, Arnold.** Shakespeare looks different at Stratford this year. *Performing Arts* 12:16-17, summer 1975. port.

G194. **Jackson, B.W.** The Avon and the Third stage. *Journal of Canadian Studies* 10:57-62, February 1975.

G195. **Kalem, T.E.** Tale of two Stratfords: Shakespearean festival, Ontario. *Time* (Canada) 105:52-53, June 30, 1975.

G196. **Pettigrew, John S.** Stratford festival theatre, 1974. *Journal of Canadian Studies* 10:49-56, February 1975.

H

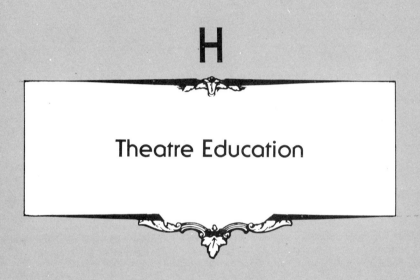

Theatre Education

H1. The work of the B.C. dramatic school. *Canadian Forum* 10:31-33, October 1929.

H2. **Gowan, Elsie Park.** There's drama in them there hills: being an account of the summer drama course at Banff. *Curtain Call* 7:14, October 1935.

H3. School of the theatre in British Columbia. *Curtain Call* 10:9, May/June 1939.

H4. **Lavell, W.S.** Applied dramatics for schools. *Curtain Call* 11:9, September-October 1939; 21-22, November 1939; 16, December 1939; 15-16, January 1940; 14, March 1940.

H5. New theatre in the Rockies. *Curtain Call* 11:4-5, March 1940. (Banff School of Fine Art).

H6. Summer school of the theatre on the Pacific coast. *Curtain Call* 11:9-10, April 1940. (University of British Columbia).

H7. Summer theatre for Queen's. *Curtain Call* 11:7, May/June 1940.

H8. **Cameron, Donald.** Banff becomes international centre of culture. *Curtain Call* 13:21-22, October 1941.

H9. **Firkins, Yvonne.** Our school theatres. *Curtain Call* 12:5, April 1941.

H10. **MacCorkindale, Archie.** Drama course in heaven. *Curtain Call* 12:8-9, March 1941. (Smithers, B.C.).

H11. **Rittenhouse, Charles.** Montreal schools go dramatic. *Curtain Call* 13:7-8, October 1941.

H12. **Gordon, K.W.** Place of drama in adult education. *Food for Thought* 3:18-23, May 1943.

H13. **Jones, Emrys Maldwyn.** The university's duty towards Canadian drama. *Culture* 7:311-324, September 1946.

H14. **Voaden, Herman.** Dramatic art in Canadian higher education. In Kirkconnell, Watson. *The humanities in Canada* by Watson Kirkconnell and A.S.P. Woodhouse. Ottawa, Humanities Research Council 1947. p. 228-236.

H15. **Cameron, Donald.** *The Banff School of Fine Arts.* Foreword by Walter B. Herbert. Toronto, Canadian Association for Adult Education, 1953. 24 p.

H16. **Cameron, Donald.** *Campus in the clouds.* Toronto, McClelland and Stewart, 1956. 127 p. illus. (Banff School of Fine Arts).

H17. **Patterson, Tom.** Stratford and education. *Food for Thought* 17:169-173, January 1957. illus. p. 189.

H18. **Hirsch, John.** National Theatre School. *Canadian Art* 19:89-90, January/February 1962.

H19. **Moon, Barbara.** Ingenue from the rockies goes to drama school. *Maclean's Magazine* 75:22-25, September 8, 1962. illus.

H20. **Russel, Robert.** The National Theatre School. *Tamarack Review* no. 27:71-79, spring 1963.

H21. **Gasse, Gilles.** La grande université . . . et le petit théâtre. *La Barre du Jour* 1:16-18, juillet/décembre, 1965.

H22. **Winter, Jack.** Theatre and university. *Edge* 2:94, spring 1964.

H23. Hour company's touring troupe of players bring live theatre to high school pupils. *School Progress* 34:36-37, September 1965. illus.

H24. **Crampton, Esmé.** *An interim review on the preparation of teachers of theatre arts.* Toronto, College of Education, University of Toronto, 1966. 76, (17) p. bibl.

H25. Where bi-culturalism works, the National Theatre School. *Performing Arts* 4 no. 4:36-41, 1966. illus.

H26. **Davies, Robertson.** There will be no "soft" degrees. *Varsity Graduate* 13:90-96, June 1967. illus.

H27. Our new man of the theatre. *Varsity Graduate* 13:89, June 1967. (Brian Parker and Leon Major).

H28. **Salmon, E.** Sense of urgency and desperation needed by university theatre. *Canadian University* 2:48-50, March-April 1967.

H29. **Beaulne, Guy.** L'enseignement de l'art dramatique. *Culture Vivante* 11:30-34, 1968.

H30. **Parker, Brian.** A flexible laboratory for the dramatic arts. Toronto, University. *Graduate* 1:48-52, summer 1968. illus.

H31. Les cahiers de la nouvelle compagnie théâtrale aideront les professeurs à mieux préparer leur classe. *Hebdo-Education* 6 e année, no. 11:54, octobre, 1969.

H32. **Peacock, Gordon.** Theatre has a place in higher learning. *Performing Arts* 6 no. 1:42-45, 1968. (University of Alberta).

H33. **Ontario Institute for Studies in Education.** *Courses of study in the theatre arts: grades 7 to 12.* Toronto, O.I.S.E. Theatre Arts Committee, 1969. 48 p.

H34. **Claus, Joanne.** Theatre New Brunswick and the Fredericton High School. *Atlantic Advocate* 61:40-41, October 1970. illus.

H35. **Meeting of Experts on Arts Education for the General Public,** Ottawa 1970. *Arts Education for the general public.* Toronto, Canadian Conference of the Arts, 1970. 50, 49 p.

H36. **Canadian Theatre Centre.** Theatre education: what-how-where? *Stage in Canada* supplement to vol. 6 no. 5, February 1971. 120 p.

H37. **Barnet, David.** The Manitoba theatre school. In Crampton, Esmé. ed. *Drama Canada.* Toronto, College of Education Guidance Centre, 1972. p. 11-13.

H38. **Boone, Terry.** The Council of drama in education. In Crampton, Esmé. ed. *Drama Canada.* Toronto, College of Education Guidance Centre, 1972. p. 28.

H39. **Charlesworth, Marigold.** The Theatre hour company. In Crampton, Esmé. ed. *Drama Canada.* Toronto, College of Education Guidance Centre, 1972. p. 14-16.

H40. **Charlesworth, Marigold.** Young people's theatre. In Crampton, Esmé. ed. *Drama Canada.* Toronto, College of Education Guidance Centre, 1972. p. 21-23.

H41. **Colbeck, James.** Ontario youtheatre. In Crampton, Esmé. ed. *Drama Canada.* Toronto, College of Education Guidance Centre, 1972. p. 29-30.

H42. **Courtney, Richard.** Developmental drama as a university discipline. In Crampton, Esmé. ed. *Drama Canada.* Toronto, College of Education Guidance Centre, 1972. p. 30-31.

H43. **Crampton, Esmé.** ed. *Drama Canada: trends in drama in education during the past 25 years.* Toronto, University of Toronto, College of Education Guidance Centre, 1972. 38 p.

H44. **Dunlop, Helen.** The dramatic arts in Ontario schools. In Crampton, Esmé. ed. *Drama Canada.* Toronto, College of Education Guidance Centre, 1972. p. 26-27.

H45. **Layman, Grace.** The educational drama program in Newfoundland. In Crampton, Esmé. ed. *Drama Canada.* Toronto, College of Education Guidance Centre, 1972. p. 16-18.

H46. **Needles, Dorothy.** Play acting in the classroom. In Crampton, Esmé. ed. *Drama Canada.* Toronto, College of Education Guidance Centre, 1972. p. 8-9.

H47. **Ripley, John.** The McGill undergraduate program. In Crampton, Esmé. ed. *Drama Canada.* Toronto, College of Education Guidance Centre, 1972. p. 31-34.

H48. **Rushton, M.** Playhouse holiday. In Crampton, Esmé. ed. *Drama Canada.* Toronto, College of Education Guidance Centre, 1972. p. 10-11.

H49. Sperdakos joins drama school. *Performing Arts* 9:4, winter 1972. (Cambrian College).

H50. **Watts, Ken.** The Ontario Collegiate drama festival. In Crampton, Esmé. ed. *Drama Canada.* Toronto, College of Education Guidance Centre, 1972. p. 7-8.

H51. **Wilson, Lorna.** The theatre arts guild. In Crampton, Esmé. ed. *Drama Canada.* Toronto, College of Education Guidance Centre, 1972. p. 23-24.

H52. National theatre school. *Performing Arts* 11:7, spring 1974. illus.

H53. **Lister, Rota.** Why not study Canadian drama? *Matrix* 1:25-26, spring 1975.

Laurence Housman's *Bethlehem,* directed by Dorothy Goulding, one of the early productions of the Toronto Children's Players (1931-1959) at Hart House Theatre, Dec. 1933. See items under children's theatre.

I

Theatre Architecture, Facilities, Stage Design, Lighting

I 1. Some Canadian theatres. *The Builder* 109:275-6, October 15, 1915. illus. (Toronto).

I 2. **Robinson, Maynard.** Stage lighting. *Curtain Call.* 6:19-20, March 1935.

I 3. **Ness, Margaret.** How to go about it: a practical clinic on play production. *Curtain Call* 9:7-11, October 1937; 13-17, November 1937; 21-23, December 1937; 15-19, January 1938; 15-18, February 1938; 16-18, March 1938; 17-19, April 1938; 15-18, May 1938.

I 4. **Craig, John.** My method of play production. *Curtain Call* 9:7-8, April 1938.

I 5. **MacLaren, F.W.** Lighting of the amateur stage. *Curtain Call* 9:7, May 1938.

I 6. **Angus, William.** Artistic stage lighting. *Curtain Call* 11:21-22, September-October 1939.

I 7. **Firkins, Yvonne.** Stagecraft for school and community players. *Curtain Call* 10:13-15, November 1938; 18-20, December 1938; 18-20, January 1939; 16-18, February 1939; 18-19, March 1939; 18-20, April 1939; 14-16, May 1939.

I 8. **Wholton, T.H.** The typical school auditorium stage criticized. *Curtain Call* 10:10, 13, May 1939.

I 9. **Woods, John.** Making your scenery look solid. *Curtain Call* 10:14, March 1939.

I 10. **Bennett, Ernest Sterndale.** Problems of production. *Curtain Call* 11:5-6, April 1940.

I 11. **Mayorga, Margaret.** If you're giving a costume play. *Curtain Call* 11:7-8, April 1940.

I 12. **Sinclair, Edith** and **Russell, John.** *Consider the play.* Winnipeg, Drama Division, Adult Education Committee, University of Manitoba, 1941. (Lectures on stage production and stage design mimeographed from radio series.)

I 13. **Cabana, Laure.** Les costumes au théâtre et leurs modèles dans la peinture. *Vie des Arts* 7:22-25, été, 1957. illus.

I 14. Stratford festival theatre, Stratford, Ontario. Architects Rounthwaite and Fairfield. Royal Architectural Institute of Canada. *Journal* 34:267-274, July 1957. illus. diagr.

I 15. Comédie canadienne. *Architecture — Bâtiment — Construction* 13:404-409, December 1958. illus. plans.

I 16. **Toupin, Paul.** Précisions et digressions sur le théâtre. *Vie des Arts* 10:40, printemps, 1958.

I 17. **Canadian Theatre Centre.** *Report on a survey of theatrical facilities in Canada.* 2 vols. Toronto, Canadian Theatre Centre, 1960-62. unpaged.

I 18. **Davies, Robertson.** Robertson Davies on architects and architecture. Royal Architectural Institute of Canada. *Journal* 37:346-349, August 1960.

I 19. **Minton, Eric.** Design for entertainment. *Habitat* 3:2-7, January/February 1960. illus.

I 20. O'Keefe Centre for the Performing Arts, Toronto. Royal Architectural Institute of Canada. *Journal* 37:461-487, November 1960. illus. plans.

l 21. **Garret, R.M.** Palace Grand Theatre. Royal Architectural Institute of Canada. *Journal* 39:61-66, April 1962. illus. (Dawson City).

l 22. **Acland, James.** Royal Alexandra Theatre. Royal Architectural Institute of Canada. *Journal* 40:30-31, November 1963. (Toronto).

l 23. Civic Playhouse (Victoria, B.C.) theatre and extensions. *Canadian Architect* 8:70-71, November 1963. illus. plans.

l 24. **Toronto. City Planning Board.** *The St. Lawrence Centre for the Arts. A Proposal.* Toronto, (1963) 24 p. illus., plans.

l 25. **Izenour, George C.** Theatre design. Royal Architectural Institute of Canada. *Journal* 41:47-48, December 1964. illus., plans. (Confederation Theatre, Charlottetown).

l 26. **Joseph, Stephen.** ed. *Actor and architect.* Toronto, University of Toronto Press, 1964. 120 p. illus. (Stratford).

l 27. *Seminar on architectural requirements for the performing arts in Canada:* sponsored by the Centennial Commission, Ottawa, June 1-2, 1964. Ottawa, 1964.

l 28. **Szmidt, Boleslaw.** Un théâtre dramatique transformable. *Architecture — Bâtiment — Construction* 19:35-42, July 1964. illus., plans (Quebec City).

l 29. **Varry, Jacques.** Théâtre du Nouveau Monde. Repentigny. *Architecture — Bâtiment — Construction* 19:33-40, November 1964. illus., plans.

l 30. **Wray, John.** Neptune Theatre. *Habitat* 7:25-27, January/February 1964. illus. (Halifax).

l 31. **Urwick, Currie.** Ltd. *An assessment of Toronto's cultural facilities and requirements:* a report for the Toronto Arts Foundation. Toronto, 1964. n.p.

l 32. Bishops University Theatre. *Canadian Architect* 11:10, November 1966. illus.

l 33. **Lebensold, D.F.** Theatre: a need for dialogue. *Canadian Architect* 11:51-53, August 1966.

l 34. **Toronto Arts Foundation, Ontario.** *Canadian Architect Yearbook* 1966. p. 84-85. illus., plans.

l 35. **Donat, Peter.** Theatre architecture: an actor's point of view. *Architecture Canada* 44:49, August 1967.

l 36. Le Grand Théâtre de Québec. *Architecture Canada* 44:48-49, October 1967. illus., plans.

l 37. **Lebensold, D.F.** Form follows function. *Opera Canada* 8 no. 3:12-13, 86, September 1967. illus.

l 38. Praise (Stratford's Avon Theatre) *Canadian Architect* 12:6, November 1967. illus., plans.

l 39. **Roux, Jean-Louis.** Montreal colloquium 67: the design of theatres. *World Theatre* 16:435-449, 1967. illus., plans.

l 40. **Varry, Jacques.** Edifice des théâtres Maisonneuve et Port-Royal. *Architecture — Bâtiment — Construction* 22:21-31, September 1967. illus., plans. (Montréal).

l 41. Manitoba Theatre Centre, Winnipeg, Man. *Canadian Architect* 13:52, December 1968. plans.

I 42. **Desjardins, Pierre W.** Orphée. *Vie des Arts* 57:59, hiver, 1969-70. illus.

I 43. **Gauvreau, Jules.** Le centre national des arts. *Vie des Arts* 56:15-16, automne, 1969. illus.

I 44. **Viau, Guy.** Le centre national des arts. *Vie des Arts* 56:17-23, automne, 1969. illus.

I 45. **Blouin, André.** Le grand théâtre du Québec. *Vie des Arts* 63:54-59, 78, été, 1971. illus.

I 46. *Le Grand Théâtre de Québec.* Québec, Editions du Songe, 1971. 32 p. illus.

I 47. **Doherty, Tom.** Building the magic box. *Performing Arts* 9 no. 2:44-45, 9 no. 3:46, 48, 9 no. 4:23-24, 1972.

I 48. **Ham, Roderick.** ed. *Theatre planning.* Toronto, University of Toronto Press, 1972. 292 p.

I 49. **Arnott, Brian.** World as a stage. *Canadian Architect* 18:24-32, February 1973. illus., plans.

I 50. **Claus, Joanne.** Theatre design. *Atlantic Advocate* 64:18-20, November 1973. port.

I 51. **Doherty, Tom.** Building the magic box. *Performing Arts* 10:35-38, fall 1973. illus., plans.

I 52. **Hood, Hugh.** Murray Laufer and the art of scenic design. *Artscanada* 29:59-64, December 72-January 73. illus.

I 53. **Laufer, Murray.** Galileo, working drawing. *Artscanada* 29:63, December 72-January 73.

I 54. **Laufer, Murray.** Louis Riel: rendering of Riel's house in Montana. *Artscanada* 29:60, December 72-January 73.

I 55. **Laufer, Murray.** Puntila: drawing for a slide in the style of Grosz. *Artscanada* 29:61, December 72-January 73.

I 56. **Laufer, Murray.** Puntila: drawing for a slide showing Puntila with knife. *Artscanada* 29:61, December 72-January 73.

I 57. Hamilton Place, Hamilton, Ontario. *Canadian Architect* 19:22-31, May 1974. illus., plans.

I 58. **Kerr, Mary.** Mandragola: a designer's portfolio. *Canadian Theatre Review* CTR 2:34-39, spring 1974. illus., port.

I 59. **Kohl, Helen.** Getting your head together for the stage. *Performing Arts* 11:40-41, winter 1974.

I 60. **Laufer, Murray.** Designing at the centre. (St. Lawrence Centre). *Canadian Theatre Review* CTR 3:42-45, summer 1974. illus., port.

I 61. **Russell, Wallace.** Light cues when sweet voices die, linger in the memory. *Performing Arts* 11:46, summer 1974.

I 62. **Smith, Peter.** Shaw festival theatre, Niagara-on-the-lake. *Canadian Architect* 19:24-28, January 1974. illus.

I 63. **Strike, Maurice.** The designer's dilemma. *Canadian Theatre Review* CTR 1:45-48, winter 1974. illus., port.

I 64. **Thom, R.J.** Shaw festival theatre, Niagara-on-the-lake, Ontario: the design process. *Canadian Architect* 19:20-24, January 1974. illus., map, plan.

I 65. **Waisman, Allan H.** Building the building. *Canadian Theatre Review* CTR 4:32-35, fall 1974. illus.

I 66. **Arnott, Brian.** Architecture and the artful stage. *Canadian Theatre Review* CTR 6:7-13, spring 1975. illus.

I 67. **Carpenter, Edmund** and **McLuhan, Marshall.** Acoustic space. *Canadian Theatre Review* CTR 6:46-49, spring 1975.

I 68. **Dennis, Wendell.** Ubu in the new world. *Canadian Theatre Review* CTR 5:129-135, winter 1975. illus.

I 69. **Joliffe, Marlynn.** The building burden. *Canadian Theatre Review* CTR 6:32-40, spring 1975. illus.

I 70. **Schloegl, Georg. F.** Good scenery involves everyone and should. *Performing Arts* 12:45, spring 1975.

I 71. **Svoboda, Joseph.** The designer's space. *Canadian Theatre Review* CTR 6:41-43, spring 1975. port.

I 72. **Wilcox, Richard Kent.** Environments. *Canadian Theatre Review* CTR 6:28-31, spring 1975. illus.

I 73. **Wilcox, Richard Kent.** Notes to the building committee. *Canadian Theatre Review* CTR 6:44-45, spring 1975.

J

Biography And Criticism
Actors, Actresses And Playwrights

J1. **Taylor, Bayard.** The author of Saul. *Atlantic Monthly* 94:411-414, October 1865.

J2. Mr. Irving's second American tour (London, Ontario, October 6). *The Theatre* (London, England) Series 4, Vol. 4: 227-235, November 1, 1884.

J3. **Rose, George Maclean.** *A Cyclopedia of Canadian Biography, being chiefly men of the time.* Toronto, Rose Pub. Co. 1886-1888. 2 v.

J4. **Lindley, Harry.** *Merely players.* Toronto, Toronto News Co., n.d. 121 p. illus. (circa 1890).

J5. **Payzant, J.A.** John Hunter-Duvar. *Dominion Illustrated* 5: 127, August 1890.

J6. Gentlemen supernumeraries in Canada, "by a Canadian journalist". *The Theatre* (London) 26: 277, November, 1895.

J7. **Thorold, W.J.** Canadian successes on the stage. *Massey's Magazine* 2: 189-194, September 1896. illus.

J8. **Thorold, W.J.** Canadian successes on the stage. (second paper) *Massey's Magazine* 2: 235-240, October 1896. illus.

J9. **Morgan, Henry James** (ed.) *Canadian men and women of the time.* Toronto, Briggs, 1898. xii, 1119 p.

J10. **Strang, Lewis C.** *Famous actresses of the day in America.* Boston, Page, 1899-1901. 2 v.

J11. **Thorold, W.J.** Some actors and actresses. Including several Canadians who are winning fame. First paper. *Canadian Magazine* 12: 116-123, December 1898. illus., ports.

J12. **Thorold, W.J.** Some actors and actresses. Second paper. The Shakespearean experiences of Miss Julia Arthur. *Canadian Magazine* 12: 237-244, January 1899. ports.

J13. **Thorold, W.J.** Some actors and actresses. Third paper. *Canadian Magazine* 12: 319-321, February 1899. ports.

J14. **Thorold, W.J.** Some actors and actresses. Last paper. *Canadian Magazine* 12: 496-502, April 1899. ports.

J15. **Burpee, William J.** Charles Heavysege. Royal Society of Canada. *Transactions* vii, Section ii, Series ii, 1901: p. 22-52.

J16. **Morris, Clara.** *Life on the stage; my personal experiences and recollections.* New York, McClure Phillips, 1901. 399 p., illus.

J17. **Morgan, Henry James.** *Types of Canadian women.* Toronto, Briggs, 1903. (Short biographies of Canadian-born actresses and of those who have acted extensively in Canada.)

J18. **Roy, Camille.** Le théâtre. In his *Tableau français.* Québec, Action sociale, 1911. p. 79-80. (List of French-Canadian dramatists.)

J19. **Casgrain, L'Abbé H.R.** *A. Gérin-Lajoie d'après ses mémoires.* Montréal, Librairie Beauchemin Lté., 1912. 141 p.

J20. **Morgan, Henry James** (ed.) *Canadian men and women of the time.* 2nd ed. Toronto, Briggs, 1912 xx, 1218 p.

J21. **Bell, Margaret.** What Canada has done for the stage. no. 1. Margaret Anglin. *Maclean's Magazine* 27: 33-35, April 1914. port.

J22. **Bell, Margaret.** Little princess of the stage. *Maclean's Magazine* 27: 33-35, May 1914. port. (Christie MacDonald).

J23. **Bell, Margaret.** May Irwin - peeress of stage widows. *Maclean's Magazine* 27:30, 97-100, July 1914. illus.

J24. **Bell, Margaret.** Rose Stahl, versatile mirth maker. *Maclean's Magazine* 27: 31-33, 123-124, August 1914. port.

J25. **Bell, Margaret.** How Hackett won a fortune. *Maclean's Magazine* 27: 37-38, 45, September 1914. port. (James Hackett).

J26. **Bell, Margaret.** Marie Dressler: the inimitable. *Maclean's Magazine* 27: 42-43, 102, October 1914. ports.

J27. **Bell, Margaret.** Viola Allen's greatest achievement. *Maclean's Magazine* 28: 47-48, 72, February 1915. ports.

J28. **Bell, Margaret.** Queen of the movies. *Maclean's Magazine* 28: 50-51, April 1915. port. (Mary Pickford).

J29. **Bell, Margaret.** Canadian Adonis of the stage. *Maclean's Magazine* 28: 29-30, 95, October 1915. port. (Matheson Lang).

J30. **Winter, William.** *Vagrant memories: being further recollections of other days.* N.Y., G.H. Doran, 1915. 525 p.

J31. **Eayrs, Hugh.** Advance of Canadian stars. *Maclean's Magazine* 30: 38-40, November 1916. illus. ports.

J32. **Steinmetz, Geraldine.** Julia Arthur comes back. *Maclean's Magazine* 29: 17-19, January 1916. port.

J33. **Stringer, Arthur.** Life of Mary Pickford. *Maclean's Magazine* 31: 19-22, 98-103, October 1918. illus.

J34. **Stringer, Arthur.** Our Mary. *Maclean's Magazine* 31: 22-25, 98-104, September 1918. illus., port.

J35. **Pringle, Gertrude E.S.** Catherine Proctor, Canadian actress. *Maclean's Magazine* 35: 64-66, September 15, 1922. ports.

J36. **Brereton, Austin.** *"H.B." and Laurence Irving.* Boston, Small, Maynard and Company, 1923. See ch. XVIII *"Typhoon and Canada"*.

J37. **Montigny, Louvigny De.** *Antoine Gérin-Lajoie.* Toronto, Ryerson Press, 1925. 130 p. (In Makers of Canadian Literature series).

J38. **Forbes-Robertson, Sir Johnston.** *A player under three reigns.* Toronto, Macmillan Company, 1925. 292 p. See chapters on American tours.

J39. **Wallace, William Stewart.** *The Dictionary of Canadian Biography.* Toronto, Macmillan, 1926. 433 p. (2nd ed. 1945 2 v., 3rd ed. 1963, 822 p.)

J40. **Crane, William H.** *Footprints and echoes.* New York, E.P. Dutton, 1927. see p. 40-43, 48, 53, 199.

J41. **Pierce, Lorne Albert.** The dramatists. In his *Outline of Canadian Literature (French and English).* Toronto, Ryerson 1927. p. 113-121.

J42. **Terriss, Ellaline,** *Ellaline Terriss by herself and with others.* London, Cassell and Co., 1928. p. 256-296.

J43. **Benson, Sir Frank.** *My memoirs.* London, Ernest Benn Ltd., 1930. 316p.

J44. **Jackson, Sir Barry.** *Sir Barry Jackson's company of British players from London, England to the Dominion of Canada 1931-1932.* London, J. Miles, 1931. xlvii p. illus. port.

J45. **Wallace, William Stewart.** The Small mystery. *Maclean's Magazine* 44: 6, July 1931.

J46. **Bellerive, Georges.** *Nos auteurs dramatiques anciens et contemporains: répertoire analytique.* Québec, Garneau, 1933. (List of French-Canadian dramatists and their work with analyses of plots.)

J47. **Ashwell, Lena.** *Myself, a player.* London, Michael Joseph Ltd., 1936. 288 p.

J48. **O'Hagan, Thomas.** *What Shakespeare is not.* Toronto, Hunter Rose, 1936. See p. 108-109. (Actors who performed Shakespeare).

J49. **Coulter, John.** On the art of the playwright. *Curtain Call* 9: 7-8, January 1938.

J50. **Prévost, Robert.** *Que sont-ils devenus?* Montréal, Princeps, 1939. 123 p. (Que sont-ils devenus ces artists de la scène . . .? Voici dix-sept entrevus . . . .qui vous révéleront ce que sont devenues des célébrités aujourdhui à leur retraite.)

J51. **Paterson, Andrew.** Dickensian mysteries from Montreal. *Dickensian* 38: 17-22, December 1, 1941. illus.

J52. **Paterson, Andrew.** The Montreal theatre and another mystery. *Dickensian* 38: 85-86, March 1, 1942.

J53. **Paterson, Andrew.** The amateur theatricals in Montreal, contemporary criticisms of Dicken's first public appearances as an actor. *Dickensian* 38: 72-74, March 1, 1942.

J54. **Brodersen, George.** Gwen Pharis — Canadian dramatist. *Manitoba Arts Review* 4:3-20, spring 1944.

J55. **Disher, Maurice Willson.** *The last romantic.* The authorized biography of Sir John Martin-Harvey. London, Hutchinson and Co. Ltd., 1948. 270 p.

J56. **Irving, Laurence.** *Henry Irving: the actor and his world.* London, Faber and Faber, 1951. (See p. 444-445, 585).

J57. **Wallace, William Stewart.** *A Dictionary of North American Authors deceased before 1950.* Toronto, Ryerson Press, 1951. 525 p.

J58. **Ness, Margaret.** On stage abroad. *Saturday Night* 68:41-42, November 15, 1952. illus. (Canadian actresses).

J59. **Williams, Bramsby.** *Bramsby Williams by himself.* London, Hutchinson and Co. Ltd., 1954. 240 p.

J60. **Wolfit, Donald.** *First interval.* London, Odhams Press, 1954. (See chapter 6.)

J61. **Hirsch, John.** In search of a theatre. *Manitoba Arts Review* 9:15-21, winter 1955.

J62. **Bossin, Hye.** *Stars of David.* Toronto, Jewish Standard, 1956. 39 p. (Jewish participation in Toronto theatre.)

J63. **Plunkett, Al.** *Al Plunkett, the famous dumbell* by Patrise Earle as told by Al Plunkett. N.Y., Pageant Press, 1956. 107 p. illus.

J64. **De La Roche, Mazo.** *Ringing the changes.* Toronto, Macmillan, 1957. 304 p.

J65. **Baillargeon, Samuel.** Le théâtre. In his *Littérature canadienne-française.* Montréal, Fides, 1957. p. 429-437. (French-Canadian dramatists since 1945).

J66. *Canadian theatrical arts guide* . . . annual pictorial directory of Canadian stage, screen, radio and television artists. 1959-1961. Toronto, Parkway Publishing. 3 v.

J67. **Trewin, J.C.** *Benson and the Bensonians.* London, Barrie and Rockliff, 1960. See Chapter 12.

J68. **Wagner, Frederick.** *Famous American actors and actresses.* N.Y., Dodd, Mead, 1961. 159 p.

J69. **Ferry, Anthony.** There's a new one man band in show business. *Maclean's Magazine* 75:21-23, 87-90, November 17, 1962. illus.

J70. **Lucia, Ellis.** *Klondike Kate.* New York, Hastings House Publishers, 1962. 305 p. illus., port.

J71. **Plain, Denis.** Nouveaux visages. *Magazine Maclean* 3:21-25, février 1963. ports.

J72. **Cohen, Nathan.** In view: Canadian actors and actresses. *Saturday Night* 80:6-7, February 1965.

J73. **Dufresne, Guy.** Dialogue sur le théâtre. *Le Barre du Jour* 1:62-64, juillet/ décembre, 1965.

J74. **Gauvreau, Claude.** Ma conception du théâtre. *La Barre du Jour* 1:71-73, juillet/ décembre, 1965.

J75. **Grandmont, Eloi De.** Mort de Jean Béraud. *La Barre du Jour* 1:19-20, juillet/ décembre, 1965.

J76. **Huard, Roger B.** Etablir une définition. *La Barre du Jour* 1:74-79, juillet/ décembre, 1965.

J77. **Levac, Claude.** Théâtre, conceptions, reflexions. *La Barre du Jour* 1:85-90, juillet/décembre, 1965.

J78. **Savoie, Claude.** Louis-Joseph Quesnel. *La Barre du Jour* 1:113-116, juillet/ décembre, 1965.

J79. **Shrive, Norman.** *Charles Mair: literary nationalist.* Toronto, University of Toronto Press, 1965. xii, 309 p.

J80. **Durang, John.** *The memoirs of John Durang. American actor 1785-1816.* ed. Alan S. Downer. Pittsburgh, University of Pittsburgh Press, 1966. illus. (See part two "Durang's tour of Canada" p. 47-93).

J81. **Sylvestre, Guy** ed. *Canadian writers — écrivains canadiens.* Revised and enlarged edition. Toronto, Ryerson, 1966. xviii, 186 p.

J82. **Lapalme, Michel.** Cinq nouveaux visages. *Magazine Maclean* 7:24-25, novembre 1967.

J83. **Nicol, Eric.** *A Scar is born: Eric Nicol takes his Canadian play to Broadway.* Toronto, Ryerson, 1968. 91 p.

J84. **Dufferin and Ava, Hariot Georgina Hamilton-Temple-Blackwood,** marchioness of. *My Canadian journal, 1872-78.* ed. by G.C. Walker. Don Mills, Longmans, 1969. xv, 325 p. illus., port. (First published London, Murray; N.Y., Appleton, 1891).

J85. **Reaney, James.** Ten years at play. *Canadian Literature* no. 41:53-61, summer 1969.

J86. **Vanasse, André.** Le théâtre de Jacques Ferron: à la recherche d'une identité. In *Livres et Auteurs Québecois.* 1969. p. 219-230.

J87. **Burger, Baudoin.** Louis Joseph Quesnel. *La Barre du Jour* 5:60-64, été 1970.

J88. **Henry, Ann.** *Laugh baby, laugh.* Toronto, McClelland and Stewart. 1970. 186 p.

J89. **Martineau, Denyse.** *Juliette Béliveau.* Montréal, Les Editions de l'Homme, 1970. 218 p. illus.

J90. **Berthiaume, René.** A propos de l'oeuvre dramatique de Michel Tremblay, un cri d'alarme lancé au peuple québecois. *Nord* 1:9-14, automne, 1971.

J91. **Bourque, Paul André.** Masculin-féminin. Le rêve triste et la triste réalité. *Nord* 1:41-48, automne, 1971.

J92. **Cloutier, Guy.** Michel Tremblay: de la revolution tranquille aux évênements d'octobre. *Nord* 1:15-17, automne, 1971.

J93. **Cloutier, Rachel; Gignac, Rodrigue; Laberge, Marie.** Entrevue avec Michel Tremblay. *Nord* 1:49-81, automne 1971.

J94. *Creative Canada: a biographical dictionary of twentieth century creative and performing artists.* Compiled by the Reference Division, McPherson Library, University of Victoria, B.C., Toronto, University of Toronto Press, 1971-72. 2 vols.

J95. **Fosty, Andrée.** En pièces détachées. *Nord* 1:18-22, automne, 1971.

J96. **Frye, Northrop.**The narrative tradition in English-Canadian poetry. In *The Bush Garden.* Toronto, Anansi Press, 1971. p.145-156. (Comment on Charles Heavysege, J. Hunter-Duvar, Charles Mair).

J97. **Harwood, Ronald.** *Sir Donald Wolfit, CBE., his life and work in the unfashionable theatre.* London, Secker and Warburg, 1971. See Chapter 13.

J98. **Herbert, John.** My life and hard times in cold, bitter, suspicious Toronto. *Saturday Night* 86:21-24, December 1971. illus.

J99. **Houde, Christiane.** Une langue qui se cherche ou de la servitude à la liberation. *Nord* 1:35-40, automne, 1971. (Michel Tremblay).

J100. **Belair, Michel.** *Michel Tremblay.* Montréal, Presses de l'Université du Quebec, 1972. 95 p.

J101. **Buitenhuis, Elspeth.** *Robertson Davies.* Toronto, Forum House, 1972. 80 p.

J102. **Carson, Neil.** George Ryga and the lost country. In New, William H. ed. *Dramatists in Canada: selected essays.* Vancouver, University of British Columbia

Press, 1972. p. 155-162. (Reprinted from: *Canadian Literature* no. 45: 33-40, summer 1970).

J103. **Carson, Neil.** Sexuality and identity in "Fortune and Men's eyes". *Twentieth Century Literature* 18: 207-218, July 1972.

J104. It's not this, not that (Mia Anderson in "Ten Women, Two Men and a Moose"). *Performing Arts* 9: 4-5, winter 1972.

J105. **Lee, Alvin.** A turn to the stage: Reaney's dramatic verse. In New, William H. ed. *Dramatists in Canada: selected essays.* Vancouver, University of British Columbia Press, 1972. p. 114-133. (Reprinted from: *Canadian Literature* no. 15: 43-51, winter 1963).

J106. **Messenger, Ann P.** Damnation at Christmas: John Herbert's "Fortune and Men's Eyes". In New, William H. ed. *Dramatists in Canada: selected essays.* Vancouver, University of British Columbia Press, 1972. p. 173-178.

J107. **New, William H.** Household locks: the plays of Simon Gray. In his *Dramatists in Canada: selected essays.* Vancouver, University of British Columbia Press, 1972. p. 163-172.

J108. **Parker, Brian.** Reaney and the Mask of Childhood. In Reaney, James. *Masks of Childhood: the Easter Egg, Three Desks, the Killdeer.* Toronto, New Press, 1972. p. 279-289.

J109. **Pontaut, Alain.** *Dictionnaire critique du théâtre québecois.* Ottawa, Leméac, 1972. 151 p.

J110. **Primeau, Marguerite.** Gratien Gélinas et le théâtre populaire au Canada français. In New, William H. ed. *Dramatists in Canada: selected essays.* Vancouver, University of British Columbia Press, 1972. p. 105-113. (Reprinted from: *Canadian Literature* no. 4: 31-39, spring 1960.

J111. **Reaney, James.** Ten years at play. In New, William H. ed. *Dramatists in Canada: selected essays.* Vancouver, University of British Columbia Press, 1972. p. 70-78. (Reprinted from: *Canadian Literature* No. 41:53-61, summer 1969).

J112. **Shrive, Norman.** Poets and patriotism: Charles Mair and Tecumseh. In New, William H. ed. *Dramatists in Canada: selected essays.* Vancouver, University of British Columbia Press, 1972. p. 27-38. (Reprinted from: *Canadian Literature* no. 20:15-26, spring 1964).

J113. **Steinberg, M.W.** Don Quixote and the puppets: theme and structure in Robertson Davies' drama. In New, William H. ed. *Dramatists in Canada: selected essays.* Vancouver, University of British Columbia Press, 1972. p. 53-61. (Reprinted from: *Canadian Literature* no. 7:45-53, winter 1961).

J114. **Tait, Michael.** Everything is something: James Reaney's "Colours in the Dark." In New, William H. ed. *Dramatists in Canada: selected essays.* Vancouver, University of British Columbia Press, 1972. p. 140-144.

J115. **Tait, Michael.** The limits of innocence: James Reaney's theatre. In New, William H. ed. *Dramatists in Canada: selected essays.* Vancouver, University of British Columbia Press, 1972. p. 134-139. (Reprinted from *Canadian Literature* no. 19:43-48, winter 1964).

J116. *Who's who in the theatre:* a biographical record of the contemporary stage. 15th ed. London, Pitman, 1972. 1952 p. (1st edition 1912).

J117. **Woodman, Ross.** *James Reaney.* Toronto, McClelland and Stewart, 1972. 64 p.

J118. **Champagne, Jane.** Alan Laing: working at putting music into theatre. *Canadian Composer* 84:cover, 4-9, October 1973. illus., port.

J119. **Garner, Hugh.** *One damned thing after another.* Toronto, McGraw-Hill, Ryerson, 1973. 293 p.

J120. **Hassan, R.F.** All you ever wanted to know about monodramas. (David Watmough). *Journal of Canadian Fiction.* Vol. 2, no. 4:100-101, 1973.

J121. **Hausvater, Alexander.** Michel Tremblay: superstar. *Motion* 2:24-25, November-December 1973, port.

J122. **Hirsch, John.** Adoption by a cold land. *Maclean's* 86:39, 55-56, April 1973. port.

J123. **Johns, Ted.** Interview with Paul Thompson. *Performing Arts* 10:30-32, winter 1973. illus., port.

J124. **MacDonald, Dick.** *Mugwump Canadian: the Merrill Denison story.* Montreal, Content Publishing, 1973. 204 p.

J125. **McLarty, James.** Chief Dan George: more than an actor. *Motion* 1:6-7, July-August 1973. illus., port.

J126. **McLarty, James.** The world according to John Herbert. *Motion* 1:16-20, March-April 1973. illus.

J127. Mia Anderson: a woman of many faces. *Performing Arts* 10:10-11, spring 1973. illus.

J128. **Moore, James Mavor.** *4 Canadian playwrights: Robertson Davies, Gratien Gélinas, James Reaney, George Ryga.* Toronto, Holt, Rinehart and Winston, 1973. 92 p.

J129. Three years ago — Doris Petrie. *Motion* 1:35-38, January-February 1973. illus.

J130. **Warkentin, G.** The artist in labour: James Reaney's plays. *Journal of Canadian Fiction.* Vol 2, no. 1:88-91, 1973.

J131. **Windeler, Robert.** *Sweetheart: the story of Mary Pickford.* London, W.H. Allen, 1973. 226 p. illus., port.

J132. **Allan, Andrew.** *Andrew Allan: a self-portrait.* Toronto, MacMillan Company, 1974. 199 p. illus.

J133. **Cook, Michael.** Introduction to "Head, guts, and sound bone dance". *Canadian Theatre Review* CTR 1:74-76, winter 1974.

J134. **Dalrymple, Andrew A.** and **Gray, Jack.** From stage to screen. *Motion* 3:12-14, November-December 1974. port.

J135. Determination never to go back. (David Freeman). *Time* (Canada) 103:10, January 28, 1974. illus.

J136. **Dudek, Louis.** A problem of meaning. (James Reaney's plays). *Canadian Literature* 59:16-29, winter 1974.

J137. From playing a bastard to being national theatre school's artistic director (Douglas Rain). *Performing Arts* 11:10, fall 1974. port.

J138. **Gass, Ken.** Directing abroad. *Canadian Theatre Review* CTR 1:56-59, winter 1974.

J139. **Gilbert, Edward.** A personal view. *Canadian Theatre Review* CTR 4:22-25, fall 1974.

J140. **Hausvater, Alexander.** Acting is my religion. (Madeleine Thornton-Sherwood). *Motion* 2:12-13, July-August 1974. illus., port.

J141. **Hirsch, John.** Directing in Canada. *Canadian Theatre Review* CTR 1:49-55, winter 1974.

J142. **Hofsess, J.** Will success spoil David Freeman? *Maclean's* 87:35, 42, February 1974. port.

J143. Jessie Ross de River award. (Chris Wiggins). *Canadian Author and Bookman* 50:20, fall 1974.

J144. **Juliani, John.** On being invited: a comment. *Canadian Theatre Review* CTR 1:65-67, winter 1974.

J145. **Juliani, John.** Soviet diary. *Canadian Theatre Review* CTR 2:24-33, spring 1974.

J146. **McCaughna, David.** A terribly personal business. *Motion* 2:16-19, July-August 1974. illus., port.

J147. **McCaughna, David.** 3 Canadian views: Peter Madden, "the night no one yelled"; Bryan Wade, "blitzkrieg"; Gary Engler, "sudden death overtime". *Motion* 3:31-33, November-December 1974.

J148. **McClement, Fred.** *The strange case of Ambrose Small.* Toronto, McClelland and Stewart, 1974. 158 p.

J149. **McLarty, James.** Time's on my side: Luce Guilbeault. *Motion* 2:12-13, January-February 1974. illus., port.

J150. **MacDonald, Dick.** Luce Guilbeault, unstereotyped actress. *Chatelaine* 47:33, 67, February 1974. port.

J151. **MacDonald, Dick.** Merrill Denison: return from obscurity. *Maclean's* 87:86, 88, June 1974. port.

J152. **Meltzer, Peter.** The many faces of Paul Gaulin. *Performing Arts* 11:47-49, spring 1974. illus.

J153. **Moore, James Mavor.** Canada's great theatre prophet! Roy who? *Canadian Theatre Review* CTR 1:68-71, winter 1974.

J154. **Mullaly, Edward J.** Canadian drama: David French and the great awakening. *Fiddlehead* 100:61-66, winter 1974.

J155. **Neary, Peter.** Of many coloured glass: Peter Neary interviews David French. *Canadian Forum* 53:26-27, March 1974.

J156. Royal bank award given to theatre man. (Jean Gascon). *Performing Arts* 11:5, summer 1974.

J157. **Thomas, Powys,** and **Chadwick, Bernard.** On being a Canadian actor: two perspectives. *Canadian Theatre Review* CTR 1:33-44, winter 1974.

J158. **Warwick, Ellen D.** The transformation of Robertson Davies. *Journal of Canadian Fiction* 3, no. 3:46-51, 1974.

J159. **Wittgens, Claudia.** In conversation with Gordon Pinsent. *Motion* 2:23-24, July-August 1974. port.

J160. **Wyers, H.** Jean Gascon receives Royal Bank award. *Canadian Banker and I.C.B. Review* 81:19, May-June 1974.

J161. **Wylie, Betty Jane.** At the heart of a loss. *Maclean's* 87:24-25, 40-41, February 1974. port.

J162. **Alianak, Hrant.** Interview with Urjo Kareda. In his *Return of the big five* ed. by Connie Brissenden. Toronto, Fineglow Plays, 1975. p. 9-24.

J163. **Anthony, Geraldine.** The forgotten man: John Coulter, dean of Canadian playwrights. *Canadian Drama/L'Art Dramatique Canadien* 1:12-18, spring 1975.

J164. **Canadian Conference of the Arts.** *Who's who: list of key persons with responsibility for arts and culture.* Toronto, Canadian Conference of the Arts, June 1975. 42 p.

J165. **Evanchuk, Peter M.** From the ashes (John Hirsch). *Motion* 4:20-21, August 1975. illus.

J166. James Reaney wins Chalmers award. *Quill and Quire* 41:4, March 1975.

J167. **Knelman, Martin.** Theatre: the outlandish joual world of Michel Tremblay. *Saturday Night* 90:79, 81-83, May 1975.

J168. **McCaughna, David.** Love is all. (Michel Tremblay). *Motion* 4:13-14, August 1975.

J169. **Mailhot, Laurent.** Le loup dans la bergerie ou le théâtre d'Yves Thériault. *Canadian Drama/L'Art Dramatique Canadien* 1:19-26, spring 1975.

J170. **Nicol, Eric.** Introduction to "The citizens of Calais". *Canadian Theatre Review* CTR 7:54-55, summer 1975.

J171. Robertson Davies. *Time* (Canada) 105:11, March 10, 1975.

J172. **Sim, Sheila E.** Tragedy and ritual in "the great hunger" and "the ecstasy of Rita Joe". *Canadian Drama/L'Art Dramatique Canadien* 1:27-32, spring 1975.

J173. **Voaden, Herman.** Murder pattern and its critics. *Canadian Theatre Review* CTR 5:61-62, winter 1975.

J174. **Wagner, Anton.** Gwen Pharis Ringwood rediscovered. *Canadian Theatre Review* CTR 5:63-69, winter 1975.

The Walker Theatre in Winnipeg, opened in 1907, was one of the large touring houses prominent on the Canadian circuits during the early 1900's. The nature of many of the shows which toured is well illustrated by this picture of *The Flirting Princess,* starring Helen Darling and Harry Bulger.

See items: B103, B105.

These two photographs were taken on Sir John Martin-Harvey's tour across Canada in 1913-14. As Martin-Harvey relates in his autobiography, "Playing 'the smalls' in Canada needs some heroism," (p 427). The photo above shows what often happened when the stage sets were too large to be stored in a Canadian theatre. The balustrade and rostrum in the foreground and the grandfather clock on top of the centre pile are from *The Breed of the Treshams,* Act 2, "Upper Room in Feversham Castle." The building is the Victoria Theatre, Regina, Saskatchewan, which later burned when Bramsby Williams, another touring actor was playing in it in 1929. The photo below shows one of the methods necessary for transporting stage equipment on Sir John Martin-Harvey's tour.

See items B131, C12, J55.

K

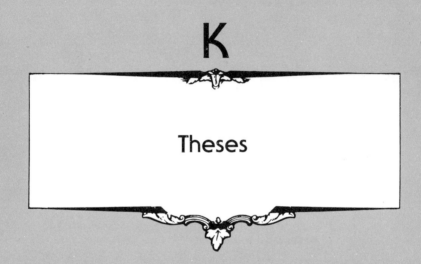

Theses

K1. **Aikens, James. R.** *Rival operas: Toronto theatre 1874-84.* Ph.D. University of Toronto, 1975. 2 v.

K2. **Amyot, Michel.** *Le drame de l'impuissance dans le théâtre de Marcel Dubé.* M.A. University of Montreal, 1963.

K3. **Asher, Stanley A.** *Playwriting in Canada, an historical survey.* M.A. University of Montreal, 1962. v, 118 p. bibl.

K4. **Audet, Marc.** *Le théâtre canadien français de 1945 à nos jours.* Maîtrise en Sciences Sociales. Laval, 1965. (1), 59, (3) p. bibl.

K5. **Barber, Teresa.** *History of the Bastion theatre 1963-1975.* M.A. University of Victoria, Victoria, B.C. 1975. viii, 417 l.

K6. **Best, James Linden.** *The post-Confederation theatres of Halifax.* M.A. University of New Brunswick, 1972. ix, 153 l. bibl.

K7. **Bilodeau, Françoise.** *Théâtre canadien-français 1900-1955.* M. Ecole de Bibliothéconomie. Laval, 1956. 94 p.

K8. **Birch, Kathleen Jane.** *The broken window pane: a study in the creative imagination in James Reaney's "Listen to the Wind".* M.A. McMaster University, 1973. 143 p.

K9. **Bisson, Margaret Mary.** *Le théâtre français à Montréal 1878-1931.* Ph.D. McGill University, 1932. 137 p.

K10. **Bolster, Charles.** *Shakespeare in French Canada.* M.A. University of New Brunswick. 1970. 203 p.

K11. **Brissenden, L. Constance.** *Canadian plays produced professionally during the 1960's in Toronto.* M.A. University of Alberta, 1971. 203 p.

K12. **Conroy, Patricia.** *A history of the theatre in Montreal prior to Confederation.* M.A. McGill University, 1936. 174 p.

K13. **Corriveau, Jeanne.** *Jonathas du R.P. Gustave Lamarche et le théâtre collégial.* M.A. Université de Montreal, 1966.

K14. **Crompton, Jack.** *L'état, le théâtre, et le public: la situation au Québec.* M.A. Laval (Etudes Canadiennes). 1972. vii, 124 p.

K15. **Cruikshank, Marion Gertrude.** *The influence of the university on the development of drama in the United States and Canada.* M.A. McGill University, 1931. ii, 75, vi, p. bibl.

K16. **Dalgleish, Gail.** *Canadian drama: history in transition.* M.A. University of Calgary, 1973.

K17. **Duval, Etienne F.** *Le sentiment national dans le théâtre canadien francais de 1760 à 1930.* Doctorat de l'Université. Paris, 1967. 438 l. bibl.

K18. **Edwards, Margaret Christian.** *Canadian drama, dramatists and players.* M.A. McGill University, 1926. 164, 10 p. bibl.

K19. **Edwards, Murray Dallas.** *The English speaking theatre in Canada 1820-1914.* Ph.D. Columbia University, 1963. v., 339 p. bibl.

K20. **Elliott, Craig C.** *Annals of the legitimate theatre in Victoria, Canada from its beginning to 1900.* Ph.D. University of Washington, 1969. 447 p.

K21. **Fitzpatrick, Marjorie Ann.** *The fortunes of Molière in French Canada.* Ph.D. University of Toronto, 1968. xxx, 518 p. bibl.

K22. **Germain, Pauline.** *Les structures dynamiques dans le théâtre de Marcel Dubé.* Maîtrise en Arts. Laval, 1964. ix, 141 p. bibl.

K23. **Gold, Muriel Nora.** *A study of three Montreal children's theatres.* M.A. McGill University, 1972. iv, 100 l. bibl.

K24. **Gustafson, David Axel.** *The Canadian regional theatre movement.* Ph.D. Michigan State University, 1971. iv, 346 l. illus.

K25. **Haynes, Nancy Jane.** *A history of the Royal Alexandra Theatre, Toronto, Ontario, Canada; 1914-1918.* Ph.D. University of Colorado, Boulder, Colorado. 1973. vii, 290 l., bibl.

K26. **Hiritsch, Basil.** *The development of Ukrainian theatre and its role in Canada.* M.A. Université de Montreal, 1962. (in Ukrainian).

K27. **Jackson, Roger Lee.** *A history and analytical study of the origins and development and impact of the dramatic programs produced for the English language network of the Canadian Broadcasting Corporation.* Ph.D. Wayne State University, 1966. 230 p.

K28. **Johnston, Viola M.** *Bibliography of one act plays by Canadian authors.* Ms. McGill University Library School, 1932. 12 l.

K29. **Klein, A. Owen.** *Theatre Royal, Montreal 1825-1844.* Ph.D. Indiana University, 1973. vi, 181 p.

K30. **McAlister, Ruth.** *Some aspects of the amateur theatre in Canada.* (One hundred years' progress demonstrated chiefly by certain local developments in the Province of Ontario.) M.A. Columbia University, 1950. 89, 16 l.

K31. **MacKinnon, Teresa.** *Theatre for young audiences in Canada.* Ph.D. New York University. 1974. 2 v. 808 p.

K32. **Maybee, Janet.** *A calendar of theatre performances in Halifax 1850-1880.* M.A. Dalhousie University, 1965. xlix, 146 p. bibl.

K33. **Moussali, Lucienne.** *Les personnages du théâtre d'André Laurendeau.* M.A. Laval, 1967. xvi, 195 p. bibl.

K34. **Oland, Sidney M.** *Materials for a history of the theatre in early Halifax.* M.A. Dalhousie University, 1966. lx, 195 p. bibl. (1749-1829).

K35. **O'Neill, Patrick Bernard Anthony.** *A history of theatrical activity in Toronto, Canada from its beginnings to 1858.* Ph.D. Louisiana State University, 1973. 794 p.

K36. **Ouellet, Thérèse.** *Bibliographie du théâtre canadien français avant 1900.* Diplôme de Bibliothéconomie. Laval, 1949. 53 p.

K37. **Pagé, Raymond.** *Le théâtre amateur en Mauricie rurale ou en voie d'urbanisation (1900-1967).* Diplôme d'Etudes Supérieures. Laval, 1970. x, 208 p. illus., maps, bibl.

K38. **Parkhill, Frances Neily.** *The Dominion Drama Festival, its history, organisation and influence.* M.A. Emerson College, 1952. 98, ii p. bibl.

K39. **Pope, Karl Theodore.** *An historical study of the Stratford Ontario Festival* *theatre.* Ph.D., Wayne State University, 1966. 266 p. illus.

K40. **Rickett, Olla Goewey.** *The French speaking theatre of Montreal 1937-1963.* Ph.D. Cornell University, 1964. iv, 144 p. bibl.

K41. **Ross, John Richard.** *A preliminary study of the historical background, educational philosophy and future development of drama in education in Canada.* M.A. University of Saskatchewan, Saskatoon, 1968.

K42. **Sansom, Wilma Louise.** *Some aspects of the development of drama in New Brunswick.* M.A. University of New Brunswick, 1953. iv, 120 p.

K43. **Scott, Robert Barry.** *A study of amateur theatre in Toronto: 1900-1930.* M.A. University of New Brunswick, 1966. xxii, 794 p. bibl.

K44. **Scott, Robert Barry.** *A study of English Canadian dramatic literature 1900-1930.* Phil.M. University of Toronto, 1969. 319 l.

K45. **Sheremeta, James D.** *Entertainment in Edmonton before 1914.* M.A. University of Alberta, 1970.

K46. **Sillito, Jolayne.** *A study of the community and university theatres in Edmonton, 1882-1964, their history, inter-relationship and influence.* M.A. Brigham Young University. 1966. 115 p.

K47. **Spensley, Philip J.** *A description and evaluation of the training methods of the National Theatre School of Canada, English acting course 1960-68.* Ph.D. Wayne State University, 1970. 409 p.

K48. **Stuart, Euan Ross.** *An analysis of production on the open stage at Stratford, Ontario.* Ph.D. University of Toronto, 1975. 333 p. plates, illus.

K49. **Tait, Michael Strong.** *Studies in the theatre and drama of English Canada.* M.A. University of Toronto, 1963. 126 l.

K50. **Turner, Edwin.** *The verse theatre of James Reaney.* Ph.D. University of Alberta, 1971.

K51. **Ursell, G.B.** *A triple mirror: the plays of Merrill Denison, Gwen P. Ringwood and Robertson Davies.* M.A. University of Manitoba, 1966. 144 p.

K52. **Watt, Frank.** *Radicalism in English-Canadian literature since Confederation.* Ph.D. University of Toronto, 1957.

K53. **Weiller, Georgette.** *Sarah Bernhardt et le Canada.* M.A. University of Ottawa, 1968. 119 p. illus.

K54. **White, Meredith Allison.** *The Canadian little theatre: a bibliography.* Ms. McGill University Library School, 1932. 14 l.

K55. **Whittaker, Walter Leslie.** *The Canada Council for the encouragement of the arts, humanities and social sciences: its origins, formation, operation and influence on the theater in Canada, 1957-1963.* Ph.D. University of Michigan, 1965. ix, 389 p. bibl.

K56. **Williams, Albert Ronald.** *A survey of the professional and major amateur presentations in Saskatoon from 1912 to 1930.* M.A. University of Saskatchewan, 1967. v, 132 p. bibl.

K57. **Young, William Curtis.** *A guide to manuscript and special collections in theatrical arts in the U.S. and Canada.* Ph.D. University of Kansas, 1970. 295 p.

L

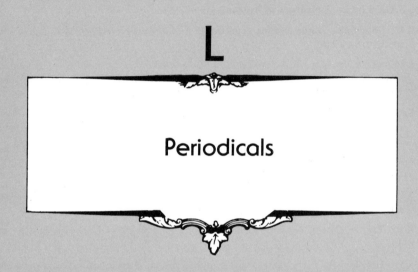

Periodicals

L1. *Act One.* Toronto, Students' Administrative Council, University of Toronto. October, 1968-February, 1969. 4 issues only.

L2. *Actors' Equity Association Newsletter.* Toronto, Actors' Equity Association. Vol. 1, 1955 + Monthly.

L3. *ACTRA News Magazine.* Toronto, Association of Canadian Television and Radio Artists. Vol. 1, no. 1, summer, 1947-summer, 1967. Quarterly.

L4. *Actrascope.* Toronto, Association of Canadian Television and Radio Artists. Vol.1, no.1, March, 1968 + Quarterly.

L5. *Actrascope News.* Toronto, Association of Canadian Television and Radio Artists. Vol.1, no.1, July, 1973 + Members only. Eight times per year.

L6. *Alive Magazine.* Guelph, Ontario, Alive Press. Vol.1, no.1, 1970 + Occasional articles on Canadian theatre and drama.

L7. *The American review of Canadian Studies.* Washington, D.C., Johns Hopkins School of Advanced International Studies, Centre of Canadian Studies. Vol.1, no.1, spring, 1971 + Reviews of books relating to theatre and drama, occasional articles about Canadian theatre and drama.

L8. *Atlantic Advocate.* Fredericton, New Brunswick. Vol.1, no.1, 1910 + Regular articles on current theatrical scene. Monthly.

L9. *Bala Summer Colonist.* Bala, Ontario, J.N. Harris (Publisher). No.1, July 9, 1936 - No.7, August 20, 1936. Contains information on Actor's Colony Theatre under direction of John Holden. (7 issues).

L10. *The Beaver.* Winnipeg, Manitoba, Hudson's Bay Company. Vol.I, no.1, October, 1920 + Occasional articles on early Canadian theatre.

L11. *Books in Canada.* Toronto, Canadian Review of Books Limited. Vol.I, no.1, July, 1971 + Reviews of plays published and of books related to Canadian theatre.

L12. **British Columbia Drama.* Victoria, B.C., School and Community Drama Branch of the Department of Education (for the British Columbia Drama Association). Vol. I, no. 1, 1948 - Vol. 2, no. 6, autumn, 1952. (?).

L13. *B.C. Drama Newsletter.* Victoria, B.C., Community Programmes Branch of the Department of Education (for the British Columbia Drama Association). Vol.I, no.1, December, 1959 - Vol.4, no.2, November, 1966.

L14. *Bulletin.* Toronto, Canadian Conference of the Arts. Vol. I, November, 1973 + Bi-monthly.

L15. *Bulletin des Recherches Historiques.* Lévis, Québec. Vol. 1, no. 1, 1895 - Vol. 70, no. 2, 1968. Occasionally articles on theatre in Quebec.

L16. **Cahiers de l'Acta.* Montreal, Association Canadienne du Théâtre d'Amateur Vol. 1, no. 1, janvier, 1962 - Vol. 3, no. 3, octobre, 1964. (?) Quarterly.

L17. *Cahiers des Compagnons.* Bulletin d'art dramatique. Compagnons de St. Laurent. Vol. I, no. 1, septembre/octobre, 1944 - Vol. 3, no. 2, mars/mai, 1947. Bimonthly.

L18. *Cahiers des Dix.* Montréal, Vol. I, 1936 + Historical review containing information on theatres and performances in Quebec and Montreal in seventeenth, eighteenth, and nineteenth centuries. See index in each volume. Published irregularly.

L19. *Cahiers des Résumés.* Montréal, Le Centre d'Essai des Auteurs Dramatiques. No. 1, janvier, 1973 + Summaries of plays chosen by Le Centre for further development. Irregularly.

L20. *Cahiers des Résumés — théâtre pour les enfants.* Montréal, Le Centre d'Essai des Auteurs Dramatiques. No. 1, octobre, 1974 + Irregularly.

L21. *Call Board.* Halifax, Nova Scotia Adult Educational Division. Vol. I, no. 1, December, 1949-January, 1960. 38 issues. Publication continued after January 1960 by Nova Scotia Drama League, Halifax, as official publication of the Nova Scotia Drama League. Contains information on current events in Nova Scotia theatres, articles on various aspects of theatre and drama, play scripts.

L22. *Call Boy.* London, London Little Theatre Association. Vol. I, no. 1, January, 1946 - Vol. 20, no. 130, March, 1967. Six times per year.

L23. *Call Sheet.* Toronto, Central Ontario Drama League. No. 1, November, 1949. No more published. Mimeographed.

L24. **Canada Council.** *Annual Report.* Ottawa, 1957/8 + .

L25. *Canadian Annual Review of Public Affairs.* Toronto. 1901 - 1937/8 ed. John Castell-Hopkins. Volumes for 1922-1932, contains surveys of little theatre movement. Continued as *Canadian Annual Review.* 1960-1970 ed. John T. Saywell. Contains annual review of theatre activity. Continued as *Canadian Annual Review of Political and Public Affairs.* 1971 + No theatre articles.

L26. *Canadian Commentator.* Toronto, W.H. Baxter Publishing. Vol. I, January, 1957 - October, 1971. Articles on current events in Canadian theatre. Monthly.

L27. *Canadian Drama/L'Art Dramatique Canadien.* Waterloo, University of Waterloo. Vol. I, no. 1, spring, 1975 + Semi-annually.

L28. *Canadian Forum.* Toronto. 1920 + Monthly review of the little theatre. January, 1929 — News of little theatres; February, 1929 - February, 1931 — The little theatre; March, 1931 - November, 1932 — Stage and Screen; from 1932 irregularly published articles in "Footlights", "The Arts in Review". Occasional reviews of books related to Canadian theatre. Monthly.

L29. *Canadian Illustrated News.* Montreal, G.E. Desbarats, Publisher. Vol. I, October 30, 1869 - December 29, 1883. Articles on Canadian theatre, illustrations, occasional playscripts. Weekly.

L30. *Canadian Literature.* Vancouver, University of British Columbia. No. I, summer, 1959 + Articles on Canadian drama and theatre. Quarterly.

L31. *Canadian Magazine.* Toronto, Canadian Magazine Limited. Vol. I, no. 1, March, 1893 - April, 1939. Occasional articles on Canadian theatre. Monthly.

L32. *Canadian Monthly and National Review.* Toronto, Adam Stevenson & Co. Vol. 1, January-June 1872 - Vol. 13, January-June 1878. Monthly. Regular article "Music and Drama" from Vol. 6, October 1874. Continued after Vol. 13 as *Rose-Belford's Canadian Monthly and National Review.* Occasional articles on theatre.

L33. *Canadian Reader.* Toronto, Readers' Club of Canada. Vol. I, no. 1, November, 1959 + Occasional reviews of theatre books and plays published. Every four weeks.

L34. *The Canadian Review.* Ottawa, Pomeroy, Carter, and Associates. Vol. 1, no. 1, February, 1974 + Reviews of theatre productions, books, plays. Occasional articles on Canadian theatre. Bi-monthly.

L35. *Canadian Review of Comparative Literature.* Toronto, University of Toronto Press. Vol. I, no. 1, winter, 1974 + 3 times per year.

L36. *Canadian Stage, Screen and Studio.* Toronto, Canadian Stage Publishing Co. Vol. I, March, 1936 - Vol. 2, no. 1, December, 1937.

L37. *Canadian Theatrical Arts Guide . . . Annual Pictorial Directory of Canadian Stage, Screen, Radio, and Television Artists.* Toronto, Parkway Publishing. Vol. I, 1958-59 - Vol. 3, 1960-61.

L38. *Canadian Theatre Centre: Directory of Membership.* Toronto, Canadian Theatre Centre. No. 1, November, 1965 - October, 1972. Irregularly published.

L39. *Canadian Theatre Review.* Toronto, York University Faculty of Fine Arts. Vol. I, no. 1, winter, 1974 + Articles on Canadian theatre and drama; reviews of books related to Canadian theatre and published plays; surveys of current theatre scene in major centres of Canada. Quarterly.

L40. *Central Ontario Drama League Newsletter.* Toronto, Vol. 1, October, 1950 + (mimeographed). Published 6 times a year. Organization changed name to Association of Community Theatres in 1975, and C.O.D.L. newsletter became *Act News.*

L41. *The Circle.* Saskatoon, Saskatchewan Child and Youth Drama Association. Vol. 1, 1968 (?) Semi-annually.

L42. *Citadel Scene.* Edmonton, Citadel Theatre. Vol. 1, no. 1, January/February, 1975. +

L43. *Cité Libre.* Montreal. Vol. I, 1950 - 1966. Became *Cahiers de Cité Libre* 1966 - 1971. Occasional articles on Quebec theatre, play scripts. Irregularly.

L44. *Chronicle.* Edmonton, Citadel Theatre. Vol. I, November, 1965/6 - 1967/8. Two seasons only.

L45. *Communiqué.* Toronto, Canadian Conference of the Arts. Vol. I, summer, 1972 + One special issue, winter, 1971-2, preceded Vol. I. Previously *Communiqué* was a 6 page newsletter sent to C.C.A. members. Quarterly.

L46. *Community Playhouse News.* Sarnia Drama League.

L47. *Cue.* Montreal, Montreal Repertory Theatre. No. I, December 1, 1930 - Vol. 32, No. 5, January, 1961. Published as programme for each M.R.T. production.

L48. *Cue Theatre Magazine.* Vancouver, I.M. Frew Publishing. Vol. I, July 1967 + Published irregularly.

L49. *Curtain Call.* Toronto. Vol. I, no. 1, November 29, 1929 - Vol. 4, no. 8, May 12, 1933. Published fortnightly (later monthly) by permission of the syndics of Hart House Theatre. Devoted to all the arts, especially in Toronto. Vol. 5, no. 1, October, 1933 - Vol. 13, November/December 1941. Published monthly. Official publication of the Dominion Drama Festival. Articles, photographs of current theatre scene,

Hart House theatre and national amateur movement; book reviews; play scripts.

L50. *Dalhousie Review.* Halifax, Dalhousie University. Vol. I, no. 1, April, 1921 + Occasional articles on Canadian theatre and drama. Quarterly.

L51. *Dominion Drama Festival and Theatre Conference Programmes.* 1933 - 1971. Title varies; published in city where conference is held. Annually. Regional festivals have similar programmes. Annually.

L52. *Dominion Drama Festival News Letter.* Ottawa, Dominion Drama Festival. No. 1, February, 1951 - March/April, 1961. Title varies; numbering irregular: to No. 46, May/June, 1959, called *Dominion Drama Festival News Letter;* succeeding issue, numbered Vol. 8, no. 4, July/August, 1959, and called *Theatre Canada:* "Official Publication of the Dominion Drama Festival"; from January/February, 1961, numbered Vol. 14, published by Dominion Drama Festival and Canadian Theatre Centre.

L53. *Drama at Calgary.* Calgary, University of Calgary. Vol. 1, November, 1966 - September, 1969. 3 times yearly.

L54. *Eastern Ontario Drama Newsletter.* Belleville and Ottawa District Offices, Eastern Ontario Drama League. Vol. 1, November, 1957 + Published irregularly.

L55. *Edge.* Edmonton. No. 1, autumn, 1963 - no. 9, summer, 1969. Small number of articles on Canadian theatre and drama.

L56. *L'Envers du Décor.* Montréal, Théâtre du Nouveau Monde. Vol. 1, Novembre, 1968 + Périodique sur la vie du théâtre. Monthly.

L57. *Equity: Equity in Canada.* Toronto. Vol. I, July 1969. One issue only brought out by Equity members.

L58. *Face to Face with Talent.* Toronto, Association of Canadian Television and Radio Artists. Vol. 1, January, 1970 + Bi-annually. Includes various members of Actors Equity Association.

L59. *Fanfares.* Stratford, Stratford Shakespearean Festival Foundation. Vol. 1, no. 1, March, 1967 + Quarterly.

L60. *The Fiddlehead.* Fredericton, University of New Brunswick. Vol. 1, 1945 + Occasional articles on Canadian theatres; book reviews. Quarterly.

L61. *Glaser Players' Bulletin.* Toronto, Uptown Theatre. Vol. 1, 1921 - 1924. Information on Vaughan Glaser Players' productions and theatre comment. Weekly.

L62. *Glitter: the Magazine of People, Places and Pleasure.* Toronto. Vol. 1, no. 1, January, 1975 + Articles on people in theatre. Published 6 times a year.

L63. *Historic Kingston.* Kingston, Kingston Historical Society. Vol. 1, October 1952 + Small number of articles on early Kingston theatre. Annually.

L64. *(Facsimile of the) Illustrated Arctic News: published on board H.M.S. Resolute.* London, Ackerman and Co. March 15, 1852. 5 issues: No. 1, October 31, 1850; No. 2, November 30, 1850; No. 3, December 31, 1850; No. 4, January 31, 1851; No. 5, March 14, 1851. A journal containing articles documenting the activities of the "Royal Arctic Theatre" established on board H.M.S. Assistance, one of three ships of Sir John Franklin's expedition, as they wintered off Griffith's Island in 1850-51. Illustrations in colour; advertisements; playbills.

L65. *In Review: Canadian Books for Children.* Toronto, Provincial Library Service. Vol. 1, no. 1, winter, 1967 + Reviews of Canadian children's plays and theatre books; in French and English. Quarterly.

L66. *International Theatre Informations.* International Theatre Institute. Vol. 1, 1959 + Title has varied (*World Premières Mondiales,* 1959-64). Occasional articles on Canadian theatre. 3 times per year.

L67. *Le Journal des Etoiles.* Montréal, Publications des Etoiles. Vol. 1, juillet, 1969 +

L68. *Journal of Canadian Fiction.* Montreal, Journal of Canadian Fiction Association. Vol. I, no. 1, winter, 1972 + Occasional articles on Canadian theatre and drama; reviews of books relating to Canadian theatre. Quarterly.

L69. *Journal of Commonwealth Literature.* University of Leeds. Vol. I, September, 1965 + Annual bibliography of Canadian literature containing a section on Canadian drama.

L70. *Julius Cahn's Official Theatrical Guide.* New York. Vol. 1, 1896. In 1912 became *Julius Cahn-Leighton Theatrical Guide.* In 1921 became *Julius Cahn-Gus Hill Theatrical Guide and Motion Picture Directory.* Contains information on a number of Canadian theatres; touring companies which worked in Canada. Annual editions; supplements.

L71. *Key to Toronto.* Toronto, Key Publishers Ltd. Vol. 1, August, 1954 + Articles on current Toronto theatre. Monthly.

L72. *The Last Post.* Montreal. Vol. I, no. 1, December, 1969 + Occasional articles on Canadian theatre and drama. Monthly.

L73. *Letters in Canada.* Toronto, 1935 + University of Toronto Quarterly. Annual review of drama; criticism of Canadian plays, except for 1947-1952, when articles included general comment on Canadian theatre. 1953 on - occasionally a review of Canadian drama and theatre; occasionally a review of books on Canadian theatre and published plays. From summer 1974 regular article on Canadian drama and theatre. French and English.

L74. *Little Theatre Gossip.* Winnipeg, The Community Players of Winnipeg. Vol. 1, no. 1, 1926 - Vol. 2, no. 4, 1928. Continued as *The Bill* Vol. 1, no. 1, 1928 - Vol. 2, no. 4, 1930. One issue unnumbered April 1933.

L75. *Livre de l'Année.* Montréal, Grolier. 1950 + Contains annual review of theatre. Later numbers give brief survey of theatre in Canada.

L76. *Marguerite G. Bagshaw Theatre Committee Newsletter.* Toronto, Toronto Public Libraries. Vol. 1, March, 1974 + Children's theatre. Annually.

L77. *Masses.* Toronto, Progressive Arts Club. Vol. 1, April, 1932 - April, 1934. 12 issues, published irregularly. Theatre reviews and articles, especially on the workers' theatre in Toronto; play scripts.

L78. *Manitoba Theatre Centre Newsletter.* Winnipeg, Manitoba Theatre Centre. Vol. 1, 1971 - 1973. 6 times yearly. Two seasons only.

L79. *Manitoba Theatre Centre: Souvenir Programme.* Winnipeg, Manitoba Theatre Centre. 1965-66, 1970-71, 1971-72. Published irregularly.

L80. *Le Maclean.* Montreal, Maclean-Hunter Ltd. Vol. 1, no. 1, mars, 1961 + Monthly article "Les Arts", sometimes dealing with theatres; occasionally feature articles on theatre. Title varies: *Magazine Maclean.* Monthly.

L81. *Maclean's.* Toronto, Maclean-Hunter Ltd. Vol. 1, no. 1, 1896 + Occasionally feature articles on Canadian theatre; book reviews; comment on current theatre scene. Title varies: *Busy Man's Magazine; Maclean's Magazine.* Monthly.

L82. *Matrix.* Lennoxville, Quebec, Department of English, Champlain College. Vol. I, no. 1, spring, 1975 + Articles on current literary and cultural scene; play scripts. Semi-annually.

L83. *Masks and Faces.* Regina Little Theatre Society. 1942 + 5 times yearly. (1942-45 mimeographed).

L84. *The Montrealer.* Montreal, Passing Show Publishing. Vol. 1, March, 1926 + Short review of current theatre events in Montreal. Monthly.

L85. *Motion.* Toronto, Canada Media Productions Ltd. Vol. I, no. 1, November/ December, 1972 + Articles on Canadian performing arts; surveys of current theatre scene in Canada; brief comments on books. Publishing and numbering irregular.

L86. **National Arts Centre.** *Annual report of the national arts centre corporation.* 1968-9 + One issue published with illustrations, pictures, and portraits, in soft cover form, June, 1973.

L87. **National Theatre School of Canada.** *Annual report.* Montreal. 1961 +.

L88. *New Frontier.* Toronto, ed. Margaret Gold. Vol. 1, no. 1, April, 1936-October, 1937. Articles on workers' theatre, current theatre scene; book reviews; play scripts. Monthly.

L89. *New Frontiers.* Toronto, "Partnership of New Frontiers". Vol. 1, winter, 1952 - summer, 1956. Articles on workers' theatre; comments on current theatrical scene in Canada; reviews of books. Monthly.

L90. *News of the Canadian Child Drama Association.* Ottawa, Canadian Child Drama Association. Vol. 1, no. 1, December, 1962 + Name of organization changed to Canadian Child and Youth Drama Association in early years. Monthly.

L91. *North Georgia Gazette and Winter Chronicle.* London, John Murray. 1821. Vol. 1, no. I, November 1, 1819 - Vol. 1, no. XXI, March 20, 1820. Journal printed on board ships employed in the discovery of the North-West Passage, 1819-1820. Ed. Captain Sabine. Contains items documenting the activities of the North Georgia Theatre established on board ship.

L92. *Nouvelle Revue Canadienne.* Montréal. Vol. 1, no. 1, février/mars, 1951 - Vol. 3, no. 3, avril/mai, 1954. "Le théâtre" — a review of theatre in Montreal every two months.

L93. *Onion: the bi-monthly paper on the arts.* Toronto. Vol. 1, no. 1, June 20, 1975 +

L94. *On Stage.* Vancouver Little Theatre Association. 1958 + Five times a year. (mimeographed).

L95. *On Stage with Canadian Players.* Toronto, Canadian Players Foundation. Vol. 1, no. 1, October, 1960 - Spring, 1964.

L96. *Open Letter.* Toronto. Series 1, no. 1, 1965 + Occasionally articles on Canadian theatre and drama. 4 times per year.

L97. *Performance Magazine of the Arts.* Vancouver, Promotion Arts Enterprises. Vol. 1, no. 1, November 1972 + Monthly.

L98. *Performing Arts Directory.* Toronto, Canadian Theatre Centre. Vol. 1, 1968. One only.

L99. *Performing Arts in Canada.* Toronto, Canadian Stage and Arts Publications. Vol. I, no. 1, March, 1961 + Surveys of current theatrical activities across Canada; calendar of up-coming events; play scripts; occasionally reviews of books and published plays. Quarterly.

L100. *Performing Arts Ontour.* Toronto, Ontario Arts Council. 1975, 216 p. Annually. Previous to 1975, this was a "kit" made up of a series of pamphlets circulated annually.

L101. *Play Bill.* Winnipeg Community Players. ed. Robert Ayre. (1930's?)

L102. *Playboard.* Vancouver, Archway Publishers. Vol. 1, no. 1, October, 1966 + Eight times yearly.

L103. *Playwrights' Space Journal.* Toronto, Playwrights Co-op. 1972. One only.

L104. *Prairie Call Boy.* Winnipeg, Drama Division, Adult Education Committee, University of Manitoba. Vol. 1, no. 1, October 1941 - Vol. 5, no. 2, January 1946.

L105. *Queen's Quarterly.* Kingston, Queen's University. Vol. 1, July, 1893 + Occasional articles on Canadian theatre and drama. Quarterly.

L106. *Quill and Quire.* Toronto, Greey de Pencier Publications. Vol. 1, no. 1, April, 1935 + Occasional articles on Canadian theatre and drama; reviews of theatre books and published plays. Minimum of 12 times a year.

L107. *Rélations.* Montréal, publiée par un groupe de Pères de la Compagnie de Jésus. Vol. 1, no. 1, janvier, 1941 + Up to 1956, occasionally contained theatre-related articles. From 1956, Georges-Henri d'Auteuil published regular article on various aspects of French-Canadian theatre. Monthly.

L108. *Saturday Night.* Toronto. Vol. 1, 1887 + Feature articles on Canadian theatre; Regular articles on current theatre scene written by Hector Charlesworth, B.K. Sandwell, among others. Monthly.

L109. *La Scène au Canada/The Stage in Canada.* Toronto, Canadian Theatre Centre. Vol. 1, no. 1, March, 1965 - Vol. 7, no. 3-4, November-December, 1972. Calendar of events in Canadian theatres; articles on Canadian theatre and drama. Monthly.

L110. *Scene Changes.* Toronto, Theatre Ontario. Vol. 1, no. 1, February, 1973 + Articles on theatre activity in Ontario; Vol. 1, no. 1, - vol. 1, no. 5. mimeographed. Monthly.

L111. *Scene Magazine.* Toronto, David B. Crombie. Vol. 1, 1963 + In 1975 taken over by Toronto Life Magazine. Published irregularly.

L112. *Simon's Directory of Theatrical Materials, Services, and Information.* New York, Bernard Simon. Vol. 1, 1956 + Subsequent editions 1963, 1966, 1970, 1975. Contains information on Canadian theatrical materials, services.

L113. *Stage.* Ottawa, Theatre Department of the National Arts Centre. Vol. 1, no. 1, October, 1974 + Quarterly.

L114. *Stage Centre.* Winnipeg, Manitoba Theatre Centre. No. 1, October, 1961 + Later referred to as "House Programme-", bearing the name "Manitoba Theatre Centre". 6 times per year.

L115. *Stage Door: Canada's Entertainment Journal.* Vancouver, James Colistro Enterprises. Vol. 1, no. 1, April 2, 1970 - Vol. 1, no. 7, May 14, 1970. Weekly.

L116. **Stage Door.* Edmonton, University of Alberta, Drama Department, Department of Cultural Affairs. 1947-48.

L117. *Stage Struck.* Sarnia, Sarnia Little Theatre. Vol. 1, no. 1, June, 1967 + .

L118. *The Stratford Festival Story.* Stratford, Ontario, Stratford Shakespearean Festival Foundation of Canada. Vol. 1, 1954 + Each issue covers history of the Festival from 1953 to the date of issue. Annually.

L119. *Stratford Shakespearean Festival Foundation of Canada: Annual Report.* Stratford, Ontario. No. 1, 1953. No reports from 1954-1957. Continued 1958-1967. Replaced by simpler "President's Report" in 1968. + .

L120. *Stratford Shakespearean Festival Programme.* Stratford, Ontario. No. 1, 1953 + Annually. Additional programmes for tours, 1967, 1975.

L121. *Tamarack Review.* Toronto. Vol. 1, no. 1, autumn, 1956 + Occasional articles on Canadian theatre and drama; book reviews. Quarterly.

L122. *Targya.* Saskatoon, Twenty-fifth Street House Publications. Vol. 1, no. 1, 1973 - Fall 1974. (no more published).

L123. *That's Showbusiness.* Toronto, Bette Laderout, ed. and pub. Vol. 1, no. 1, October, 1971 + .

L124. *Théâtre. (Revues Théâtre).* Montréal, Théâtre du Rideau Vert. Vol. 1, no. 1, octobre 15, 1960 - Vol. 9, no. 7, mai, 1969.

L125. *Theatre B.C.* Vancouver, Promotion Arts Enterprises for the British Columbia Drama Association. Vol. 1, no. 1, 1975 + 6 times yearly.

L126. *Theatre Canada Newsletter.* Ottawa, Theatre Canada. Vol. 1, no. 1, October, 1971 + .

L127. *Théâtre/Québec.* Montréal, Centre d'essai des auteurs dramatiques de Montréal. Vol. 1, no. 1, 1969-70. (Two issues only)

L128. *Théâtre Vivant.* Montréal, Centre d'essai des auteurs dramatiques de Montréal. Vol. 1, no. 1, novembre, 1966-1969. (7 numbers only)

L129. *Theatre World.* New York, Daniel Blum. Vol. 1, 1944-5 + Includes annual record of Stratford Shakespearean Festival Company from its first year in 1953. Annually.

L130. *This Magazine.* Toronto, Red Maple Publishing Company. Vol. 1, no. 1, 1966 + Occasional articles on Canadian theatre and drama. Title changed from *This Magazine Is About Schools* in May/June, 1973. Bi-monthly.

L131. *T N M*. Montréal, Fondation du Théâtre du Nouveau Monde. Vol. 1, no. 1, octobre/novembre, 1964 - 1968.

L132. *Toronto Calendar Magazine*. Toronto, Calendar Magazine Limited. No. 1, April 11, 1969 + Brief calendar of theatrical activity in Toronto. 16 times per year.

L133. *Toronto Life*. Toronto, Key Publishers Limited, Vol. 1, no. 1, November, 1966 + Brief survey of current theatrical events in Toronto. Monthly.

L134. *Toronto Theatre Review*. (A capsule review . . . for the year 1913). Toronto, Page Publications, 1973. 1 issue only. (Prepared by Gwen Sands Dempsey). illus.

L135. *Touring Directory of the Performing Arts in Canada*. Ottawa, Touring Office of the Canada Council. Vol. 1, 1975. 314 p. Lists attractions, facilities, services, sponsors, for dance, music, theatre. Annually?

L136. *University of Toronto Quarterly*. Toronto, University of Toronto. Vol. 1, October, 1931 + Occasional articles on Canadian theatre and drama. See also *Letters in Canada*.

L137. *Vancouver Little Theatre News*. ed. A.P. Crocker. Published in 1930's.

L138. *Vie des Arts*. Montreal. No. 1, janvier/février. 1956 + Infrequent articles on French-Canadian theatre.

L139. *World Literature Written in English*. Texas, Modern Languages Association. Vol. 1, no. 1, April, 1962 + Occasional reviews of Canadian theatre books. Twice yearly.

L140. *West Coast Review*. Burnaby, British Columbia, Simon Fraser University. Vol. 1, no. 1, winter, 1971 + Occasional articles on Canadian theatre; play scripts.

L141. *York Theatre Journal*. Toronto, Department of Theatre, York University. Vol. 1, winter, 1971 + Published irregularly.

Garrison "Penny Readings" at the Soldier's Institute in Halifax, June 1872. See items listed under Garrison Theatricals.

M

Bibliography of
Theatre Bibliographies

M1. **Morgan, Henry James.** *Bibliotheca Canadensis or a manual of Canadian literature.* Ottawa, Desbarats, 1867. xiv, 411p. (Reprint, Detroit, Gale Research co, 1968).

M2. **Pence, James Harry** (comp.). *The magazine and the drama: an index.* N.Y. Burt Franklin, 1896. 190 p. (Reprint Dunlap Society, 1970).

M3. Recent publications relating to Canada. *Canadian Historical Review.* University of Toronto Press. Vol. 1, no. 1, March, 1920 + Bibliography in each issue.

M4. Presentable plays for use in Canada. *Ontario Library Review* 13: 14-46, August 1928, p. 44-46 Canadian plays.

M5. **Bellerive, Georges.** Nos auteurs dramatiques. *Canada Français* 20: 748-757, avril 1933. (List of French-Canadian plays up to 1933, including date of first performance and publication.)

M6. **Robert, George H.** Nos auteurs dramatiques by George H. Robert and P.E. Senay. *Canada français* 21: 237-243, novembre 1933. (Completes list of Bellerive above.)

M7. **Tremaine, Marie.** *A bibliography of Canadian imprints 1751-1800.* Toronto, University of Toronto Press, 1952. xxvii, 705 p. (See section on Quebec theatre).

M8. **Canadian Association for Adult Education.** *Canadian plays and playwrights; a selective bibliography of Canadian plays.* Toronto C.A.A.E., 1957. (English language only).

M9. **Milne, William Samuel.** *Canadian full-length plays in English: a preliminary annotated catalogue.* Ottawa, Dominion Drama Festival, 1964. viii, 47 p.

M10. **Milne, William Samuel.** *Canadian full-length plays in English (11): a supplement to the preliminary anotated catalogue.* Ottawa, Dominion Drama Festival, 1966. vii, 39 p.

M11. **Watters, Reginald Eyre.** *On Canadian literature, 1806-1960: a check-list of articles, books and theses on English Canadian Literature, its authors and language.* Toronto, University of Toronto Press 1966. ix, 165 p.

M12. **Du Berger, Jean.** *Bibliographie du théâtre québecois de 1935 à nos jours.* Québec, Université Laval, Dept. des études canadiennes, 1970. L8 l.

M13. **Lemire, Maurice and Landry, Kenneth.** *Répertoire des spécialistes de littérature canadienne-française.* Archives de littérature canadienne. Université Laval, 1971. 93p.

M14. **Young, William C.** *American theatrical arts: a guide to manuscript and special collections in the United States and Canada.* Chicago, American Library Association, 1971. ix, 166p.

M15. *Brock bibliography of published Canadian stage plays in English, 1900-1972,* by Richard Cummings and others. St. Catharines, Ont., Brock University, 1972. 85 p.

M16. **Gray, Jack.** Drama. In Fulford, Robert ed. *Read Canadian: a book about Canadian books.* Toronto, J. Lewis and Samuel, 1972. p. 246-252.

M17. **Harrison, Cynthia.** *Women in Canada 1965-72: a bibliography.* Hamilton, Ont. McMaster University Library Press, 1972. 51p.

M18. **Kalman, Rolf** ed. *A collection of Canadian plays.* Toronto, Bastet Books, Simon and Pierre Publishers, 1972-75. 4 vols.

M19. **Klinck, Carl F.** (compiler). Post graduate theses in Canadian literature: English and English-French comparative. *Journal of Canadian Fiction* 1:68-73, summer, 1972.

M20. **Watters, Reginald Eyre.** *A checklist of Canadian literature and background materials 1628-1960* 2nd ed. rev. and enl. Toronto, University of Toronto Press, 1972. xxiv, 1085 p.

M21. **Barnwell, Stephen.** Post graduate theses in Canadian literature: English and English-French comparative. *Journal of Canadian Fiction* II, no. 2:78-82, 1973.

M22. *Canadian theses/thèses canadiennes, 1947-1960.* Ottawa, Information Canada, 1973. 2 v.

M23. **Conolly, L.W. and Wearing, J.P.** N.C.T.R.:. a bibliography for 1972. *Nineteenth Century Theatre Research* 1:109-124, autumn, 1973.

M24. **Deschamps, Marcel.** *Dossier en théâtre québecois* Vol. 1. *Bibliographie.* Jonquière, Que., Presses collégiales de Jonquière, 1973. xii, 230 p.

M25. *First supplement to the Brock bibliography of published Canadian plays.* St. Catharines, Ont., Brock University, 1973. 44 p.

M26. **Gnarowski, Michael.** *A concise bibliography and select reference guide to Canadian literature.* Toronto, McClelland and Stewart, 1973. 126 p.

M27. **Holden, David F.** *An analytical index to Modern Drama, Vol. 1-13.* Toronto, Hakkert Publishing, 1973. 220 p.

M28. **McCallum, Heather.** *Research collections in Canadian libraries: II Special Studies: I Theatre resources in Canadian collections.* Ottawa, National Library of Canada, 1973. 113 p. illus.

M29. **Nesbitt, Bruce.** Canadian literature/littérature canadienne, 1972: an annotated bibliography/une bibliographie avec commentaire. *Journal of Canadian Fiction* II, no. 2:97-159, 1973.

M30. **New, William H.** Annual bibliography of Commonwealth literature: Canada. *Journal of Commonwealth Literature* 8:59-86, December, 1973.

M31. **Peel, Bruce.** *A bibliography of the Prairie Provinces to 1953.* 2nd. ed. Toronto, University of Toronto Press, 1973. 808 p. (section entitled "Drama", pages 593-594).

M32. **Schoolcraft, Ralph N.** *Performing arts books in print: an annotated bibliography.* New York, Drama Book Specialists, 1973. 761 p.

M33. **Tougas, Gérard** (compiler). *A checklist of printed materials relating to French-Canadian literature/ Liste de référence d'imprimés relatifs à la littérature canadienne française.* 2nd ed., rev. and enl., Vancouver, University of British Columbia, 1973. 174 p.

M34. **Barnwell, Stephen.** Post graduate theses in Canadian literature: English and English-French comparative. *Journal of Canadian Fiction* 3, no. 2: 87-92, 1974.

M35. **Carpenter, Charles A.** Modern drama studies: an annotated bibliography. *Modern Drama* 17:67-120, March, 1974.

M36. **Conolly, L.W. and Wearing, J.P.** N.C.T.R.: a bibliography for 1973. *Nineteenth Century Theatre Research* 2:93-112, autumn, 1974.

M37. **New, William H.** Annual bibliography of Commonwealth literature: Canada. *Journal of Commonwealth Literature* 9:54-94, December, 1974.

M38. **New, William H.** *Critical writings on Commonwealth literature: a selected bibliography to 1970.* University Park, Pennsylvania State University Press, 1974. 432 p.

M39. **Schafer, D. Paul.** *A selective bibliography of Canadian and international readings in arts administration and cultural development.* Toronto, Canadian Conference of the Arts, 1974. 24 p.

M40. **Armitage, Andrew, and Tudor, Nancy.** *Canadian essay and literature index: 1973.* Toronto, University of Toronto Press, 1975. 445 p.

M41. **Canada. Public Archives.** *Union list of manuscripts in Canadian repositories.* Rev. ed. Ottawa, 1975. 2 vols. (1st edition 1968 contains some entries not in revised edition)

M42. **Canadian Conference of the Arts.** *Reading list on the arts in Canada.* Toronto, Canadian Conference of the Arts, 1975. 10 p.

M43. **Carpenter, Charles A.** Modern drama studies: an annual bibliography. *Modern Drama* 18:61-116, March, 1975.

M44. **Juliani, John.** The iconoclast's space primer. *Canadian Theatre Review* CTR 6:56-57, spring, 1975.

M45. **Magee, Eleanor, and MacDonald, Ruth.** Recent Canadian reference books: a selected list. *Atlantic Provinces Library Association Bulletin* 39:25-27, spring, 1975.

M46. **Nesbitt, Bruce.** Canadian literature/littérature canadienne: 1973 An annotated bibliography/une bibliographie avec commentaire. *Journal of Canadian Fiction* 3, no. 4:103-142, 1975.

M47. **Wagner, Anton** (ed.) *National playlist.* Toronto, Playwrights Co-op. Vol. 1, no. 1, February 1975 + quarterly.

Index

Burton, Jean. E 2.

Business and the Arts (see also Financing). C 220, C 234, C 237, C 244, C 269, C 280, C 566, C 601, D 226, D 241, J 156, J 160.

Cabana, Laure. I 13.

Calgary (see also Theatre Calgary; Alberta Theatre Project). C 183, C 582, C 591, C 597, C 608.

Calgary Conference on the Visual Arts, 1969. C 183.

Callbeck, L.C. C 303, C 304, C 305, C 306, C 307, C 308, C 329, C 330.

Callwood, June. G 60.

Calvert Trophy. F 38.

Cambrian College, (Sudbury). H 49.

Cameron, Donald. H 8, H 15, H 16.

Cameron, Duncan. C 264.

Cameron, Margaret M. B 12.

Camosun College (Victoria B.C.) C 642.

Campbell, D.E. C 215.

Campbell, Douglas. C 359, C 360.

Campbell, Loughlin. C 57, E 22.

Campbell, Mrs. William. B 88

Camus, Albert. D 95.

Canada Council. C 118, C 149, C 191, C 231, C 248, C 264, K 55, L 24, L 35.

Canadian Association for Adult Education. M 8.

Canadian Broadcasting Corporation. A 12, K 27.

Canadian Child and Youth Drama Association; (see also Canadian Child Drama Association; regional branches of CCYDA). C 199.

Canadian Child Drama Association. L 90.

Canadian Conference of the Arts. C 158, C 172, C 177, C 183, C 216, C 217, C 224, C 265, C 266, C 267, J 164, L 14, L 45, M 42.

Canadian Mime Theatre (see also Mime). C 483, C 505, C 524.

Canadian Players (Foundation). C 282, C 359, C 360, C 365, L 95.

Canadian Playwright's Series: Samuel French. C 38.

Canadian Theatre Centre. C 126, C 190, C 191, C 192, C 276, H 36, I 17, L 38, L 98, L 109.

Canadian Theatre Conference (Face to Face). C 272.

Canadian Theatre Review. C 516, C 517, C 518.

Canadian Theatres: Professional. A 43, C 235.

Cansino, B. C 556.

Caplan, Rupert. C 25.

Cappon, Daniel. C 178.

Card, R. C 425.

Cariboo Dramatic Society. B 113.

Carpenter, Charles A. M 35, M 43.

Carpenter, Edmund. I 67.

Carr, Judith. C 537.

Carson, Neil. C 387, C 388, C 390, C 391, C 392, C 393, C 394, G 160, G 161, G 165, J 102, J 103.

Casgrain, L'Abbé H.R. J 19.

Cash, Gwen. E 107.

Centaur Theatre (Montreal). D 229, D 235.

Central Ontario Drama League. L 23, L 40.

Centre d'Essai des Auteurs Dramatiques de Montréal. D 172, D 179, D 237, L 19, L 20, L 127, L 128.

Chadwick, Bernard. J 157.

Chadwick, Stella. E 29.

Chalmer's Foundation. C 239, C 445, J 166.

Champagne, Jane. C 198, J 118.

Champlain College (Lennoxville, Que.) L 83.

Charbonneau, Jean. D 3, D 4.

Charlesworth, Hector Willoughby. B 73, C 45, C 65, L 108.

Charlesworth, Marigold. H 37, H 38.

Charlottetown (see also Confederation Centre). C 303, C 304, C 306, C 316, C 339, C 343, C 347.

Children's Theatre. C 162, C 199, C 200, C 207, C 236, C 290, C 350, C 380, C 519, C 574, C 578, D 106, D 184, K 23, K 31, L 20, L 65, L 80.

Chilliwack, B.C. C 626.

Chocolate Cove (New Brunswick). E 34.

Christie, H.G.F. C 28, C 35.

Church and the Theatre. B 2, B 3, B 5, B 11, B 15, B 18, B 22, B 74, C 169.

Chusid, Harvey. C 168.

Cinema and theatre. D 189, J 134.

Cirque Royale (Québec). B 54, B 56.

Citadel on Wheels (Edmonton). C 576, C 595.

Citadel Theatre (Edmonton). C 573, C 574, C 575, C 578, C 588, C 593, C 596, C 602, L 41, L 43.

City Stage (Vancouver). C 644.

Civic Playhouse (Victoria, B.C.). I 23.

Clark, Barrett H. C 36, C 46, C 47.

Clarke, Cecil. G 43.

Claus, Joanne. C 309, C 331, C 332, C 333, C 334, H 34, I 50.

Clifford E. Lee Award. C 584, C 609.

Closingchild, Thomas D. C 617.

Cloutier, Guy. J 92.

Cloutier, Rachel. J 93.

Clowns, C 486.

Coburn, John. C 89.

Cohen, Nathan. C 110, C 115, C 120, C 156, C 364, G 44, G 61, G 123, G 156, J 72.

Colbeck, James. H 41.

Colby, Mel. F 40.

Coleman, Francis A. D 22.

Colgate, William G. B 83.

Colicos, John. F 53.

Colombier, Marie. B 117.

Colonnade Theatre (Toronto.) C 409, C 440.

Comédie-Canadienne (Montréal.) D 49, D 51, D 95, I 15.

Community Arts Survey Committee, (Vancouver.) C 611.

Community Players of Winnipeg. L 72, L 101.

La Compagnie de Jésus (Montreal.) L 107.

Les Compagnons de Saint-Laurent (St. Laurent) (Montréal.) D 18, D 20, D 22, D 26, D 28, D 175, L 17.

Confederation Centre, (Charlottetown.) I 25.

Conolly, L.W. M 23, M 36.

Corona Barn Theatre (Montreal.) E 38.

Conroy, Patricia. K 12.

Constantineau, Gilles. D 101.

Constantinidi, Mela. C 426.

Cook, Michael. J 133.

Corriveau, Jeanne. K 13.

Cotnam, Jacques. D 240.

Coulter, John. C 49, C 61, C 66, C 75, C 93, F 30, F 31, J 44, J 163.

Council for Business and the Arts. C 234, C 237, C 280.

Courtney, Richard. C 199, C 200, H 42.

Coventry, Alan Freeth. E 42.

Cowan, James. C 152.

Cowan, James A. B 127.

Cowan, John. F 36.

Cowell, Mr. Sam; Mrs. Sam. B 132.

Coxwell, Mona. C 48, C 59.

Craig, Irene. B 104, E 102, E 104.

Craig, John. I 4.

Crampton, Esmé. H 24, H 43.

Crane, William H. J 40.

Crean, Susan M. C 218, C 427.

Crest Theatre (Toronto). C 366, C 370, C 374, C 386, C 516, C 517, C 518, C 520, C 531, C 536.

Crighton, Dorothy V. C 612, E 112, E 114, E 115, F 7.

Criticism. C 133, C 170, C 232, D 13, D103, D 131.

Croft, Frank. B 140, C 132.

Crompton, Jack. K 14.

Crosby, Laurel. C 282.

Cruickshank, Marion Gertrude. K 15.

Cultural Policy. C 225, C 226, C 227, C 242, C 243, C 245, C 246, C 248, C 632.

Cummings, L. G 106.

Cunningham, Jack. D 119.

D ◆

Dafoe, Christopher. A 44, C 538, C 550.

Dale, E.A. E 43.

Daley, Frank. F 54.

Dalgleish, Gail. K 16.

Dalhousie University. L 50.

Dalrymple, Andrew A. J 134.

Dansereau, Jeanne. D 143.

Darcy, J. D 69.

D'Auteuil, Georges Henri. D 36, D 42, D 48, D 54, D 64, D 65, D 66, D 67, D 68, D 82, D 98, D 100, D 137.

Davies, Robertson. C 94, C 268, C 526, G 16, G 33, G 34, G 45, G 46, G 62, G 72, G 85, G 124, G 132, H 26, I 18, J 101, J 113, J 128, J 171, K 51.

Davis, Donald. C 520, G 174.

Davis, Montgomery. C 573.

Dawson City, Yukon (see Palce Grand Theatre).

De La Roche, Mazo. J 64.

Dempsey, Gwen Sands. L 134.

Denham, Paul. A 31.

Denison, Merrill. B 67, C 18, C 26, C 201, E 35, E 44, E 45, E 46, E 48, J 124, J 151, K 51.

Dennis, Wendell. I 68.

Deschamps, Marcel. M 24.

Desjardins, Pierre W. I 42.

Desrochiers, Pierre. D 120, D 144.

Dickens, Charles. B 119, B 122, J 51, J 52, J 53.

Dickson-Kenwin, G. C 70.

Direction Canada. C 216, C 217, C 222, C 224, C 462.

Disher, Maurice Willson. B 132, J 55.

Doat, Jan. A 32.

Dobbs, Kildare. G 114, G 146.

Doherty, Brian. C 474.

Doherty, Tom. I 47, I 51.

G

H

Halifax (see also Neptune Theatre; 2nd. Stage; Pier I). B 25, B 26, B 27, B 28, B 33, C 150, C 286, C 290, C 314, C 320, C 327, F 43, K 6, K 32, K 34.

Halpenny, Francess. E 88.

Halpert, Herbert. C 296.

Ham, George H. B 84.

Ham, Roderick. I 48.

Hamblet, Edwin, C. D 191, D 200.

Hamelin, Jean. A 11, D 50, D 71, D 72, D 73, D 86, D 167.

Hamilton, Ont. (see also Players Guild of Hamilton; Hamilton Place). B 93, C 438, C 447, E 79.

Hamilton Place. C 447, I 57.

Hardy, Alison Taylor. E 74.

Hardy, Helen Avery. C 6.

Harper, J. Russell. B 29, B 30.

Harrington, George M. B 72.

Harrison, Cynthia. M 17.

Hart House (see also issues of Curtain Call (L 49)). C 392, E 41, E 43, E 45, E 49, E 50, E 51, E 52, E 53, E 55, E 56, E 57, E 58, E 59, E 61, E 62, E 80, E 89, F 3.

Hartnoll, Phyllis. A 18, A 29.

Harvey, Ruth Walker. B 105.

Harwood, Ronald. J 97.

Hassan, R.F. J 120.

Hatch, Robert. G 134.

Hatfield, G.D.H. F 44.

Hausvater, Alexander. D 214, D 215, D 216, D 231, J 121, J 140.

Haworth, Peter. C 618, C 620.

Hay, Peter. C 245, C 246, C 247, C 631.

Haymarket Theatre (Quebec City). B 54, B 63.

Haynes, Nancy Jane. K 25.

Heald, Joseph. C 632.

Heavysege, Charles. J 1, J 15, J 96.

Hénault, Gilles. D 87, D 102, D 103, D 104, D 105, D 124.

Hénaut, Dorothea Todd. D 154.

Henderson, Roy D. E 99.

Hendry, Thomas B. C 164, C 173, C 174, C 205, C 206, C 224, C 225, C 248, C 539, C 551, C 552, F 61, G 182.

Henry, Ann. C 541, C 542, J 88.

Herbert, John. J 98, J 103, J 106, J 126.

Herity, J.O. E 64.

Hesse, Jurgen. C 621, F 52.

Hesson, Hilda. E 91, E 96.

Hewes, Henry. C 406, G 49.

Hicklin, Ralph. C 146, C 368.

Hicks, Rivers Keith. B 8.

Hillebrand, Harold Newcomb. B 130.

Hiritsch, Basil. K 26.

Hirsch, John. C 553, H 18, J 61, J 122, J 141, J 165.

Hoare, John Edward. C 7, E 23.

Hofsess, J. J 142.

Holden, David F. M 27.

Holden, John. (see Actor's Colony Theatre).

Holman Opera Company. J 40.

Home Theatre (of the Canadian Players, British Columbia). E 108, E 110.

"Honest Ed" (see Mirvish, Ed).

Hood, Hugh. C 369, I 52.

Hoos, Peter. D 43.

Houde, Christiane. J 99.

Houle, Jean Pierre. D 18.

Houle, Leopold. D 13, D 14, D 17.

Houle, Renée. A 15.

Hour Company (Theatre Hour Company) (Toronto). H 23, H 39.

House, A.W. G 21.

Howard, Irene. C 625.

Hull, R. A 34.

Howard, Rhena. C 560.

Howe, Jonas. B 24.

Huard, Roger B. J 76.

Hudson's Bay Co. L 10.

Hull, Quebec. B 18, D 171.

Hunter, Martin, C 180.

Hunter-Duvar, John. J 5, J 96.

Huron County Playhouse (Grand Bend, Ont.) C 452.

Hutchison, Percy. B 133.

Hutt, William. F 53.

Hyland, Frances. C 607.

Imperial Capitol Theatre (Saint John, N.B.). C 284.

International Theatre Institute. C 274, L 66.

Indians and Drama. A 45, B 81, C 349, C 619, C 650.

Irish Arts Theatre (Toronto). C 407, C 448.

Irving, Sir Henry. J 2, J 36, J 56.

Irving, Laurence. J 36, J 56.

Irwin, May. J 23.

Isaac, Winifred. B 147.

Izenour, George C. I 25.

Jack, Donald. C 367.

K

L

Mermaid Theatre (Wolfville, N.S.). C 298, C 337.

Messenger, Ann P. J 106.

Mezei, Stephen. C 259, C 409, C 451, C 452, C 453, C 454, C 581.

Micheli, Carla. C 195.

Michener, Wendy. C 123, C 124, C 288.

Middleton, Gilbert. C 623.

Middleton, Jesse Edgar. A 2, B 85, B 91.

Miller, J.E. E 86.

Miller, M.J. C 490.

Milne, William S. F 35, M 9, M 10.

Mime (see also Canadian Mime Theatre). C 483, C 505, F 86.

Minton, Eric. I 19.

Mirvish, Ed. C 402.

Mitchell, Betty. E 101.

Mitchell, Roy. J 153.

Moiseiwitsch, Tanya. G 46, G 80.

Molière, Jean Baptiste Poquelin. K 21.

Moncton, N.B. C 307.

Monsarrat, Nicholas. G 8.

Montagnes, Ian. E 89.

Montigny, Louvigny de. D 11, J 37.

Montreal (see also Les Compagnons de St. Laurent; Corona Barn Theatre; Lakeshore Summer Theatre; Brae Manor Theatre; Theatre Royal; Masquers Theatre; Théâtre du Nouveau Monde; Montreal Repertory Theatre; Théâtre du Même Nom). B 34, B 35, B 36, B 37, B 39, B 41, B 45, B 47, B 49, B 50, B 51, B 52, B 53, B 116, B 118, B 119, B 120, B 121, B 122, B 123, B 130, B 131, D 2, D 6, D 9, D 10, D 25, D 37, D 43, D 61, D 85, D 115, D 118, D 123, D 126, D 128, D 129, D 154, D 177, D 179, D 197, D 201, D 215, D 216, D 218, D 224, D 229, E 35, H 11, I 39, I 40, K 9, K 12, K 23, K 40.

Montreal Masquer's Club. E 98.

Montreal Repertory Theatre. E 36, L 47.

Moon, Barbara. C 361, D 44, D 93, G 51, H 19.

Moore, Dora Mavor. C 361.

Moore, James Mavor. C 87, C 91, C 111, C 117, C 125, C 184, C 185, C 208, G 78, J 128, J 153.

Moore, Jocelyn. E 66.

Morgan, Henry James. B 82, J 9, J 17, J 20, M 1.

Morgan-Powell, Samuel. B 129, C 22.

Morley, Malcolm. B 64, C 39, C 43, C 80, E 19, E 24, E 112, F 8, F 9, F 10, F 11, F 12, F 13, F 14, F 25, F 26, F 27.

Morris, Clara. J 16.

Morris, Royden. G 144.

Morse, Barry. C 382.

Mortimer, P.J. C 455.

Moussali, Lucienne. K 33.

Mulcahy, Sean. (see Press Theatre, St. Catharines).

Mullaly, Edward J. C 251, C 299, C 317, C 318, C 319, J 154.

Mullane, George. B 26.

Mulligan, Louis. D 24.

Mullock, A.C. E 90.

Mulvany, C. Pelham. B 78.

Mummers Theatre Troupe. C 336, C 342.

Mumming. C 296.

Muskoka (see Muskoka Summer Theatre; Actor's Colony Theatre).

Muskoka Summer Theatre. C 493.

N

Naramata, B.C. (see also Aikins, Carroll; Home Theatre, B.C.). E 107.

National Arts Centre (Ottawa). C 153, C 404, C 405, C 411, C 441, C 442, C 444, C 480, C 488, D 205, I 43, I 44, L 86, L 113.

National Theatre and Drama (see also issues of Curtain Call and related periodicals). C 7, C 8, C 10, C 15, C 17, C 19, C 20, C 23, C 24, C 25, C 26, C 27, C 28, C 29, C 30, C 32, C 35, C 36, C 41, C 42, C 43, C 44, C 46, C 47, C 49, C 58, C 62, C 64, C 66, C 67, C 72, C 73, C 74, C 75, C 79, C 83, C 85, C 95, C 97, C 99, C 103, C 104, C 111, C 119, C 122, C 141, C 145, C 150, C 197, C 201, C 203, C 206.

National Theatre School (Montreal). C 494, H 18, H 20, H 25, H 52, K 47, L 87.

Nau, T. G 185.

Neary, Peter. J 155.

Needles, Dorothy. H 46.

Nelson, B.C. C 651.

Nelson, Keith D. C 273.

Neptune Theatre (see also Halifax, N.S.). C 287, C 288, C 289, C 291, C 294, C 297, C 300, C 302, C 305, C 322, C 326, C 340, C 346, I 30.

Nesbitt, Bruce. M 29, M 46.

Ness, Margaret. C 100, C 101, E 26, I 3, J 58.

New, William H. A 36, C 209, C 229, J 107, M 30, M 37, M 38.

New Brunswick. C 293, C 295, C 299, C 317, K 42.

New Play Society (Toronto). C 355, C 361.

New School (Toronto). C 495.

Newfoundland (see also St. John's). C 296, C 328, E 33, F 60, H 45.

O

P

Playwrights Co-op (Toronto). C 527, L 103.

Plunkett, Al. J 63.

Plunkett, Patrick Mary. G 88.

Poirier, Pascal. A 1, B 40.

Political theatre (see also Workers Theatre, Cultural Policy). A 35, A 40, A 47.

Pollock, Sharon. C 345.

Pontaut, Alain. J 109.

Pope, Karl Theodore. K 39.

Popular Theatre. C 123, C 124.

Port Royal - Theatre of Neptune. B 8, B 10, B 16, B 19, B 20, B 21, B 23.

Port Stanley, Ont. E 69.

Portman, Jamie. C 569, C 582, C 597.

Posner, Michael. C 210.

La Poudrière (Montréal). D 88, D 93, D 232.

Power, Tyrone. B 145.

Pratt, Martha. C 347, C 348.

Prendergast, Tannis. E 103.

Press Theatre (St. Catharines, Ont.) C 501.

Prévost, Robert. J 50.

Price, C. C 401.

Pride, Leo B. A 38.

Primeau, Marguerite. D 60, J 110.

Prince Edward Island (see also Charlottetown). B 31, C 306, C 311, C 348.

Pringle, Gertrude E.S. J 35.

Proctor, Catherine. J 35.

Progressive Arts Club (Toronto). L 82.

Puppet theatre (see also issues of periodicals such as Curtain Call (L 49). A 42, A 46, C 40, C 254, C 426, C 641.

Pyper, Nancy. E 21, F 23, F 28.

Q

Quebec City. B 38, B 42, B 54, B 56, B 57, B 58, B 59, B 60, B 61, B 62, B 63, B 130, I 28, I 45.

Queen's University. H 7, L 105.

Quesnel, Louis-Joseph. B 42, J 78, J 87.

R

Raby, Peter. G 10.

Racine, Jean. D 87.

Radio Drama. C 82, C 130.

Raeburn, Alan. C 412.

Rain, Douglas. J 137.

Rainbow Stage (Winnipeg). C 554, C 558.

Ramsay, Alexander. E 20.

Reaney, James. G 25, G 117, J 85, J 105, J 108, J 111, J 114, J 115, J 117, J 128, J 130, J 136, J 166, K 8, K 50.

Redlight Theatre (Toronto). C 502, C 523, C 529.

Reid, Kate. F 53.

Regina (see also Globe Theatre; Regina Little Theatre Society). C 568.

Regina Little Theatre Society. L 81.

Regional Theatre. C 156, C 257, C 537, C 604, K 24.

Rémillard, Jean-Robert. D 132.

Revue (Theatre). D 168.

Rhodenizer, Vernon Blair. A 4.

Rhys, Charles Horton. B 114, B 142.

Richards, Stanley. E 84, G 136.

Rickett, Olla Goewey. K 40.

Ringwood, Gwen Pharis. J 54, J 174, K 51.

Ripley, John. H 47.

Rittenhouse, Charles B. D 25, H 11.

Rivard, Y. C 583.

Robb, Edith. D 220.

Robert, George H. D 5, M 6.

Robert, Guy. D 79.

Roberts, Sheila. C 627.

Robertson, George. C 130.

Robertson, Heather. C 154.

Robertson, J.L. E 31.

Robertson, John Ross. B 79.

Robinson, Cyril. C 289, C 290.

Robinson, Maynard. I 2.

Robson, Frederick. C 3, C 5.

Rochette, Gilles. D 107.

Rockwell, Kate: Klondike Kate. J 70.

Roquebrune, Robert de. B 11.

Rose, George Maclean. J 3.

Ross, John Richard. K 41.

Ross, Mary Lowrey. C 139.

Roux, Jean Louis. D 39, D 169, D 180, I 39.

Rowe-Sleeman, Alice. C 67.

Roy, Camille. J 18.

Roy, Elzéar. B 43.

Roy, Joseph Edmond. B 6.

Roy, Pierre-Georges. B 56, B 57, B 58, B 59, B 60, B 62, B 63.

Royal Alexandra Theatre (Toronto). C 379, C 410, I 22, K 25.

Royal Arctic Theatre. B 139, L 64.

Royal Commission on Book Publishing (Ontario). C 214.

Royal Commission on National Development in the Arts Letters and Sciences 1949-1951 (see also Massey Report). C 94, C 95, C 268.

Vancouver East Cultural Centre. C 643.

Vancouver Little Theatre. E 119, L 94, L 137.

Vancouver Repertory Theatre. C 614.

Varry, Jacques. I 29, I 40.

Vaudeville. B 146.

Vaughan Glaser Players. L 61.

Viau, Guy. I 44.

Victoria, B.C. (see also Bastion Theatre; Victoria Little Theatre; Civic Playhouse; Camosun College). B 110, C 612, C 622, F 7, F 27, K 20, L 12, L 13.

Victoria Little Theatre. E 118.

Vigneault, Jacques. D 142, D 158, D 170, D 182.

Voaden, Herman A. C 24, C 68, C 72, C 522, H 14, J 173.

Volinska, John (see also Drao Players). C 371.

Voltaire, François Marie Arouet de. B 59.

W

Wade, Bryan. J 147.

Wagner, Anton. A 40, A 47, J 174, M 47.

Wagner, Frederick. J 68.

Waisman, Alan. I 65.

Waldo, Lewis Patrick. B 13.

Walker, Adrian. A 30.

Walker, Frank Norman. B 98, B 137.

Walker Theatre (Winnipeg). B 103, B 105.

Wallace, Bob. C 510.

Wallace, William Stewart. J 39, J 45, J 57.

War and the Theatre. C 57, C 63.

Warehouse Theatre (Winnipeg). C 556.

Warkentin, G. J 130.

Warrick, Paddy. C 344.

Warrington, Irma. C 283.

Warwick, Ellen D. J 158.

Waterdale Associates (Edmonton). C 592, C 593, C 600.

Waterloo (County), Ont. B 96.

Waterston, Elizabeth. A 41.

Watmough, David. J 120.

Watson, Freda. C 64.

Watson, Wilfred. C 197, C 212, C 213, C 571.

Watt, Frank. A 10, K 52.

Watters, Reginald Eyre. M 11, M 20.

Watts, Ken. H 50.

Weales, Gerald. G 91.

Wearing, J.P. M 23, M 36.

Weaver, Robert L. C 149.

Webber, John E. C 4, C 9.

Webling, Peggy. B 126.

Webster, J. C 345.

Webster, Margaret. B 144.

Weiller, Georgette. K 53.

West, Richard. F 45.

Wetmore, Donald. B 20, E 32.

White, C.A. C 281.

White, Harvey. C 301.

White, Joy Roberts. C 585, C 586.

White, Meredith Alison. K 54.

Whittaker, Herbert. A 13, A 26, C 97, C 103, C 105, C 116, C 128, C 167, C 417, C 536, D 27, D 46, F 39, G 92.

Whittaker, Walter Leslie. K 55.

Wholton, T.H. I 8.

Wich, Sylvia. E 33.

Wiggins, Chris. J 143.

Wilcox, Richard Kent. I 72, I 73.

Williams, Albert Ronald. K 56.

Williams, Bramsby. J 59.

Williams, Norman. C 113.

Wilson, Lorna. H 51.

Wilson, Marian M. F 56.

Windeler, Robert. J 131.

Windsor, John Best. C 622.

Windsor, (Ont.). F 27.

Wingfield, Alexander H. B 93.

Winnipeg (see also Manitoba Theatre Centre; Walker Theatre; Warehouse Theatre; Winnipeg Masquer's Club; Winnipeg Little Theatre; Community Players of Winnipeg). A 44, B 103, B 104, B 105, C 538, C 542, C 545, C 547, C 548, F 10, F 20, F 21, F 24.

Winnipeg Little Theatre. E 91, E 92, E 96, E 103.

Winnipeg Masquer's Club. E 98.

Winter, Jack. C 363, D 61, D 62, G 111, G 112, G 122, H 22.

Winter, William. J 30.

Winters, Kenneth. C 540.

Wittgens, Claudia. C 449, J 159.

Wojciechowska, Cécile Cloutier. D 195.

Wolfit, Sir Donald. J 60, J 97.

Wolfville, N.S. (see also Mermaid Theatre). C 285, C 321.

Women's Alumni Theatre (Toronto). E 88.

Women in the Arts. A 48, C 194, M 17.

Women's Theatre Cooperative (Vancouver). C 629.

Wood, Ted N. C 386.

Woodcock, George. C 214.

Woodman, Ross. J 117.

Woods, John. I 9.

Woodstock (Ontario) Little Theatre. E 83.

Photo Credits

p. 14 Garrison Theatricals: *Canadian Illustrated News,* Oct. 5, 1872. University of Toronto, Thomas Fisher Rare Books Library.

p. 24 Edmund Kean: U. of T., Thomas Fisher R.B. Lib.

p. 25 John Howard drawing: Baldwin Room, Metropolitan Toronto Central Library.

p. 26, 28 Royal Lyceum sketches: Baldwin Room, M.T.C.L.

p. 27 Royal Lyceum playbills: Theatre Section, M.T.C.L.

p. 29 Military drama: *Canadian Illustrated News,* Feb. 23, 1878. U. of T., Thomas Fisher R.B. Lib.

p. 30 St. Mary's College: *Canadian Illustrated News,* May 28, 1870. U. of T.,Thomas Fisher R.B. Lib.

p. 31 Peterborough Opera House, May Bell: Theatre Section, M.T.C.L.

p. 64 Tamahnous Theatre: *Canadian Theatre Review Yearbook 1974,* Toronto, CTR Publications, 1975.

p. 77 *Les Belles-Soeurs:* Le Théâtre du Rideau Vert, Montréal.

p. 85, 86 Hart House: U. of T., University Archives.

p. 91 Toronto Progressive Arts Club: *Canadian Theatre Review* # 10.

p. 92 Stratford: A. Rogers, Central Photography, Theatre Section, M.T.C.L. Collection Herbert Whittaker.

p. 108 Children's Players: Theatre Section, M.T.C.L.

p. 124 Walker Theatre: Theatre Section, M.T.C.L.

P. 125 Martin-Harvey: *The Autobiography of Sir John Martin-Harvey,* London, Sampson Low, 1933, courtesy of MacDonald and Jane's Publishers Ltd., London, England and Mr. Eric Jones-Evans, Fawley, Hants., Eng.

p. 139 Garrison "Penny Readings": *Canadian Illustrated News,* June 15, 1872. U. of T., Thomas Fisher R.B. Lib.